TOWARDS
FINANCIAL
SELF-RELIANCE

A handbook on
Resource Mobilization for
Civil Society Organizations
in the south

Richard Holloway

AGA KHAN FOUNDATION

CIVICUS
World Alliance for Citizen Participation

Earthscan Publications Ltd, London and Sterling, VA

First published in the UK and USA in 2001 by
Earthscan Publications Ltd

Copyright © Aga Khan Foundation, 2001

ISBN: 1 85383 773 3

Typesetting by JS Typesetting, Wellingborough, Northants
Printed and bound in the UK by Clays Ltd, St Ives plc
Cover design by Danny Gillespie

For a full list of publications please contact:

Earthscan Publications Ltd
120 Pentonville Road
London, N1 9JN, UK
Tel: +44 (0)20 7278 0433
Fax: +44 (0)20 7278 1142
Email: earthinfo@earthscan.co.uk
http://www.earthscan.co.uk

22883 Quicksilver Drive, Sterling, VA 20166–2012, USA

A catalogue record for this book is available from the British Library

Library of Congress Cataloging-in-Publication Data

Holloway, Richard, 1945-.
    Towards financial self-reliance : a handbook of approaches to resource
  mobilization for citizens' organizations / Richard Holloway.
        p. cm.
    "Aga Khan Foundation".
    Includes index.
    ISBN 1-85383-733-3 (pbk.)
    1. Fund raising. 2. Nonprofit organizations—Finance. I. Aga Khan Foundation.
  II. Title.

HG177 .H65 2001
658.15—dc21   00-050401

Earthscan is an editorially independent subsidiary of Kogan Page Ltd and publishes
in association with WWF-UK and the International Institute for Environment and
Development

This book is printed on elemental chlorine-free paper

Contents

PART ONE: SETTING THE SCENE

PART TWO: WAYS OF MOBILIZING RESOURCES

PART THREE: DECIDING WHICH WAY TO GO

List of Case Studies, Figures and Boxes

CASE STUDIES

FIGURES

BOXES

Foreword

On 16–17 October 2000, some 300 leading citizens of Pakistan came together in Islamabad in a major national conference. The head of state set the stage. Government ministers, many other senior public officials, and leaders from business, the media and civil society organizations (CSOs) vigorously conferred for two days and, at the climax of their deliberations, launched a new national organization. What was the topic that had captured the Pakistani national imagination in late 2000? It was not Kashmir, nuclear proliferation, or even the process of political democratization. It was indigenous philanthropy, and, specifically, indigenous philanthropy as a resource for sustainable development.

Nor is Pakistan the only developing country to take concrete action 'towards self-reliance' in this way. Over the past decade more than two dozen countries in what Richard Holloway terms the global 'South' have established formal programmes to promote indigenous philanthropy. The fledgling Pakistan Centre for Philanthropy is but the most recent of these.

I believe that these and related events signal a major point of arrival for the organizations of civil society in the developing world. In turning to their own societies for support, civil society organizations established for public benefit – to facilitate self-help among the poor, to educate, to promote health, to enable artistic and cultural expression – are doing far more than raising funds where they live. They are, as the commentaries from leading development practitioners around the world that are published with this handbook indicate, grounding themselves irrevocably in their own societies. Given the imbalances of power, wealth and cultural presence in our world today, this is a far more difficult step than one might imagine. Yet moving 'towards self-reliance' is, paradoxically, the best way to move ahead in today's 'globalized' world.

The expert commentaries published in this handbook bear special notice. Should the reader wonder how leading development practitioners estimate the utility of the handbook in specific settings in Africa, Asia and Latin America, the answers are here. The commentaries add invaluable insights 'from the field' that the astute reader will be able to apply in her or his own unique setting. I urge you not to make the error of only reading the commentaries from your own region!

This handbook is published as part of the Aga Khan Foundation's (AKF) NGO Enhancement Programmes, which aim to support effective citizens' organizations in the public interest. Our work in the field of organizational effectiveness is expanding and the set of products, services and networks that are being developed from the materials authored by Richard Holloway indicate our programme directions.

This handbook is a freestanding how-to guide. A trainer manual supplements it for those who wish to facilitate a workshop course using the materials from the handbook. The trainer manual may be downloaded from the Internet at: http://www.ngoenet.org/public. The materials are also being produced as an interactive, multimedia learning resource that is accessed either by CD-ROM or the web. This 'plugged-in' version of the Holloway materials will be enhanced and customized for different settings with local donor directories and useful electronic tools such as references to donor management systems. It will blend into the various tools and resources that will be permanent features of the website, which will host discussion forums on resource mobilization and collect and share experiences from the field. In this way, we hope that a richly textured medium of exchange and learning will evolve and help us all in the quest for self-reliance.

Ultimately, this entire enterprise is about building relationships that can advance our common efforts to be effective resource mobilizers. AKF has benefited from a number of seminal relationships in bringing this enterprise to this point. The Global Citizens' Alliance, CIVICUS, AKF's co-sponsor in this publication, has been a creative and resourceful partner. Earthscan is a rare commercial publisher with its strong commitment to our social mission and a disciplined eye for production quality. Several support organizations actively field tested and reviewed these materials, notably the Karachi- and Zanzibar-based NGO Resource Centres, and the South Asia Fundraising Group. Twenty leading development practitioners from Latin America, Africa and Asia have written commentaries on the handbook. The Ford Foundation's India office sponsored the South Asia review process, along with AKF (India). All of these contributions are acknowledged with the deepest gratitude.

Looking forward, AKF plans to build on this growing network to fashion a set of distribution and support partnerships for the full set of Holloway-related materials – the handbook, trainer manual, multimedia electronic course and resource kit, and website. AKF invites individuals and organizations that would like to learn more or might like to become part of this network to contact AKF at ngoe@akdn.ch.

David Bonbright
Director, NGO Enhancement Programmes
Aga Khan Foundation
January 2001

Preface

BACKGROUND

In 1996 Bruce Shearer and Leslie Fox were asked by CIVICUS to compile and edit a book on the subject of resource mobilization for civil society organizations. The published book was called *Sustaining Civil Society – Strategies for Resource Mobilisation* (CIVICUS, Washington DC, 1997). The contributions to this book came from all over the world, and, for the most part, supplied their text by mail.

I was one of the contributors to the book, co-authoring the chapter on 'Accessing Government Resources'. At the CIVICUS Assembly in Budapest in 1997, all the contributors finally met, talked about the book, and talked of what more needed to be done. It was generally agreed that the book needed to be turned into usable training materials so that the ideas in the book could be made widely available to what CIVICUS called civil society organisations.

I had been doing training courses for civil society organizations (CSOs) in Asia and Africa on the subject of resource mobilization, and had been an associate and resource person for the workshops of the Resource Alliance (previously known as the International Fund Raising Group – IFRG), but had always felt the lack of a conceptual framework for CSO resource mobilization work. Following the Budapest meeting, I studied the book intensively, appreciated greatly its conceptual framework, and developed the materials from it into a four-day training course. Thus I tried it out initially in Delhi with South Asian CSOs through the January 1998 Development Management Course of Participatory Research in Asia (PRIA). Modifying it on the basis of that experience, I tried it again in a very different context in Budapest in May 1998 at the International Fund Raising Workshop for Central and Eastern European CSOs through the Civil Society Development Foundation. Finally, I modified it again for Jamaican CSOs in June 1998 through the training programme in fundraising provided by the Social Investment Fund of Jamaica.

From these three experiences of South Asia, Central Europe and Jamaica I boiled down the essential elements of the book to produce a four-day training course for Southern (and Eastern) CSOs in resource mobilization – and added to it, where necessary, from other sources. The most valuable parts of the CIVICUS book are, in my opinion, the conceptual framework of the three ways to access resources (Accessing Existing Wealth, Generating New Wealth and Mobilising Non-Financial Resources) and the fine case studies assembled by Lee Davis. My thanks to CIVICUS for allowing me to adapt it.

The Aga Khan Foundation, through its programmatic interest in strengthening civil society, was interested in accessing this material for its own programmes and wanted the materials to be available more widely than simply through contracted training courses. The Aga Khan Foundation therefore asked me to produce my training materials in the form of a handbook and a linked trainer manual that would help civil society organizations in the South to learn more about the different approaches to resource mobilization. These were prepared in a 'beta' edition for the 3rd Biennial CIVICUS Global Assembly in Manila in September 1999, and distributed to participants with a request that it be 'tried and tested'. In addition, the Aga Khan Foundation organized a number of field trials and professional peer reviews of the beta edition. I received subsequently many useful comments from those who had read it and tried it out, and these have been incorporated in the text.

The result is the handbook that you have in your hands. The trainer manual presents the material in this handbook in the format of a four-day course, and includes overheads, handouts, exercises and guidelines for trainers/facilitators. It is available free to anyone who wants to use it at the website: http://www.ngoenet.org/public. Both the handbook and the trainer manual are being developed further into an interactive CD-ROM version and a web-based 'learning resource' that will allow prospective resource mobilizers to enter a course of instruction in their own time, and at their own pace and place. Users of any of these materials are invited to join the resource mobilization discussion forums and electronic newsletters (listservs) facilitated by the Aga Khan Foundation via the same website. I look forward to contributing to the website, but the expectation is that it can become a peer-to-peer learning environment in which you the practitioners will answer each other's questions, share case studies, and build new tools to advance the field.

How to Use this Handbook

This handbook is produced by a practitioner in the field of promoting civil society organizations for social change, and is addressed to other practitioners who also work in this field. Examples of good (and sometimes bad) practice are taken from the experience of the author, augmented by the case studies from the CIVICUS book. The analytical framework (mostly expressed in Chapter 1) derives from the author's experience and valuable inputs from Alan Fowler and David Bonbright.

The book introduces the reader into a variety of approaches to resource mobilization, suggests key areas to think about if the reader were to try such approaches with his/her own organization, provides case studies of organizations from all over the world that have used such approaches, and suggests (at the end of the book) further reading where more information can be gained as well as resource organizations that can help further. The reader is assumed to be a person who is connected to the work of CSOs in the South and East and who is interested to know more about the financial self-reliance of such organizations. Experience has taught me that such people may vary from those for whom this is a completely new (and challenging) field and who need to get a feel for the range of possible options, to those who have already accepted the need for financial self-reliance, and are looking for more information and ideas.

As mentioned before, the book arose from a training workshop. For those CSO support organizations who would like to use the material for a training workshop, there is a companion volume – the trainer manual – which provides a facilitator's guide to the text, a complete set of materials to turn into overheads, a complete set of handouts, and instructions for exercises. This trainer manual is for a four-day workshop that ends with time for participants to plan which of the approaches they will choose, and how they will plan to implement it. As mentioned before this is available on the web at: http://www.ngoenet.org/public I suggest that the handbook be provided to participants at the end of the training workshop as a record of the workshop and as a reference book for the future.

I would be very happy to get email feedback from anyone using the handbook or the trainer manual. My email address is: holblenk@cbn.net.id

USE OF TERMS

Civil Society Organization

The term civil society organization (and its acronym CSO) is used to refer to the organizations that are the target of this book. This is a positive descriptive term that states what we are talking about (as opposed to the negative term 'non-governmental organization' or NGO), and reflects increasingly common usage. I would like to stress, however, that this term does cause confusion in some quarters, because of the word 'civil', which refers to citizens and is not a normative term for 'civilized' or 'civil' meaning 'polite'. Citizens, associating neither for power or profit, are the third sector of society, complementing government and business, and they are the people who constitute civil society organizations. The book advocates greater use by citizens, working through CSOs, of the domestic citizen resource base, and less reliance on foreign funding. (Note, however, that the terminology may be different in the case studies, which are taken from other publications.)

NGOs

The term 'NGO' is generally avoided in this handbook, despite the fact that it is currently a common term. It is used to describe a subset of the larger world of CSOs. While CSOs can encompass grass-roots organizations, citizens' movements, trade unions, cooperatives and NGOs, and other ways in which citizens associate for non-politically partisan and non-profit motives, 'NGOs' generally refers to the formal registered public benefit development organizations which are often largely foreign-funded. They do not have to be foreign-funded (and this book advises them not to be), but at present that is their situation. In eschewing the term 'NGO', this handbook emphasizes the need for development-oriented CSOs to shift from foreign aid dependence to the local citizen base.

Southern

The term 'Southern' is used to mean 'coming from countries in the South and East' – what are otherwise referred to as 'developing countries' and 'countries in transition'. Civil society organizations in the North may find the materials useful as well, but the handbook is directed intentionally at CSOs in the South, many of whom have become dangerously dependent on foreign funding.

Resource Mobilization

This term is used to be more comprehensive than the usual 'fundraising'. 'Fundraising' suggests that someone else has funds – and approaches need to be devised to access their funds. 'Resource mobilization' includes two other concepts: first, that non-financial resources are also important; and second, that certain resources can be generated by the CSO (or by CSOs acting together) rather than accessed from other sources.

Acknowledgements

The other sources that I have used to expand and deepen the materials in the CIVICUS book (and whose value I gratefully acknowledge) are:

NGOs Funding Strategies by John Bennet and Sarah Gibbs, INTRAC, Oxford (1997)
A One Day Orientation to Alternative Financing by Richard Holloway, Pact Zambia, Lusaka (1996)
Striking a Balance – Enhancing the effectiveness of non-governmental organisations working in the field of international development by Alan Fowler, Earthscan, London (1997)
Towards Greater Financial Autonomy – a guide for voluntary organisations and community groups by Piers Campbell and Fernand Vincent, IRED, Geneva (1989)
The Unit of Development is the Organisation, not the Project by Richard Holloway, Johns Hopkins University School of Advanced International Studies, Washington, DC (1997)
The World Wide Fundraisers Handbook – a guide for Southern NGOs and Voluntary Organisations by Michael Norton and published by the Directory of Social Change in collaboration with the Resource Alliance, London (1996)
The Virtuous Spiral: A Guide to Sustainability for Non-governmental Organisations in International Development by Alan Fowler, Earthscan, London, 2000
The many publications of the Program for Non-Profit Organisations of the Johns Hopkins Institute for Policy Studies, Baltimore, USA (www.jhu.edu)

Apart from books, this publication has gained greatly from comments received by readers and users of the earlier 'beta' edition. Many of these comments, particularly from the Resource Alliance (formerly the IFRG) and South Asian Fund Raising Group (SAFRG), are gratefully acknowledged and incorporated (thanks to Murray Culshaw, Roshni Sharma, Jasreet Mahal, and Nidhi Bhasin). I also received a great deal of help in editing from Nadia Keshavjee of the Aga Khan Foundation, and in general inspiration and encouragement from David Bonbright of the same organization.

Thus, with the permission of CIVICUS, and with thanks to Miklos Marschall, past executive secretary of CIVICUS, and Kumi Naidoo, present Executive Director of CIVICUS, this handbook (and the companion trainer manual) is produced under contract to the Aga Khan Foundation and offered to all CSOs who have realized the urgent need for CSO financial sustainability and for less dependence on foreign donors – and who are looking for materials to use. I hope that the materials in this handbook prove to be useful, functional, realistic – and that they lead to large numbers of Southern development CSOs diversifying their funding sources.

Richard Holloway
Indonesia
January 2001

About the Supporting Organizations

AGA KHAN FOUNDATION

The Aga Khan Foundation, created under Swiss law in 1967, is a private, non-denominational development agency. Its mission is to promote creative and effective solutions to problems that impede social development, primarily in Asia and East Africa. It has branches and independent affiliates in 12 countries. Common Board membership ensures consistency of policy and approach.

The Foundation focuses on a small number of specific development problems by forming intellectual and financial partnerships with organizations sharing its objectives. Most Foundation grants are made to grass-roots organizations testing innovative approaches in the field.

With a staff of only 148 worldwide, a host of cooperating agencies and thousands of volunteers, the Foundation reaches out to vulnerable populations on four continents, irrespective of their race, religion, political persuasion or gender. In 1999, it funded 106 projects in 13 countries and spent US$82 million.

CIVICUS

CIVICUS: World Alliance for Citizen Participation is an international alliance dedicated to strengthening citizen action and civil society throughout the world. Our vision is of a worldwide community of informed, inspired and committed citizens who are actively engaged in confronting the challenges facing humanity. CIVICUS' special purpose, therefore, is to help nurture the foundation, growth, protection and resources of citizen action throughout the world and especially in areas where participatory democracy, freedom of association of citizens and their funds for public benefit are threatened. CIVICUS' goals include promoting an enabling architecture for civil society, promoting citizen participation in civil society and helping build the global civil society movement.

List of Acronyms and Abbreviations

AKF	Aga Khan Foundation
AMO	alternative marketing organization
BFRG	Bangladesh Fundraising Group
BIRDEM	Bangladesh Institute of Research of Diabetes and Endocrine Metabolic Disease
CBO	community-based organization
CDS	Child Development Society
CEO	chief executive officer
CHIN	Children in Need
CIDA	Canadian International Development Agency
CIVICUS	World Alliance for Citizen Participation
CSO	civil society organization
CSR	Corporate Social Responsibility
EU	European Union
GRO	grass-roots organization
HIPC	Highly Indebted Poor Countries (Initiative)
IDRC	International Development Resource Centre
IFRG	International Fund Raising Group (now known as the Resource Alliance)
IGA	income-generating activity
IMF	International Monetary Fund
INAISE	International Association of Investors in the Social Economy
IRED	Innovations et Reseaux pour le Développement
ISP	Internet Service Provider
MFI	microfinance institution
NGO	non-governmental organization
NORAD	Norwegian Agency for Development
OECD	Organization for Economic Cooperation and Development
ORAP	Organization of Rural Associations for Progress
Oxfam	Oxford Committee for Famine Relief
PLWAs	People Living With Aids
PSP	Payment Service Provider
SAFRG	South Asia Fund Raising Group
SAP	Structural Adjustment Programme
UNDP	United Nations Development Programme
UNICEF	United Nations (International) Children's (Emergency) Fund
USAID	United States Agency for International Development

Part One

Setting the Scene

Chapter 1

The Larger Picture

As many commentators on civil society have written, it makes a lot of sense to think of the political economy of the modern society in three basic sectors – the state, business and a third sector defined by citizen self-organization. The state's distinctive competence is the legitimate use of coercion; the business sector's competence is market exchange; and the third sector's competence is private choice for the public good. Citizens mobilize through values that they share with other citizens and through shared commitment to action with other citizens.

Civil society is the dynamic equilibrium relationship among these three actors. As Salamon and Anheier (1999) have put it:

> *[A] true 'civil society' is not one where one or the other of these sectors is in the ascendance, but rather one in which there are three more or less distinct sectors – government, business and nonprofit – that nevertheless find ways to work together in responding to public needs. So conceived, the term 'civil society' would not apply to a particular sector, but to a relationship among the sectors, one in which a high level of cooperation and mutual support prevailed.*

The citizen sector becomes operational through citizens organizing themselves for action for the common good. Formal organizations that result will be stronger if they address social problems together with government and business – and the most effective civil society organizations will be those that have a strong base in many different kinds of citizens in their country.

This handbook sets out to do two things – to change the way that civil society organizations think about their own scope and potential; and to provide tools that civil society organizations can use in mobilizing (mostly) domestic resources. The book is also interested in foreign resources that build self-reliance and sustainability. This challenges the prevailing orthodoxy of the aid system, which creates more and more dependency on foreign resources, and retards the development of an indigenous citizen resource base.

This handbook is based on the following beliefs:

- The existing pattern of support for civil society organizations in the South, which is largely based on foreign funding, is neither desirable nor sustainable.

- A variety of domestic resources are potentially available to Southern civil society organizations, but have not been adequately researched, attempted, or mainstreamed by them.
- Local or domestic support, expressed through local funding, is fundamentally important for the long-term sustainability of civil society organizations and their programmes.

For these reasons it is important for Southern civil society organizations to learn more about the different strategies for resource mobilization that are available to them.

This handbook will introduce you to 12 different approaches for resource mobilization, each of which will have its own rationale, and each of which will have its own advantages and disadvantages. Using these different approaches will not only change where your money is coming from, but may also change the way that your CSO thinks of itself and operates. The advantages and disadvantages may appeal to your organization in different ways.

THE NEED FOR RESOURCES

Civil society organizations need resources so that they can be effective and sustainable. As organizations look for strategies to mobilize resources, they should be guided by these two important principles, and assess the various possible alternatives from these two standpoints.

The place to start with any CSO or group of CSOs is where they are at present. To set the scene for new ideas in resource mobilization, each CSO should look at, and list, its present resources. Then, for each one, it should give its origin, advantages and disadvantages from the point of view of effectiveness and sustainability. The result of this exercise is likely to show the CSO that it is relying on a very restricted number of resources. For many development CSOs, the exercise reveals a heavy reliance on grants from Northern donors, and that many of the grants have disadvantages of different kinds from the perspective of effectiveness and sustainability. The main advantage of such grants, on the other hand, is that they are available, that such funds are indeed offered, and that they are usable by the CSO community. Because they exist, such grants have become the norm. Other forms of resource mobilization seem strange. Because they are unfamiliar it is assumed they are difficult.

The other result of this exercise, particularly when practised with a large group of different CSOs, is that it will throw up a number of different experiences beyond grants from Northern donors. These experiences will probably be of less importance financially than the foreign grants, but will allow participants to appreciate the range of other possibilities that exist, and allow interorganizational learning based on actual experience.

Resources, particularly money, are not value neutral or value free. They bring certain baggage with them, depending on their origin and culture. Some CSOs will have strong reactions to some kinds of resources (like, for instance, resources from the corporate community), but will accept the possibility of resources from individuals. Other CSOs will start from different perspectives. The important point at present is to be open to a range of possibilities and to suspend critical judgement until you have understood them better.

The CSO world is very likely to change. Some of these changes are already taking place, particularly the drying up of funds from Northern NGOs. Existing patterns of resources to Southern CSOs will likely fall into one or more of the following categories:

- They will not be available to your organization in the future.
- They have significant disadvantages that outweigh their advantages.
- They seem less attractive in relation to some other resources.

The Characteristics of CSOs

This handbook is based on the premise that there is a continuing need for effective, ethical, committed and sustained CSOs, whose main purpose is to improve the situation of the poorest and most disadvantaged people in the South. It is taken as a given that CSOs can do things which neither of the other national development actors – the government and the corporate sector – can do on their own. If this premise is accepted, it is obvious that CSOs need resources to allow them to have an impact on their chosen field of work, and to sustain them so that they can continue to have such an impact. The question is which resources and how they can be acquired.

While most CSOs indeed have as their purpose the improvement in the lives of the poorest and most disadvantaged, there are increasing numbers of 'pretender' organizations who call themselves by the name of CSOs, but whose purpose is different. Such organizations are created for personal income or private interests, or as a front for governments or businesses. Precisely because such pretenders are challenging the CSO world, and because such 'bad apples' can spoil the reputation of the citizen sector as a whole, it is valuable to reiterate the most important characteristics of civil society organizations before we look at what such CSOs need, and how such needs can be met.

Civil society organizations created in the public interest, both North and South:

- are driven by values that reflect a desire to improve lives;
- contain elements of voluntarism (ie are formed by choice, not by compulsion, and involve voluntary contributions of time and money);
- have private and independent governance;

- are not for anyone's profit (ie they do not distribute profit to staff or share-holders);
- have a clearly stated and definable public purpose to which they hold themselves to be accountable;
- are formally constituted in law or have an accepted identity in the culture and tradition of the country.

WHAT DO CSOs NEED?

What do such organizations need in order to be effective and sustainable? There are five basic requirements:

1   Good programmes that actually do improve lives and can be shown to do so, as opposed to programmes that claim to do so, but which actually have not had the impact desired.
2   Good management which will make sure that any resources are efficiently put to the service of the good programmes. Good management also means a proactive practice of performance accountability, including rigorous public reporting.
3   A commitment to sustainability: CSOs need to appreciate that their mission is unlikely to be achieved quickly and that they need to be involved over the long haul. CSOs need to be marathon runners rather than sprinters.
4   The financial resources to support the good programmes, the good management and the sustainability mentioned above.
5   Local support, which includes:
    - a supportive political, legal and fiscal environment in which they are enabled to exist and flourish;
    - good human resources to work for the NGO;
    - a good reputation built on the credibility they have acquired from their good programmes;
    - supporters from a variety of different sources (local development agencies, national governments, specific groupings in society, the general public);
    - and, specifically, well-placed champions who can defend them when they are under attack, and promote them when they have something of wide significance to offer.

THE PRESENT PATTERN OF CSO RESOURCES

Before we look at the different ways of mobilizing resources that may or may not suit your organization's circumstances, it is useful to get an overview of the ways

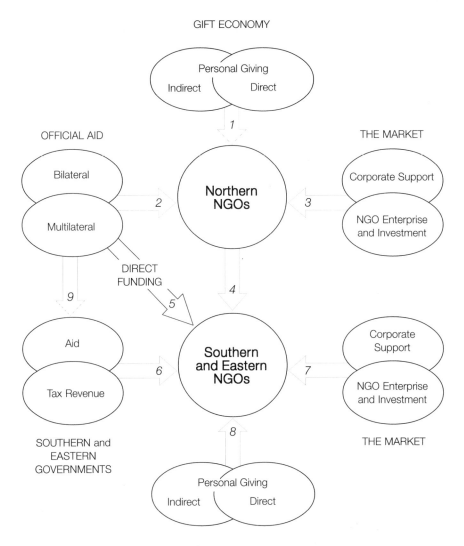

GIFT ECONOMY

Personal Giving

Indirect   Direct

1

OFFICIAL AID

THE MARKET

Bilateral

Northern NGOs

Corporate Support

2

3

Multilateral

NGO Enterprise and Investment

DIRECT FUNDING

9

5

4

Aid

Southern and Eastern NGOs

Corporate Support

6

7

Tax Revenue

NGO Enterprise and Investment

SOUTHERN and EASTERN GOVERNMENTS

8

THE MARKET

Personal Giving

Indirect   Direct

Source: Alan Fowler (1997) *Striking a Balance*, Earthscan Publications, London
Note: Use of NGO not CSO

Figure 1.1 *Striking a Balance*

that resources come to CSOs in the world. Figure 1.1 illustrates how both Northern and Southern CSOs receive their funding.

In the South, CSOs can expect the possibility of resources from the following:

1   Northern governments
   • Directly as bilateral assistance (Channel 5).
   • Indirectly as multilateral assistance (Channel 5).

- Via Northern CSOs (Channel 4).
- Via their own governments as bilateral assistance relayed to CSOs (Channel 6).
2   Northern CSOs directly (Channel 4).
3   The market
   - From businesses (Channel 7).
   - From CSO's enterprises, including investments (Channel 7).
4   Citizens
   - Directly as gifts (Channel 8).
   - Indirectly as support (Channel 8).
5   Their own governments directly, national and local (Channel 6).

Research done by the Johns Hopkins Institute for Policy Studies in a number of countries in the North suggests that the greatest flow of resources for Northern CSOs comes from government, followed by the market, followed by the gift economy. This reflects the pattern of government contracting of CSOs to supplement their work for them, and the large number of Northern CSOs (particularly foundations) that have large investments.

The same Institute for Policy Studies has done some research in a limited number of Southern countries. It is clear that the largest amount of resources available for CSOs is from Northern CSOs, and increasingly from Northern governments directly. All the other sources of support, however, are potentially available to CSOs, even if, at the present, they have not availed themselves of them. It is useful to think how CSOs could construct their own unique mixture of government, market and citizen support to help their work. Think of the resources that come into your own organization, or an organization that you know, in the terms described above, and think of these both in terms of financial and non-financial resources.

The Existing Pattern of Resources for CSOs

At present it is likely that the subset of CSOs oriented towards development work are dependent on a limited range of resources. The greatest dependence is very likely to be on foreign grants, and it is likely that the funds which make up these grants come from Northern CSOs or from Northern bilateral donors. The grants most likely come in the form of projects – time-limited, fixed budget funding for carefully defined activities. Figure 1.2 gives a visual picture of the situation experienced by many CSOs. It illustrates:

- A CSO with only two sources of funding – foreign project funding, and much smaller local fundraising.

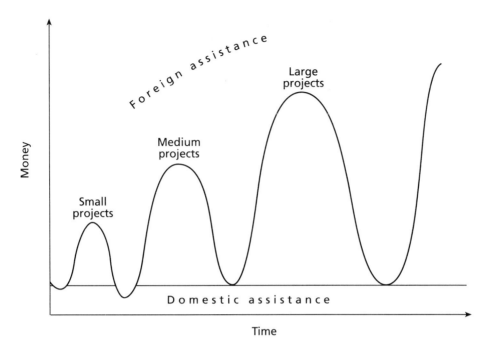

Figure 1.2 *The Usual Situation of CSO Financing*

- A CSO whose dependence on foreign funding increases over time, and the proportion of whose local funding, while it remains steady in absolute terms, decreases relative to foreign funding. It may even decrease in absolute terms.
- A CSO dependent on and vulnerable to time-limited project funding, which brings it back to zero after each project grant is expended.

Such dependence is not new for CSOs, but because the amount of grant money that is being offered by Northern donors has increased greatly during the 1990s, the dependence is getting greater and more widespread. At the same time some types of foreign funding, particularly funding by Northern CSOs, has been decreasing – and CSOs are vividly aware of their vulnerability due to their reliance on a few funding sources. From time to time the total amounts of foreign funding that is available to CSOs in a particular country may increase for a while, due to a disaster or a move towards policies cherished by foreign donors, but the trend, on average, is down.

Many CSOs have been shaken into awareness of how precarious their situation is. For a long time CSOs assumed that they would continue to be funded from Northern sources ad infinitum; indeed, some new CSOs defined themselves as 'NGOs' specifically to attract foreign funding. While it is true that many CSOs have frequently complained about the limitations and frustrations of relying on Northern donors, not many have decided to do without them or find alternatives to them.

While foreign funding is becoming more precarious, there are a few situations where the opposite is happening. Where large CSOs can help donors to disburse large amounts of money in ways that are administratively convenient to them, Northern donors actively seek them.

Dealing with Northern donors has become part of the learned experience and knowledge base for CSOs. They have learned which donors do what, how they want proposals written, what words of what development fashion are important to whom, and how to deal with the occasional donor visits. The care and maintenance of Northern donors has become an important skill for those who work for CSOs. It is expected that development-oriented CSOs will be supported by funding from foreign countries.

Let us look, by analogy, at the situation of CSOs in the North when they first started, and were working on very similar subjects as the present civil society organizations in the South, such as child rights, cooperatives, environmental health, women's rights, and the care and welfare of those marginalized and forgotten by society. There was no foreign source of funds for such organizations as Dr Barnardo's, the early friendly societies and cooperatives, the Anti-Slavery Society, or the Votes for Women organizations, when they were first starting. If there had been, they might have developed very differently. Instead they relied on building societal awareness of the problems they identified, seeking contributions from well-wishers, building up their financial assets, and trying to change injurious government and business policies.

By contrast, many CSOs in the South have been nurtured from birth by funds from Northern sources, often to the exclusion of funds from any other source. They are very dependent on such sources, and if the funds from such sources dry up, they are left very vulnerable to closure. Very few of these Northern resources to Southern CSOs have been in the form of financial investments that build long-term financial strength – they have nearly always been time-limited funding for specific projects which ceases once the project is over. In addition to this, the Northern funds have often been made available with a number of conditions. Some of these conditions have been unhelpful and distracting from the main task of the CSOs.

WHY NOT JUST RELY ON FOREIGN FUNDING?

The first four of the requirements mentioned above (good programmes, good management, commitment to sustainability, financial resources) may be met by foreign funding, given helpful and serious foreign donors, but there are strong reasons why foreign funding cannot help you with the fifth (local support), which is essential, however, for an organization's long-term sustainability.

Some of these reasons are:

1   Foreign funding does not build local support for your work, nor does it build local supporters. As long as you are seen as being supported by foreign funds, local people will not feel the need to help you with funds or other kinds of support. They will assume that you have money from overseas, and that you can buy whatever you need. Moving people from that preconception to one in which they feel that your worthwhile work is worth their support, is very difficult.

2   Foreign funding makes you politically vulnerable to accusations that you are only doing the work because you are paid to do so, or because you are obeying the instructions of some foreign power that may have some concealed motives to the detriment of your country. Development is a political process, and foreign funding provides ammunition to detractors – especially those in government – that you are being used politically by foreigners.

3   Foreign funding throws into sharp contrast the very basic contradiction that development CSOs promote and urge self-reliance among the groups that they work with, but do not themselves practise what they preach. If self-reliance is an important aspect of development, then the development CSOs should pay as much attention to it as the people with whom they work.

A Statement of Belief

As CSOs look hard at the questions involved in resource mobilization and accept that there are alternatives to the approaches that they have been practising to date, a leap of faith is required. CSOs need to be convinced that if they wean themselves from foreign funding, support of some other kind will be possible, and that they will be able to mobilize the resources they need to do the work they think needs doing.

The credo is that if Southern civil society organizations pursue a mission and perform functions that are valuable to society, if they communicate this well to the public, business and government, and if they undertake well thought-out efforts to obtain the resources needed to perform these functions, then, in most circumstances, such resources will be available.

CSOs have to think this concept through, given their knowledge of their own societies, and given their assessment of their own abilities to make strategic changes in their ways of operating. The examples given in this handbook are designed to add to their thinking, and to enable them to accept that article of faith. Specific ways to implement the credo which fit their strategic analysis of themselves and their society are the subject of Part Three of this handbook.

Part of this strategic analysis will mean considering the risks to their organizations of pursuing an alternative financing approach. Will they be diverted from their mission? Will they be able to acquire the management skills necessary? Are they prepared for the increased accountability and transparency to the public? Another part will mean considering the benefits of being supported by your own efforts or by your countrymen and women – mobilizing mass support for improved policies and practices; educating people about the real situation and the ways to solve it; attracting large volunteer commitment and contributions to your work.

This credo, of course, does not suppose that all CSOs will continue to be supported in the manner to which they have become accustomed. Many CSOs do not perform functions that are valuable to society, and many of them are not competent at mobilizing resources. Many CSOs have been artificially sustained by foreign funding that they have not used well, and probably did not deserve to have in the first place. Readers probably have many examples of unhelpful CSOs.

Let us be clear that many CSOs will not continue to exist in the future. Many people who are involved with the citizen sector will not cry on this account since the rising tide of foreign funding for local CSOs over the last 20 years has lifted not only bona fide development CSOs, but many free riders who contribute little or nothing to society. These foreign aid parasites will be the least likely to develop a local citizen base. This is not to say that there are enough CSOs to respond to the existing need. There is a huge need for more active citizen participation in public benefit activities, and this should translate into more civil society organizations. The credo is, however, that if you do good work, and if you are competent at requesting support for your good works, you will likely be supported by the resources of your own country – with such support perhaps being supplemented by foreign funding, but in no way dependent on it.

Chapter 2

Overview of Possibilities

WHAT ARE THE ALTERNATIVES?

Conceptually there are three categories of ways to mobilize resources:

1   Accessing existing wealth (from private and public sources). There *is* wealth out there – with individuals, institutions, governments, businesses – and the name of the game is persuading them to give it to your organization.
2   Generating new wealth (through market-based approaches). It is possible for your organization to generate wealth by using the market in one way or another.
3   Capitalizing on non-financial resources. With local support, good will and a good reputation, many people will be prepared to gift time and goods to your organization.

Let us look at these categories one by one.

ACCESSING EXISTING WEALTH FROM PUBLIC AND PRIVATE DONORS

Before we look at the individual strategies for capturing existing wealth, it is important to reflect on how this might be different from what CSOs are doing at the present.

Capturing existing wealth is basically what aid-dependent CSOs have been doing up to now. They have been applying for the wealth of (specifically) Northern CSOs and Northern governments, and trying to capture it for their own purposes. There has been much talk of partnership in the relations between CSOs and Northern donors, but to varying degrees of mutual respect and mutual inter-dependence, funding relations basically obey the golden rule – those who have the gold, make the rules.

There has been much posturing around the central point that Northern donors would like to have their funds used in certain ways and for certain purposes as they determine, and CSOs would like to use the Northern donors' funds in ways that they determine. Where those interests and purposes coincide, real partnership can occur, but increasingly it is becoming a world where Northern donors are only prepared to contract CSOs to do what the Northern donors have decided needs doing.

The present situation is that:

- There is a decreasing pool of Northern resources.
- There is increasing competition for such resources (both between CSOs and, where such funds originate with bilateral donors, between Southern CSOs and Northern CSOs).
- The present practice has given us a legacy of dependency in which CSOs make their applications and wait for Northern donors to agree or disagree. The decisions are not made locally, and are not under local control.

In the future we need to shift our ways of relating to existing sources of wealth, both Northern and Southern: new thinking is required. We look towards a future where:

- There will be strategic joint ventures between CSOs and sources of existing wealth (whatever they be) in which both sides plan together for mutual benefit and both sides win, rather than the South being dependent on the North.
- There will be increasing attempts to build institutional sustainability so that CSOs, after capturing some of the existing wealth, build up their own wealth, rather than have to keep trying to capture wealth time after time.
- Philosophies and practice of partnership will become common in which all contributors think through what needs to be done and what their various comparative advantages are. Various parties' needs for resources, and access to the existing wealth, will be more transparent, involve more local decision-making, and will give mutual benefit to all parties, rather than CSOs trying to find the right code which will unlock the safes of wealthy organizations or individuals.

The following are suggestions for the resources to be mobilized through accessing existing wealth:

1　Indigenous foundations.
2　Individual philanthropy.
3　Grass-roots CSOs.
4　Government.
5　Foreign development agencies.
6　Businesses.

GENERATING NEW WEALTH

Coupled with the acceptance that CSOs will always operate through acquiring wealth from others has been the reluctance on the part of CSOs to generate wealth themselves. CSOs have often been involved in helping others to generate wealth for themselves – as in vocational training, small-scale credit, entrepreneurship training etc – but they have not often seen that they also have the opportunity to generate wealth for their own organization.

In some cases they have not known how to do it, in other cases they worry that such endeavours and enterprises will take them away from their own mission, and in some cases they have felt a distaste for the world of business, and have not wanted to enter that world.

There are, however, plenty of examples where CSOs have been able to generate money, both through enterprises that are linked to their mission, and enterprises that are entered into purely as a source of revenue. Provided they have been clear why they are doing it, what human resources are needed and how it should be managed, many CSOs have found income through enterprises.

The following are suggestions for mobilizing resources through generating new wealth:

1 Production and trade.
2 Conversion of debt.
3 Establishing and operating microcredit programmes.
4 Tapping social investment.
5 Building reserve funds.
6 Using the Internet.

CAPITALIZING ON NON-FINANCIAL RESOURCES

This category is a cross-cutting theme which runs through all the ways of accessing existing wealth or generating new wealth. Whichever way of mobilizing resources that you decide to use, always remember that there are some relevant non-financial resources that can be tapped. The ways of mobilizing non-financial resources include:

- Volunteer time.
- Volunteer skilled labour.
- Goods and materials.
- Experience.
- Seconded professional personnel.
- Training.

- Access to public policy fora.
- Access to services provided for non-profit organisations.
- Champions.

Since these ideas are cross-cutting and will not be dealt with separately in the chapters that deal with each particular approach to mobilizing resources, it is useful to spend some time on them here.

Volunteer Time

Elements of voluntarism is one of the fundamental characteristics of CSOs (see p5). In most CSOs this breaks down into:

- Free time being given by the Board of Governors (also called Trustees, Executive Committee etc, depending on what legal form is employed in your country).
- Free labour and discussion time being given by beneficiaries of the CSOs' programmes, often in the name of participation.

Volunteer time is more than just this: it means that supporters of the work of your organizations offer to give their time and expertise freely for the good of your organization. Depending on their abilities, this can involve a great variety of ways in which they can help your organization.

Of all the tasks that need to be done to keep your organization moving, many of them can be done by people who are not professionally trained to do the main work of your organization, whatever it is. Such work may be on the administrative side (typing, filing, mailing), on the fundraising side (organizing events, collecting funds, building up membership), or in a variety of fields where general work needs to be done (driving, telephoning, message taking).

Identifying people who have time and are willing to give it to your organization is not always easy, particularly when most people are short of money and need to be paid. Sometimes people find your organization and offer to help because of the reputation of your organization. Working out the ground rules between paid staff and volunteer staff is an important aspect of managing volunteers.

Volunteers provide their services free, and for this reason their contribution to your organization is sometimes undervalued by those managing CSOs. Volunteers have needs as well, and the good CSO manager takes time to learn these needs and to care for and maintain their commitment.

Volunteer Skilled Labour

This refers to skilled people who are willing to make a small contribution of their time and skills to help your organization (to help with the book-keeping, to service/ repair the vehicle, to write a brochure, to produce architect's plans for a building, to install a solar water heater, or a hundred other jobs where you need professional skills). Again, such people will be willing to give their services free if they admire and value the work that you are doing and you can show them a way in which they can contribute without too high a cost to themselves.

Another factor is that people will be willing to give your organization their time freely if they believe that you need it. If they believe that your organization has plenty of money and can pay for their services, they will not be too enthusiastic to give their time free.

Goods and Materials

This involves both second-hand materials and equipment (like computers, printers and furniture when a business office is replacing existing stock with new) and also gifts in kind (like paper, paint, engine oil, food, or anything else which your organization regularly or occasionally needs). Firms in particular can be persuaded more easily to help with something that they deal in, at less cost to themselves, than asking them to help by donating money. Again, it is important to have a good reputation, but also to let it be known that you are interested in receiving second-hand goods. Always be ready to acknowledge your givers publicly so that they get the recognition and publicity they deserve.

Experience

Organizations could benefit from people who have experienced some of the problems and possibilities that you are facing in your organization, and who are prepared to give you the benefit of their experience. Lawyers, probation officers, auditors, salesmen, public relations officers, media people and many others might be able to give you extremely valuable advice at certain times that you need it, if they are motivated to help your organization, and are aware that you would be interested in receiving their help.

Seconded Professional Personnel

One possibility worth pursuing is to talk to existing firms and ask them if they are prepared to second staff to your organization for a while. Such people would work for your organization, but be paid by their original employer, and keep their position in the original firm. Depending on the work that your organization does, this might fit the firm's need to broaden the experience of young managers, or it might more fit the need to find work for older employees near retirement. Some firms see such secondments as their philanthropic duty, particularly if the head of the firm has a religious background in which notions of duty to society play a large part. To have a professional accountant work for your organization, or a farm manager, even if it is only for a few months, can be a tremendous help. If your organization was mounting for instance a fundraising drive, or an income-generating business, a seconded professional could be invaluable.

A different category of personnel comes from the academic community. It is entirely possible that the work your CSO is doing will be of interest (or can be made of interest) to academics interested in that field of work. Such academics can study your organization, can provide you with data and insights, and can be involved in 'participatory action research' ie research carried out with clients or beneficiaries of your CSO which leads to further action.

Training

Here the possibilities are of outsiders coming to train your staff, or your staff being able to undergo some training outside your organization, both opportunities being provided by some organization or person free of cost. This could have a tremendous effect on your staff's morale, and be something for which you could never afford to pay.

Access to Public Policy Fora

Sometimes your organization's work would be enormously enhanced if you could get certain policies or practices changed – possibly government policies (local or national), possibly local business practices, but you cannot get yourself into the circles where such matters are discussed and such decisions are made. Strategically placed people who are well-disposed towards your organization can introduce you to, for instance, the land allocation board, the juvenile court, the agricultural extension services, the district officer, senior government and corporate personnel, and politicians, and at least allow you to present your case in the place where important decisions are made. This may also mean international policy fora where international agreements on fishing or drug use are discussed.

This can be one of the most important long-term voluntary gifts that a person can make to your organization, but it is not generally thought of as 'volunteering'.

Access to Services Provided for Non-Profit Organizations

In some countries, particular services are provided free for non-profit organizations, and your CSO may be able to access them. This could be space for public service announcements on the radio or television, free advertisements in the media, certain occupations or products reserved for clients of CSOs, tax concessions, free listing in telephone books, etc. This often requires research to discover what services are offered.

Champions

A variant on someone who can get you access to public policy fora is someone of position, reputation and authority who can champion your organization, speak for it, endorse it when necessary, and, perhaps most of all, defend it when it is in trouble. Relations between CSOs and the state are often tricky in many countries, and to have a 'godfather' (or 'godmother') who is highly placed and who can vouch for the bona fides of your organization and its purpose, can be very valuable (even life-saving in some circumstances, either for the staff or the beneficiaries of your organization).

Apart from a politically well-positioned 'godfather/mother', the support of a publicly known celebrity can be very beneficial to your CSO. It will likely get your CSO known, but there is the problem of the celebrity's celebrity waning!

Whatever other fundraising or income-generation strategies that you employ, always think of ways to acquire people's time or gifts of goods beyond money. Make it your practice to stop and think what goods and services could help your work, and then draw up a strategy to access them through some form of donation that will supplement your other resource mobilization strategies.

Chapter 3

Why Should Anyone Help a Southern CSO?

The purpose of this handbook is to widen the range of options that a CSO considers when trying to mobilize resources, and, in most cases, this means widening it in the direction of domestic resources. CSOs set up with foreign aid are relatively experienced in the world of foreign financing of local organizations, and they know something of the complex reasoning why foreign organization 'x' should support local organization 'y', but what is new terrain is how to attract support of your own countrymen and women.

A new challenge for most CSOs when they think of mobilizing a wider range of resources is to work out why a citizen or a business or a government in your own country might support the work of your organization. This requires thinking about the psychology and the culture of your country and the giving behaviour of its people.

In many cases, giving is traditionally linked to religion – of whatever kind. All major religions have institutionalized charitable behaviour, and have praised and recognized charitable giving as admirable and worthwhile behaviour. Part of the work that needs to be done is to expand people's horizons of charitable giving so that it moves from the personal to the organizational.

SOME POSSIBLE REASONS

Let us look at some of the reasons why people in your own country might give money to a civil society organization.

Because it is Doing Good Work

Here a potential donor moves into becoming an actual donor because he or she thinks that your organization is doing good and worthwhile work that should be supported. Such topics as helping the disabled, helping children, helping the aged are topics that most people would consider worth supporting, but, depending on how you present yourself and who you present yourself to, your organization may well find people who think that working with AIDS sufferers, with the illiterate or with homeless people is the kind of good work that they would like to support.

Because it is Doing Good Work More Effectively than Others

Here it is assumed that there are a number of different organizations that are working in the same field, but that your organization has shown itself as being more effective than others. Since people or organizations that are giving money are generally interested in seeing value for their money, a more effective organization is likely to attract donors more than one which does not seem so effective, even if they are both working on the same topic.

Because it is Honest and Responsible

This deals with an organization whose reputation as an honest and responsible organisation is the selling point for that organization. Potential donors assume that they are doing good work, although they may not know very much about what they are actually doing. Their reputation and image is the aspect of them that persuades people or organizations to give.

Because it is Attractive and Persuasive

This refers to an organization that is very clever at 'selling' itself or its cause to the public, or to a potential donor organization. Its advertisements of itself and its work are snappy, bright, eye-catching, fashionable and persuasive. The cause that it is promoting is obviously part of the persuasion, but what persuades a potential donor to become an actual donor is the attractive and persuasive way in which the ideas or the organization are communicated.

Because it Appeals to a Particular Interest in a Potential Donor

Here the organization has targeted its appeal to a particular group or a particular section of the population that they believe will be interested in and sympathetic to that organization's cause. If you are seeking funding for AIDS sufferers, there is a good chance that people who have gone through the experience of having a relative die of AIDS, or people who themselves have AIDS, would be willing to support your work. If you are seeking funding for working with cancer victims, it is likely that those who have had the experience of a member of their family dying of cancer will be interested in helping your cause. The skill lies not just in deciding who may be sympathetic to your cause, but finding them and making the appeal. This can apply more widely than the causes mentioned above. A business that suffers from the extra costs involved in making corrupt payments may well be interested in supporting work to fight corruption.

Because it is Potentially Useful to a Potential Donor

An organization may make an appeal that others can see as having some advantage for themselves. Banks may consider that microfinance programmes are useful to them because today's recipient of microcredit may well become tomorrow's bank customer and thus fund microcredit activities. A business wanting to break into a new market or a new country may want to support something in that new country that will show it to be a public-spirited organization. A government may well want to show itself on the international stage as doing something in a particular field – eg slum rehousing, or biodiversity, or environmental conservation – and your organization may offer them that chance. Your organization thus may be able to offer potential donors a chance to help themselves, and from this appreciation both parties can benefit.

Another spin-off of this approach of enlightened self-interest is that the commercial firm or government may well learn about the social problems and issues of society through their association with your CSO, and become an advocate on your behalf, as well as a possible donor.

Because They are Asked

This may seem very obvious, but opinion polls conducted by fundraising agencies have shown consistently that the reason why people and organizations have not given to a particular cause or organization is that they have not been asked. If you do not ask, you do not know if people or organizations will respond.

In many cases people are concerned about a particular issue, like, for instance, AIDS orphans or street children, or drug addicts, or prostitutes, but do not know how to make a contribution that will make a difference. Your organization may offer them such a chance, and they will respond favourably because they have been looking for such a chance, but nobody had asked them previously. You do not know who will be your supporter unless you start asking, and you may well be surprised.

Because it Has No Other Source of Funds and May Collapse

This is obviously not a strategy that can be used frequently or people will assume that your organization is very badly managed, but urgency and a sense of crisis is sometimes a persuasive argument in fundraising.

Although these arguments have been listed separately, they are very much interwoven. A person who is inclined to support a programme fighting alcoholism because his/her uncle was alcoholic will not support your organization, even if it is working in this field, if he/she does not believe that your organization is well managed and effective. A potential donor who is entranced by your persuasive and attractive advertising may not contribute if the cause you represent – eg birth control – is against his/her religious convictions.

The purpose of this section is to help you to realize that the arguments you advance to foreign donors for support of your organization and your programmes and projects may need to be reworked and reassessed when the target for funding is a local business, a local government or local people.

COMMUNICATING TO ORDINARY CITIZENS

When you are dealing with people in your own country, and your donor (or potential donor) is Mrs Phiri (eg an individual) or Abu Bakr Cement Company (eg a firm), or the Ministry of Community Development (eg a government department), or the Brightwell Foundation (eg a local foundation) – please substitute here names from your country – there is a different psychological dynamic from when you are dealing with foreign funding agencies like Oxfam or the Norwegian Agency for Development (NORAD), or the United Nations Development Programme (UNDP) or the World Bank.

Apart from the content of the language, it is very common for CSOs to talk to their donors in English, or whatever is the language of the donors. It is also very common for CSOs to give themselves English names (or names in the language of the donors). Not only do CSOs need to learn to communicate in words and phrases that the ordinary people of their country can relate to, but they may also need to learn to communicate their work in the vernacular of their country (which most people understand) rather than English.

The name of your organization is fundamentally important. Does the name actually say what you do? Can everyone understand it easily? What language is it in? Do you think that it needs to be changed to appeal to national, as opposed to international people?

When the most common way of being funded is foreign donors, CSOs need to learn the elements of this language, and to be able to use it. If CSOs are trying to raise funds or mobilize resources from people who are not part of this circle, they will need to learn how to speak in the language of ordinary people. They will need to learn how to communicate what they do (and what they want support for) in words that people understand.

Those involved in the development business will recognize that the field of development has developed its own jargon, its own 'insider' language, and its own shorthand for communicating between professionals in the field. Key words or phrases like 'empower' or 'stakeholder' or 'beneficiary' have become common currency in a language that is shared between development financiers and development practitioners, but are not in common usage among the public.

The most important statement about your organization – the one that will not only provide the essence of your identity and your purpose, but will also be the one that has greatest currency in your country – is the mission statement. Most CSOs have appreciated the need for a mission statement as a short, informative statement of what their organization does (and thus, by implication, what it does not do). It is an important exercise to write it down and look at it in the context of this new audience.

A clear mission is very important for a CSO on many levels: it is important because it shows clear thinking in the organization, and it is important to communicate that to others. Think about the mission like this:

1   The mission is something that is created by the organization and by the constituency that the organization represents – it is *their* product and the statement of their purpose for the organization's existence. This is the organization's reason for being, and which needs to be communicated to potential supporters.
2   The mission is the way that the organization focuses and mobilizes its resources – human, organizational, and financial. By that statement, all concerned with the organization know the purpose for which they are working, organizing, and seeking funds.
3   It is the compass against which you plot your forward journey, and your requirements for funding. You are requesting or creating funds so that they fit and advance the mission – you are not creating the mission to fit the funds that are available.

After you have worked on your mission statement, ask others if it communicates clearly to them what your organization does. Ask people completely outside the development business what it means to them. Does it communicate well? Can you translate it into the vernacular of your country, or your region? Is that possible without many changes? If you translate the vernacular version back into English (or your 'colonial' language), what does it look like? Is it very different from the original mission statement?

The chances are that your mission statement is not something that can easily be understood by the man or woman in the street, or on the footpath. If you are hoping to appeal to them, you may well need to rethink your mission in terms that they can understand.

Is it possible for you to produce a one-line slogan for your organization that tries to encapsulate its essence in an even more condensed form? Try to create a slogan or phrase for your organization that grasps its essence, like an advertising slogan, eg DHL International: 'We carry out your promises'; *Daily Post*, Lusaka: 'The paper that digs deeper'; M-Net, South Africa: 'We won't stop the magic'. The corporate world is usually good at slogans, but the CSO world can also create effective slogans – Action Aid: 'Giving people choices'; Christian Aid: 'We believe in life before death'. Can you develop a phrase that communicates clearly and attractively to local people what your organization does?

Educating Ordinary Citizens

Apart from using good communication as a tool for resource mobilization, CSOs are in a very good position to educate the public about the issues in society for which they will subsequently be asking for assistance. One of the very important roles of CSOs is to expose wrongs, to inform the public and authorities of the real situation of the poor and disadvantaged, and to challenge society's ignorance, prejudice, or rejection. CSOs using good communication skills will be able both to inform and educate the public and also to seek their support (part of which will be financial). An organization in Indonesia exposed the terrible conditions under which children in North Sumatra were forcibly marooned on exposed fishing platforms in the sea where they had to catch fish for their masters/employers or not get fed. Their very competent exposure not only aired the issue, but brought them a considerable income from those who were previously unaware of the situation.

CSOs have a lot to learn from journalists who are expert at putting over a story in language that people can understand, and in ways that command people's interest. CSOs may like to think about how they can involve journalists in their causes.

Diversity

It will be obvious by now that one of the great differences in moving from financing that comes from international development agencies to financing that springs from local sources is an increase in diversity. You will need to engage a great variety of diverse parties to assure yourself of support from inside your country, and you will also need to develop skills that allow you to communicate with them in ways that they will understand.

In order for us to work on each of the 12 approaches for accessing existing wealth or creating new wealth, we will need to engage with some of the following range of people:

- The people who you are assisting – hopefully the people who will become your partners in trying together to improve their lives.
- The local community who live around the people who you are trying to help.
- The wider public in your country.
- Specialized groups within the public – like industrial workers, bankers, or women, or coffee farmers, or veterans.
- The business community, or particular business houses.
- The media.
- Academia or the intelligentsia.
- The government, at both national and local level: both regimes (political parties), the legislature, the executive, and the judiciary.

In your engagement with these diverse parties, let us be absolutely clear what we are trying to do. We are trying:

- to educate them;
- to encourage them to support our work;
- to persuade them to give funds to enable us to do the work that we have said we want to do.

Two Kinds of CSOs and their Different Dynamics

At this point it is important to note the difference between the two kinds of CSOs – the organizations that support and benefit their members, and the organizations that support and benefit others ('third parties'). It is important to make this clear since these two kinds of organizations use funds in different ways:

1   **A member-benefiting organization**

This mobilizes funds from different sources for an organization that manages programmes to benefit members of the organization. This is the case of a community-based organization (CBO) or a mass membership organization (sometimes called a people's organization).

2   **Third-party benefiting organization**

This mobilizes funds from different sources for an organization that is managing programmes whose beneficiaries are other people, not the members. This is the case with most NGOs who are basically intermediary organizations – taking funds from one group or groups and utilizing them, through its intermediary position, for the benefit of others who need help, or on a clearly identified cause.

It is important to clarify the difference between these two organizations to your prospective donors who otherwise might be surprised. For both types of organization there must be a clear 'public benefit', irrespective of the immediate beneficiaries, otherwise there would be no principled reason for people to give.

It is important to tell people what you are raising the money for. It is also important that people understand what their money will be used for if they give it. The CSO has the fiduciary responsibility (which is legal language for the trust that people have given you) to spend their money on what it told people it would spend the money on, and on nothing else.

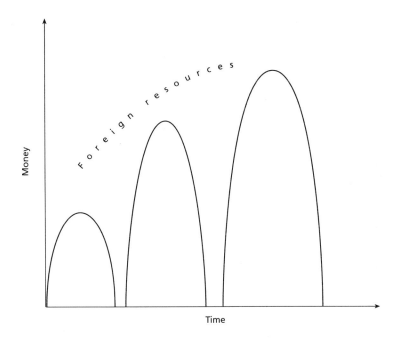

Figure 3.1 *A CSO that Derives its Financing from a Single Source*

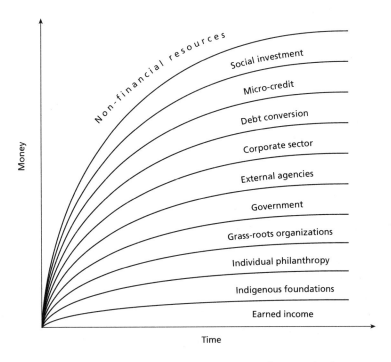

Figure 3.2 *A CSO that Derives its Financing from Multiple Sources*

The rest of this handbook will illustrate how a CSO can derive its financing from a variety of different sources. Figures 3.1 and 3.2 give a schematic (and highly simplified) view of the difference between a single source and a multiple source organizaton. The first point, therefore, is that there are a variety of approaches for resource mobilization. The second is how they can be identified and used. The rest of this handbook looks at each of these approaches and at some of the issues involved in these 12 different approaches.

Part Two

Ways of Mobilizing Resources

Chapter 4

Revenue from Earned Income

Being 'Businesslike'

Most people who are asked to define 'businesslike' would produce words like 'efficient', 'hard-working', 'professional', and 'competent'. In discussing how CSOs can operate like businesses, it is necessary to think about business behaviour and patterns of thought. Producing goods and services to sell and thus create income – either for an individual or for an organization – requires a businesslike approach, in the literal sense of the word. But this produces a problem: it is well known that most people who are involved with CSOs are not familiar with business principles and business practice. CSO people have rarely had to face the kinds of decisions and the ways of working that are common with businessmen and businesswomen. Some CSO people claim to abhor actively such behaviour. And yet, if CSOs are going to get involved in earning income for themselves, they must start thinking and behaving like business people.

Two aspects of the problem then surface:

1   How much experience do CSO people have with business?
2   Do CSO people want to behave like business people?

If CSO people have a very negative impression about running a business, they are unlikely to take this idea up as a way of creating income for their organization.

Consider two exercises:

1   The first is simply to ask people that you know who work in CSOs to tell you what involvement they have ever had with business, either directly, or through relatives (were their parents involved in business?), and what kind of business it was. Ask those who have had involvement with business what problems they (or their relatives) faced in the business world.
2   The second is to ask the same people what they would name as the characteristics of business people.

It is likely that the results of these exercises will demonstrate that:

- very few CSO people have had experience of business (most people working in the sector have come from social work, religious life, the civil service, academia);
- very few people have any idea of the kinds of problems that businesses face;
- some CSO people have negative impressions of business people.

It is not uncommon for people working in the citizen sector to talk about business people as ruthless, selfish, and corrupt. On the other hand, some people will put forward very positive characteristics of business people – like the fact that they are hard working, good decision-makers, far-sighted. It is important for all who are working in the sector to think and talk about their perceptions of business, and hopefully to agree that there is no reason why a respectable and admirable person cannot be involved in business, and no reason why they and their organizations cannot be involved in business.

The Issue of 'Profit' and 'Non-Profit'

As soon as any discussion starts on the issue of CSOs running businesses, CSO people are very likely to raise the issue of their non-profit status. This is not just a legal issue – 'can a CSO make a profit?' – but also a philosophical one that is often based on unclear ideas about what 'profit' is. This, in turn, reflects the lack of familiarity that most CSO people have with the world of business. It is important to make a few definitions clear:

1   For an ordinary profit-making business, the word 'profit' means an excess of income over expenditure that is distributed to private hands, either to the owners of the business or the shareholders in the business.
2   For a CSO, any income is reinvested, or ploughed back into the work of the organization in line with its objectives. It is not 'profit' because the work is never finished. The income is always used for the work of the CSO, and it is not distributed for private gain.

Therefore a CSO can try hard to get as much income as it can for its operations, and this is not profit, since it is never distributed to people beyond the work of the organization. A non-profit organization can indeed (and should) raise or generate income, but this does not compromise its non-profit status.

This is not difficult for most people to understand because they have seen people selling T-shirts or crafts to raise money for an organization, but it is made more complicated by public and government attitudes, and by CSO practice.

When governments set up the laws or statutes under which CSOs are legally registered, they have usually tried to make a distinction between civil society organizations and businesses, and one of those distinctions is that CSOs are non-profit making. The statutes should state, 'non-profit distributing', but unfortunately they usually do not, and few government officials are prepared to listen to the arguments from the CSO side to clarify this point.

The public, which, as mentioned earlier, has become increasingly worried about NGO pretenders masquerading behind a social purpose, is quick to be suspicious about businesses that are run by CSOs. The public is inclined to see this as another way in which CSO people are enriching themselves, rather than helping other people. It is important that there are clearly different registration procedures between businesses and CSOs; it is also important that CSOs try to raise or generate revenue – but this must be done openly and transparently with clear public information.

CSO people are used to revenue-generating enterprises for their beneficiaries (often enterprises run on charity rather than on business principles, like schools for the blind selling embroidery, or vocational training centres selling furniture) in which the income is used to run the programme. They are not, however, so accustomed to generating revenue for the organization itself to pay for its administrative and running costs separate from individual programmes.

Because of these problems of perception and attitudes, CSOs – and those who are involved with CSOs (like government) – need to be made aware of the legitimacy and rightness of CSOs generating money for their own operations. The laws will be different in different places, but CSOs need to argue the point with whatever authorities that make the rules, that:

- CSOs should try to generate income.
- CSOs should not be prevented from doing so by restrictive legislation, as long as the income is not distributed to private individuals as if it were a business.
- CSOs should not be expected to rely on foreign contributions.

DIFFERENT WAYS OF EARNING INCOME

With those general problems clarified, let us look at the four different ways in which CSOs can earn income:

- Building income together – as part of a community economic activity.
- Recovering (all or part of) the costs of programmes.
- Income from enterprises that are linked to the CSO's mission.
- Income from enterprises that are not linked to the CSO's mission.

Let us take these one by one.

Building Income Together as Part of a Community Economic Activity

Here a CSO has helped to establish an income-generating activity (IGA) for its target group – eg chicken farming, or pottery. In the usual way of things, the target group people earn their income from this activity, and the organization's role is to set it up and provide the required training. What is suggested here is that the CSO has a share in the activity, either by way of a share of the income, or itself runs a part of the operation, just like one of the target group people. Just as the IGA earns the target group some income, so it does the CSO.

There are two incidental factors that contribute to the value of this strategy:

1   It encourages the CSO to make sure that the IGA is, in fact, generating income. This may seem obvious, but many CSOs continue to run highly subsidized 'enterprises', without checking if they are actually generating revenue in excess of costs. CSO stories are replete with unsaleable baskets, and loss-making craftware. If the IGA makes no money, the CSO makes no income.
2   If the CSO is taking a part of the income, it forces the CSO to consider what part of the income is going to the producers. It is not unknown for a CSO to set up an IGA that is actually exploitative of the producers, either because of ignorance of market pricing, or possibly avarice. An income for the organization should not mask the exploitation of the producers.

Illustrations of this way of earning an income are: CORR – The Jute Works from Bangladesh, and Jairos Jiri Association from Zimbabwe (see p35).

Cost Recovery

Many CSOs are confused by the idea of cost recovery. They sometimes say, 'Since CSOs are meant to work with the poor, and many of them are set up to provide services to people who cannot afford to buy these services, how can they possibly expect the poor to pay (wholly or partially) for these services?' Experience has shown that the poor are not absolutely poor, and that they can pay for some of the costs of services, provided those services are services that they need and want, and provided that they are delivered in ways that they can have some control over. It is true that the very poorest may well not be able to pay, but there is room for cross-subsidizing – ie charging enough from the ordinarily poor, so that free (or highly subsidized) services can be offered to the poorest.

Some CSO people object to cost recovery from political or ideological convictions. They feel that just as the state should offer free services to the poor, so should CSOs. They see such organizations as an aspect of the welfare state.

Other CSO people have a different ideological perspective – that the market economy is what should be promoted, and that in a market economy everything has a cost.

Case Study 4.1 *CORR – The Jute Works*

CORR – The Jute Works started life in Bangladesh after the War of Independence in 1972 to offer some way of providing income to the large number of widows in the aftermath of war. It capitalized on the local crop, jute, and the skills of village women in making pot holders (thika) from the jute fibre – a skill that was purely functional in the village context where such hanging-pot holders were an essential part of handling liquids. CORR – The Jute Works saw an export market opportunity in this skill by buying the thika from the women to sell overseas as decorative plant-pot holders. It arranged the women into groups and gave them training in new products and techniques, bought their output, and placed it overseas through alternative marketing organizations and a mail order catalogue.

The sales of the craft work were divided: part of the income went back as a dividend to the producers (and this was used by the women's groups for a variety of useful activities like improved water supplies or tree planting); part went to pay for the administrative costs of CORR – The Jute Works; and another part was put into a reserve fund. From time to time, depending on the size of the reserves, CORR – The Jute Works would fund development activities for the women's groups beyond the craft operations, such as latrine building.

CORR – The Jute Works was living and expanding on the backs of the craft production of the women, but was doing so in a way that enabled the organization to be both self-sustaining and a source of further funds. CORR – The Jute Works has not taken foreign funding since its third year of operations (1975). The most difficult aspect of its operation is keeping up with the buying patterns of the people in the countries to which they export, and feeding these ideas back to the manufacturers. The enterprise (and the organization) will only continue if they remain smart entrepreneurs who research the market and produce for it, being prepared to change as the market dictates.

Source: The Worldwide Fundraiser's Handbook: A Guide to Fundraising for Southern NGOs and Voluntary Organisations, DSC and Resource Alliance (1996)

The most persuasive arguments in favour of cost recovery come from some people's experience that people (poor or otherwise) do not value services that are free: if they have to pay for them, they will not only value them more, but will use them more effectively.

It is fairly straightforward to argue that services that help people to make money should be paid for, and nearly all microcredit schemes, for instance, almost as an article of faith, demand a service charge (see Chapter 13, Microcredit Programmes). Some vocational training programmes also require payment for the courses undertaken, sometimes up-front, and sometimes from the income earned following the course when the graduate is gainfully employed.

It is also fairly straightforward to argue that services that help people to become more productive and thus to earn more for themselves should be paid for. Thus,

---

CASE STUDY 4.2 *JAIROS JIRI ASSOCIATION*

The Jairos Jiri Association, probably the largest organization of its kind in Africa, serves more than 10,000 disabled people annually in Zimbabwe. It has a wide range of programmes including schools and psycho-therapy treatment centres for children, a scholarship programme to assist secondary and post-secondary students, a training centre and farm for agricultural education, and outreach and follow-up integration programmes: altogether there are 16 centres all over the country.

One of the Association's main activities is the provision of specialized education plus vocational training for the disabled. It operates five craft shops, two furniture factories and a farm that produces food for nearby residents and graduated trainees. These craft shops provide a great opportunity for disabled people to obtain skills and to produce high quality goods including furniture, artificial limbs, wood, metal, and leather crafts and china.

In addition to serving as training centres and as a way to publicize the Association, the craft shops generate a considerable amount of revenue for the Association. Jairos Jiri began to generate income in 1959 to support its programmes. The goods produced by the disabled clients are sold in goodwill stores to the general public, including tourists. The Association covers 43% of its expenses from the revenues of these shops. They started their operations with external donor funds (about US$200,000) and have been producing profit since establishment.

One important lesson from Jairos Jiri is that the stores could not be managed as part of the charitable programmes. According to the Executive Director, they should have been operated as a separate business activity from the beginning, adopting business principles and strategies.

Source: Sustaining Civil Society – Strategies for Resource Mobilisation, CIVICUS (1997)

---

for example, literacy programmes, health and rehabilitation programmes, and land reform programmes are likely to increase individuals' earning powers, and such individuals could pay for the services either up-front, or with deferred payments once the greater income is earned.

If programmes, however, are dealing with the absolutely poor, or are providing services that have no earning potential (like tree-planting, post-disaster relief, help to people living with AIDS, birth control, early childhood development or orphans), it is difficult to think how the CSO can recover even part of the costs. In such cases there seem to be three possibilities:

- Applying the argument that people will find the money if they value the service.
- Part-cost recovery where the service has to be paid for but at a highly subsidized price.

- Cross-subsidies where the price of services is set at a level where the ordinary poor can afford it, but where enough income is earned to offer free services to a smaller number of the absolutely poor.

A CSO that is serious about thinking through cost recovery ideas needs to be entrepreneurial (Can tree-planting make money? Can condoms earn money?), but at the same time very pragmatic. If the service is priced beyond what the poor can afford, they will not use it, and the CSO's mission will be perhaps jeopardized. Some governments that have applied International Monetary Fund (IMF) structural adjustment programmes with cost recovery on clinic services, for instance, have found that the programme results in people dying at home because they cannot afford the costs of visiting the clinic.

An illustration of this way of earning an income is PROSALUD in Bolivia.

CASE STUDY 4.3 *PROSALUD – SELF-FINANCING HEALTH SERVICES*

PROSALUD's objective is to function without outside support, recovering its costs from the sale of its health services and products. In the health sector, recovering costs by charging fees for health services delivered to low-income families is often considered impossible. Charging fees that are high enough to cover the costs of services appears to discriminate against the very poor, who live on the edge of subsistence and often have no money on hand to pay for services or goods of any kind.

This conventional wisdom, however, seems to be belied by the PROSALUD experience in Bolivia. PROSALUD already has a growing system of health facilities in operation that are self-financing through the fees that it charges. Clients are predominantly low-income families. Services include free preventative health care and child survival interventions. Curative services are provided free of charge to families that cannot pay (between 8 and 13% of PROSALUD's patients). PROSALUD has conclusively demonstrated the feasibility of self-financing primary health care services, even in a country as poor as Bolivia.

Source: The Worldwide Fundraiser's Handbook – a Guide to Fundraising for Southern NGOs and Voluntary Organisations, DSC and Resource Alliance (1996)

Enterprises Linked to the CSO's Mission

Here the question that the CSO has to ask itself is: 'Are there any activities related to the organization's main work (or mission) which can make money from a different market?' For instance, is it possible to market for a price to a richer group of clients the same services that the organization is providing free to its target group? If the CSO is, for instance, running a nursery to produce fruit tree seedlings, can these be sold to wealthier farmers as well as given free to the target group?

Or, for instance, is there some new saleable product or service possible using the CSO's core experience? Consider this example of a CSO working with AIDS in a central African country: most of its work was free AIDS testing and counselling to the public. It realized, however, that shame and confidentiality were an important aspect of People Living With AIDS (PLWAs) and some people did not want to be seen coming to their free down-town clinic. It therefore offered a two-tier service in two different locations – their usual free clinic which was open to the public, and a more confidential service in another more secluded site, for which people paid. The income from the latter subsidized the costs of the former.

The CSO, however, had the skills to carry out the work of both the original mission, and the new variation of the mission. It was expanding its work in order to generate revenue, but in the general area in which it had experience.

Illustrations of this way of earning an income are Pact in the USA, and Yayasan Bina Swadaya in Indonesia.

CASE STUDY 4.4 *PACT: HEALTH INSURANCE FOR NGOs*

Pact, a US NGO, has a health insurance plan for its employees, as do many other US NGOs. The particular health plan is a good one and very well run. Pact found that other US NGOs were asking it for advice on running their own health plan, and were very receptive to Pact offering to include their organization into the Pact health plan. Soon Pact was earning a modest but important income from providing health insurance facilities for a number of other US NGOs. It knew how to do it, it could relatively easily scale up, it had a number of other interested potential customers, and it could do the work without undermining its services to its own employees.

Source: The Worldwide Fundraiser's Handbook – a Guide to Fundraising for Southern NGOs and Voluntary Organisations, DSC and Resource Alliance (1996)

CSOs need to do some brainstorming to consider what resources they are offering, and what they own, and then to think entrepreneurially if and how they can find some way in which these resources can make money for them. Is it possible that the CSO's set of skills and equipment be packaged differently and appeal to a different market? Can, for instance, the CSO's photocopier operate commercially in the evenings and at weekends? Can the CSO's computers be used in commercial training courses as well as be used for its administrative business? Can the CSO's accounting system be sold to others? Can the CSO's surveys of its working areas be sold to banks, advertising agencies, and government programmes?

An adventurous mind will find entrepreneurial possibilities in unlikely places: simply being in a place that others consider exotic is, for instance, a potentially saleable resource, as we can see from *Alternative Tourism* in Box 4.1.

CASE STUDY 4.5 *YAYASAN BINA SWADAYA*

Yayasan Bina Swadaya in Indonesia is an organization specialising in improving the lives of small farmers and fishermen through savings, credit, and the formation of cooperatives. Its early work was to encourage rural poor farmers to save their money and take out credit to expand their small self-employment possibilities. The Yayasan (which means 'Foundation') charged a service fee for the credit that went some way towards paying for the costs of the credit scheme. The Yayasan found that many of its customers wanted to raise chickens, but that obtaining day-old chicks was a real problem. It therefore went into the business of hatching and producing day-old chicks and selling them, making a small profit, to its customers. It found that other people apart from its target group also wanted this service and so it also started to sell day-old chicks in the market place. It started a small extension newspaper for its target group on improving farming practices, and found that this newspaper filled a need for a farmer's magazine that existed beyond its immediate target group. It also geared up its production for the market place. It then found that its skill and experience of running its original savings and credit operation was at a premium for other development agencies, and that other organizations wanted to know how this could be done. The Yayasan started a consultancy service, offering its senior employees on short-term hire to other development agencies.

Through its work with foreign development agencies it realized that there was a market for the kind of knowledge about Indonesian life that was part of its essential way of working, and so it offered alternative tourism services to the supporters of foreign development agencies. Everything that it did to make money was a spin-off from its original mission, based on skills developed in the course of activities connected to that mission.

Source: The Worldwide Fundraiser's Handbook – a Guide to Fundraising for Southern NGOs and Voluntary Organisations, DSC and Resource Alliance (1996)

Income from Enterprises not Linked to the CSO's Mission

Here the CSO is looking for anything that earns good returns on capital. To be successful, however, the organization should think of the following points:

- It should not require too high a degree of business acumen, since, as we have seen previously, CSOs are usually inexpert in this field. CSOs would not be advised to go into, for instance, the retail marketing trade or import/exports, but they might go into renting property or a meeting-room. Of course, if the CSO can acquire or hire business skills, this need not be a problem.
- It should not be anything that compromises the existing work of the CSO. An organization working with alcohol abuse or drug addiction would not be advised to open a bar, however lucrative it might be. The public would not consider the CSO to be serious.

BOX 4.1 ALTERNATIVE TOURISM

The usual kind of tourist is one who craves creature comforts familiar back home, but likes them packaged in an exotic setting. They are often unaware of the actual environment in which they spend their holidays since hotels and tour operators decide what they see and experience for them. There is, however, a small but increasing number of tourists for whom a visit to a foreign country is an 'alternative' opportunity to learn more about that country, including the reality of life 'behind the scenes'.

Basically there are two kinds of NGOs who have appreciated that they have special knowledge and experiences which are marketable and can earn money – those who offer tourists an introduction to the realities of life in a particular country – and can organize exposure tours to villages and aspects of rural and urban life that other tourists would miss (these are offered in India and Thailand, for instance): and NGOs who are involved in environmental matters who offer eco-tourism, that is specialized visits to places of particular environmental interest often combined with exposure to particular environmental problems (these are offered in Nepal and Madagascar, for instance). As with much tourism, the ethical problems arise not as a matter of principle, but when the numbers involved escalate. It is difficult for the most sensitive and committed tour guide to bring the 500th tourist to look at the misery of the rubbish mountain pickers of Bangkok, as it is difficult to preserve the wilderness conditions required for the interesting biological diversity in Madagascar under the visits of very many tourists, however pure the motives of the tour organizer.

Source: The Worldwide Fundraiser's Handbook – a Guide to Fundraising for Southern NGOs and Voluntary Organisations, Resource Alliance and DSC (1996)

- It should not be something that drains human resources from the main work of the CSO.

On the positive side, CSOs should look for ideas that capitalize on the free skills and experience of well-wishers to the organization. If someone offers the CSO a building, then it could go into the property renting business; if anyone were able to advise the CSO reliably that there was both a source and a market for second-hand clothing, then the CSO could go into that business.

A very important point for the CSO to consider is whether the income-generating activity can be compartmentalized away from its main work, and avoid interfering with it. If a CSO gets into a business unconnected with its mission, there is a strong tendency for the business to sap the strength of the organization's main work.

Positive and negative sides of this way of earning income are shown by the Zambian Red Cross and PROSHIKA in Bangladesh.

CASE STUDY 4.6 *ENTERPRISES OF THE ZAMBIAN RED CROSS*

The Red Cross in Zambia raises 87% of their income from the rental of offices and flats. The Red Cross has owned the original Red Cross building since at least 1964. They have also, in the past, received ownership of six flats that they have rented out since then. In 1991 they approached Finnish Red Cross for a loan in order to build a second building. Finnish Red Cross agreed, and when the building was finished in 1992/3, the World Bank rented the office space on the third floor (they have subsequently moved to larger premises).

Rental from the office space brings in a substantial amount of money, which is usually paid for a year in advance. The rent from flats is on a monthly basis. All of their administrative and most of their continuing project support come from rental together with smaller amounts of other domestic fundraising. For special projects of relief work, the Red Cross applies for funding from outside sources, typically their sister agencies (eg British or Finnish Red Cross, or their umbrella agencies International Committee of Red Cross and Red Crescent Societies). Mrs Munkanta says: 'We do not have the headache of chasing funds. We are able to operate in a more secure financial environment, which has allowed us to follow through with programmes and be innovative. You still have problems with flats being unoccupied or dealing with the demands of tenants, but it is generally a good experience.'

Source: Depending on Ourselves – Zambian Experiences in Domestic Fund Mobilisation by Hull and Holloway, Pact Zambia (1996)

CASE STUDY 4.7 *PROSHIKA, BANGLADESH*

PROSHIKA, a large Bangladeshi NGO, was helped by CIDA to buy a bus company that it intended to run as an income-generating enterprise. No-one in PROSHIKA had ever managed a bus company before, and the inter-city bus business in Bangladesh is not only very competitive, it is also pretty lawless as businesses try and capture passengers from each other. PROSHIKA soon got bogged down in problems of maintenance, ticket collection, cash flow problems, and, in the end, found that it was taking much too much of the senior management's time – time that should have been spent on the economic and social development work that PROSHIKA was set up to do.

Added to this the business itself was not making much money – certainly not enough to justify the management time that was being spent on it. Sensibly PROSHIKA divested itself of its bus company and stuck to what it was good at. It is now generating income for itself from a service fee on its large credit programme, by running an Internet service provider, and by renting out a spare floor in its own office block.

Source: The World Wide Fundraiser's Handbook – a Guide to Fundraising for Southern NGOs and Voluntary Organisations, by Michael Norton, DSC and Resource Alliance, London (1997)

Issues to Consider in CSO Revenue from Earned Income

Experience suggests that the following issues are likely to be important obstructions to the CSO's ability to earn income from enterprises.

The Conflict between a CSO Culture and a Business Culture

As an earlier exercise discovered, CSO people and businesspeople have different characteristics. It is well to recognize this rather than to expect CSO people to move easily between cultures. Some of the most successful CSO enterprises have worked because they have managed to attract competent businesspeople to the CSO who are prepared to work for a wage rather than a share of the profits. The organization has allowed them to run the enterprise according to their own experience, separate from its main work.

It is also true that a move into income generation may not be well received by some of the staff of your organization, who may consider that this was not the reason they joined, and opt to leave. The new ideas need to be discussed fully within the organization.

The Lack of Business Management Skills and Experience

This has been remarked on before. CSOs need either to engage in an enterprise that does not require such acumen, like renting buildings, or to hire in such expertise that will be paid from the income of the enterprise.

Planning/Allocating Human and Financial Resources

If a CSO is deciding to go into business by starting an enterprise, it must decide what part of its financial resources, and what part of its human resources (ie its staff) should be allocated to the enterprise. On the one side, the CSO may not be able to use any of its present financial resources because of its donors' regulations, and may need to fundraise separately for the enterprise (see later): on the other side, it may also find that its staff are not happy to be moved from working with street kids to running a printing press. The CSO manager needs to think through carefully the management implications, and also make sure that the board understands and agrees to the ideas. There are important questions to decide on, such as: 'Should the enterprise be managed as a separate entity?', 'What profit levels should be demanded?', 'To whom should the enterprise report?'

Access to Capital

Where can the CSO hope to get the capital with which to start an enterprise? This is a crucial matter for an organization, and one that often causes pessimism in a CSO that is otherwise interested in earning income.

There are a variety of answers to this:

- From money raised by the CSO separately from foreign sources, eg subscriptions, membership, local fundraising, and interest on investments.
- From funds specifically requested from foreign donors.
- From gifts in kind – eg a building.
- From a bank loan – just like entrepreneurs.

If a CSO is trying to get funds from foreign donors to start an enterprise, it must be understood that many donors do not yet think in these terms. They have not yet dealt with the paradox that they are trying to encourage the growth of CSOs and their self-reliance, but they are reluctant to invest in self-sustaining income-generation schemes for CSOs by which they may become self-reliant. Some donors are enlightened and are prepared to think in these terms (particularly Northern foundations), but many need to be educated by CSOs about the importance of such funding (see pp 83–89, Resources from Foreign Development Agencies).

Relations with Foreign Donors

Donors logically should be delighted that CSOs are thinking entrepreneurially, and should be very interested to invest in their enterprises in order to allow the CSOs to be financially self-reliant. Sadly, very few think like this, and some back up their position by reference to previous miserable failures in this area. It is often the case that previous attempts were poorly prepared.

In some cases foreign donor agencies have skills available to help CSOs because another section of the agency deals with small-scale industry and entrepreneurship development. There is usually a divide between the two fields, however, and CSOs wanting to start enterprises are not linked to these resources of the agency, since it comes under another department.

If a foreign donor is interested to support the entry of a CSO into an enterprise, it will ask the same sorts of questions that have been posed in this section; these are all important questions that the CSO should be asking itself in any case:

- Will the enterprise interfere with the main mission of the organization?
- Will the enterprise be profitable?
- Will the enterprise attract unwelcome or hostile comment?
- Will the CSO be able to run the enterprise?

Once the foreign donor has decided to support a CSO profit-making enterprise, it may have a variety of other support mechanisms with which it can help – funding, technical assistance, business assistance, sourcing of markets (for export goods), bank guarantees, and others.

Interdonor meetings at both a national and international level to discuss their responses to CSO enterprise creation are very much needed – too much of the present thinking about, and response to, the issue is ad hoc and unplanned.

Public Perception

If your CSO's name becomes more associated in the public's mind with, for instance, property rental than working with street kids, you may have a problem with the public's perception of your organization and what it does. The public and the government may be more than usually suspicious that your organization is a money-making scam for its directors. You will need either to be less overt about the income-generating side of your operation (eg call it by another name) or to spend some time educating the public that every time they rent your property they are helping street kids.

Legal Status

Following on from the points made earlier about the government's muddled understanding of CSOs that try to earn income, there may be complications about the legal status. In the UK, it is common for CSO income-generating businesses to be set up legally as tax-paying businesses with the profits then 'covenanted' – ie pledged, or legally agreed to be passed over to the original CSO. Such an arrangement clearly and transparently shows anyone that the enterprise is not for personal profit.

It is likely that initially all CSO-owned businesses will attract tax. Unless there is some blanket law to allow such enterprises to be given tax-free status, each CSO will probably have to argue the case for tax-free status enterprise by enterprise. The CSO should use the argument that the income earned will be used to deal with social problems for which the state would otherwise have to use its own resources, and thus ought to be rewarded by the state by releasing it from contributing to the state's income through tax.

CSOs will find that these ideas have to be argued against a possibly hostile audience, and that success is likely to be achieved by strength in numbers and influential champions (see p18, 'Champions' under 'Capitalizing on Non-Financial Resources'). One important resource that has become available recently to CSOs is the *Handbook on Good Practices for the Legal Environment for Non-Governmental Organisations*, produced by the World Bank and the International Centre for Not-for-Profit Law. This book, produced to provide advice to governments and the World Bank offices, is especially useful on the tax issues involving the NGO sector (see 'Further Reading').

Competition with the Business Sector

Part of the hostility to a CSO business and its requests for tax-free treatment is likely to come from the existing business community, particularly when the CSOs enter fields that compete with them – property, service provision, trading. Such people will not see why you should be able to undercut their prices because you do not have to pay tax, or because you are subsidized in some way. They regard this as unfair competition.

It is unlikely that CSOs will be too threatening to the business community, but this may be a problem in particular cases. There seem to be two ways of approaching this problem:

1   By educating the business community about the value of what your CSO is doing, and getting them on your side.
2   By persuading the government to declare that certain kinds of enterprises are reserved for CSOs and community organizations – this is the case, for instance, in Nepal for the handloom weaving of traditional Nepali men's hats, and in the USA, for the manufacture of car licence plates.

This problem, however, may be quite the opposite: businesses may be encroaching into areas that were previously considered to be the preserves of CSOs, which seems to be the pattern emerging in the USA.*

---

*   'The Nonprofit Sector at a Crossroads: The Case of America' by Lester M Salamon. In *Voluntas: International Journal of Voluntary and Nonprofit Organisations*, vol 10, no 1 (1999)

Chapter 5

Indigenous Foundations

WHAT ARE FOUNDATIONS?

Foundations are structures that are set up so that funds can be accumulated and made available in perpetuity to specific kinds of recipients as grants and/or loans to be used for specified purposes. Some countries have foundations that implement programmes directly as well as make grants to third parties who implement programmes.

Most cultures and traditions have created something similar to a foundation structure, very often for religious purposes. The original benefactor gives funds or a source of funds (like property or even a business) to the foundation and the income earned from that asset is available for the foundation to spend for its specified purposes.

Depending on the legal tradition in the country concerned, such funding structures may be called trusts as well as foundations, but they are basically structures whereby an individual or organization makes available funds for on-granting, on-lending, or operations for philanthropic purposes.

Such foundations may be set up by individuals, by business corporations, or by governments, but once they are set up they have a specific governance structure and are governed by the statutes under which the foundation or trust was established. They no longer belong simply to the individual, business or government, although the statutes, to a greater or lesser degree, may keep the control with the original benefactor. The Ford Foundation, for instance, which operates all over the world as a development agency and funder, was set up by the family of Henry Ford, the originator of the Ford Motor Company. For a long time, however, neither the Ford Motor Company nor the Ford family have been in charge of the Ford Foundation. It is governed by a self-perpetuating Board of Trustees made up of citizens who have been chosen for their particular skills and experience.

Foundations and trusts, however, are not features only of developed countries in the West. Charitable and philanthropic trusts exist in Japan, Korea, India, Pakistan, Bangladesh, Sri Lanka, South Africa, and in many countries of the world. They are a valuable feature of philanthropic life and need to be encouraged. Islam, wherever it is practised, has a well-developed version of the philanthropic foundation in *waqf* (see p 49).

What we are interested in accessing are indigenous foundations and trusts – structures that have been set up by nationals of the country to make funds available for a variety of purposes, some of which the CSO could access. In order to ascertain what foundations exist in your country, try the exercise of asking people you know who work in CSOs what foundations they know of, what their origins are, what their main interests are, and what CSOs have ever accessed their funds.

It is very likely that the majority of foundations or trusts that are known about are religious in nature, formed for the upkeep of mosques, temples, and churches, but it is possible that the business community, or a few wealthy individuals, and perhaps the government, have set up independent trusts and foundations for particular purposes.

WHY ARE FOUNDATIONS CREATED?

It is also a valuable exercise to discuss among people you know who work for CSOs what the motives may have been for the establishment of the trusts and foundations that you have in your country. If you know what the motives may have been, it may give you an advantage when you negotiate with them.

Some motives might be:

- Individuals (particularly successful businessmen/women) coming to the end of their lives and wanting to give back to society some of the income they have earned/raised during their lives – perhaps thus earning credits for the after-life.
- Individuals who want a particular interest of their own to be enabled to continue – eg traditional music, women's education, archaeology.
- Businesses wanting to prove themselves good corporate citizens and give back to society some of the profits they have earned/accrued, and preferring a separate organization to manage this rather than operating it from inside the business.
- Governments wanting to set up a structure that will not be a political football that is dependent on which party is in power, but a structure that will continue independently.

The question of the 'particular purposes' for which a foundation or trust is set up is one of the key factors when CSOs think of accessing funds from foundations or trusts. Since it is their money, the originators of the foundation or trust are entitled to specify in the founding legal documents exactly what their money shall be spent on, and this has to be followed by the governing trustees or directors. It is essential, therefore, that CSOs interested in accessing indigenous foundation funding should find out what the declared purposes of a foundation or trust is, rather than waste time pursuing funding that is reserved for a category (like children, or the aged), which may not be part of their work.

Accessing Foundations' Wealth

Depending on the legal system in the country and how it is operated, there are usually two kinds of trusts – private trusts (often set up by families to govern the inheritance of their property or to pay for their children's education) to which the public does not have access, and public trusts that anyone or any organization who meets the purposes of the trust or foundation can access.

Such public trusts, moreover, are bound to declare publicly how their funding has been spent, thus allowing the public to check whether they are consistent with the purposes of the original statutes (and have not been hijacked by a particular interest). The problem often for CSOs is to find out what foundations exist, what their purposes are, and what their money has been spent on. In some countries there are directories of foundations, but not by any means in all countries. A valuable job for a CSO coordinating body is to research and produce such a directory if it does not exist.

Such a directory should also clarify what are the procedures whereby people and organizations can apply for funds from an indigenous trust or foundation. It is important for CSOs to identify trusts and foundations in which there is a match between the two missions so that they do not waste each other's energy by making requests for grant support that obviously have no probability of success.

On the other hand, there are times when CSOs may wish to negotiate with the trustees/directors of the trust or foundation to persuade them that the CSO's particular cause is worth supporting, even if it seems outside the original purposes of the foundation. One way to do this is to argue that the original statutes had not considered a particular problems (like AIDS) and that the foundation should be made more relevant to current problems. Another way is to persuade the trustees/ directors that there are a variety of ways to deal with an identified problem (like, for instance, orphans), and that your way of working (for instance, home-based care, or adoption) is as valid and worth funding as the more traditional ways of dealing with the problem (eg building orphanages).

This approach is particularly possible with foundations that have been established for religious purposes. Within Islam, for instance, believers are encouraged to donate funds called *zakat*. Such funds are often used to buy food and clothes for the poor. Modernizing spirits within Islam have pointed out that such contributions do nothing to build self-reliance or diminish the number of the poor – the same people are there the next year for the same kinds of handouts. They have suggested that the *zakat* funds could be used to create a foundation for microcredit operations that would lend money to the poor to start their own businesses and, hopefully, escape from their poverty.

Depending on the way that religious practices are observed, it may be possible to persuade those responsible that religious trusts that have been set up to advance religion (often by building churches, temples or mosques) should also use their money for more developmental purposes (like health or education).

One example of an indigenous form of foundation in Islamic countries is the tradition of *waqf*. *Waqf* is a donation made by someone of property to Allah, and managed on that person's account by a group of trustees. It is often a gift of land or property, and the bequest is frequently rented out so that the income can be used for a charitable purpose. *Waqf* donations are frequently used to pay for the running costs of orphanages, religious schools, and clinics. The institution has many advantages – the donation is registered by a 'waqf board' and is tax free and the management is recognized as being a charitable duty for which no fee is charged.

So far we have been talking of mobilizing resources by accessing the wealth of indigenous foundations or trusts. Another (and in the long term, equally important) strategy is to encourage people or organizations with resources in your country to establish trusts and foundations, and to make available such resources for development purposes. Local foundations for local purposes are a valuable contribution to the philanthropic culture of a society, and CSOs could well benefit from them if they are set up. The USA has nourished a tradition of the community foundation, which is a foundation focused on community needs and supported by local contributions from individuals, businesses, and local government. Many Central and Eastern European countries have seen this model as being relevant to their own situations.

The case studies that illustrate indigenous foundations are Fundación para la Educación Superior, Colombia, and the Healthy City Foundation, Banska Bystrica, Slovakia.

CASE STUDY 5.1 *FUNDACIÓN PARA LA EDUCACIÓN SUPERIOR (FES), COLOMBIA*

FES was founded in 1964 to help a public university meet its cash flow and programme expenses. Given that Government disbursements were habitually late, the University was forced to borrow from local banks at high interest rates. At the same time funds received from foreign foundations were deposited in local banks without earning interest. These donors advised the university to set up a mechanism to promote donations from alumni and the local business community. The president and trustees selected 12 prominent civic and business leaders in Cali to establish a private foundation and an office for fundraising and development.

FES became independent in the early 1970s and its reach broadened. A Vice-President for Social Development was established to make grants, conduct research, and create seed programmes outside the original university.

FES's programmes provide financial support to NGOs and research organizations in the form of donations directly, and donations to Permanent Endowment Funds. These typically consist of money ear-marked for a specific purpose which FES matches with a 50% contribution and for which it serves as a financial manager. In 1994 there were 400 such funds, worth nearly US$22 million. FES's programmes focus on health, education, economic and social development, environment, children and youth and civil society support. To date, FES has distributed more than US$50 million in grants.

Source: Sustaining Civil Society – Strategies for Resource Mobilisation, CIVICUS (1997)

CASE STUDY 5.2 *HEALTHY CITY FOUNDATION,*
BANSKA BYSTRICA, SLOVAKIA

The Healthy City Foundation grew out of an earlier foundation in Banska Bystrica that went through an organizational crisis and survived through re-birth as a community foundation. Initial funding came from the city government which was persuaded that a community government would serve the public interest. Other support has come from external foundations, local corporations and individuals. The Foundation's budget is small – about US$30,000 per year and it has an endowment of some US$50,000. It is estimated that an endowment of US$500,000 is needed to support its programmes completely and sustainably.

The Foundation provides support to local civil society organizations that are working to improve the quality of life in and around the city. The amounts given are often small – less than US$300. Its programmes include environmental, neighbourhood, rural, women's and youth programmes. The youth programme is particularly innovative in that a programme advisory committee has been established from high school volunteers.

Source: Sustaining Civil Society – Strategies for Resource Mobilisation, CIVICUS (1997)

Chapter 6

Individual Philanthropy

Who Do You Give To?

CSOs are interested in accessing contributions from individuals to help their organizations, but if CSO staff, board and volunteers have never solicited funding from individuals, they should be aware that it involves interesting new psychological dynamics and a variety of learned skills. In order to understand something of the dynamics and skills involved in individual giving, it is useful for those who are soliciting gifts to reverse roles, consider themselves as givers, and examine what happens when they are asked to give.

A useful exercise is to ask people you know who work for CSOs to tell you of all the approaches that they have received formally and informally from people and organizations for donations over the last six months. They should say what was the organization (or person), and what they were asking for.

From this exercise, we can get a picture of the ways in which individual philanthropic giving is carried out in your country, and what are people's motivations. This may provide some interesting ideas.

Following that exercise it is both interesting and useful to discuss the ways in which philanthropy is culturally understood in your country. It is likely to be a combination of religious principles and kin, clan or tribal affiliations. Probably people in your country will feel that it is legitimate both to be asked to give and to give for the disadvantaged (particularly the disabled, and the victims of natural disasters) and for extended family members. How much further traditions of giving extend beyond that will probably be culturally specific to different countries. Possibly people in your country do not have a well-developed tradition of giving money, but are much more comfortable with giving food, shelter or in-kind gifts. An interesting local variant in Pakistan and Bangladesh is the Islamic tradition of giving skins from animals that have been sacrificed at religious festivals. These skins are given to orphanages or other charitable or religious organizations to be sold for income to meet running costs.

It will be interesting to see whether giving to organizations (as opposed to people) is an accepted cultural tradition in your country, and, if so, to what kinds of organizations, and under what conditions.

ORGANIZATIONS SOLICITING FOR FUNDS

When the discussion moves to organizations soliciting individuals for money, you are departing to some extent from traditional practices. You are asking for the disinterested giving of someone's own resources to an organization (not a person, and not necessarily a person you know) as an expression of solidarity with fellow human beings, even though they may be strangers (and may not be people who you have ever thought of helping before). This is, in many countries, a new way of thinking.

In some countries the joint family and the community have been the traditional caring mechanism. In other countries, particularly those that have evolved from a centrally planned economy, the state has been considered to be the agency that looks after the needy beyond the extended family, and foreign donors to be the agency which helps the state to do so. In the past, funding from both governments and donors has blocked both the need and the opportunity for people to give to people.

If you consider it possible in principle in your country for organizations to solicit funds from individuals, there are skills to be learnt. In order for you to make a good income for your organization from individual philanthropy, you will need to:

- Deal with large numbers of potential and actual donors.
- Learn special techniques required to identify them and ask them for resources.
- Have many people working for your organization as volunteers to solicit donations.
- Nourish and sustain those who have given in order to persuade them to give again.
- Have a simple and understandable message.

While CSOs are interested in receiving money primarily (because there are so many things that money can be used for), solicitations for individual philanthropy can equally well result in people being prepared to give your organization personal time, their sweat, goods and materials, or their good advice.

Many people consider that fundraising means begging individuals to give to something that you are committed to, while they may not be. Most people consider that this involves some form of persuasion of otherwise uncommitted, or even reluctant people. Many people feel unhappy and uncomfortable with the idea that they are trying to persuade others to give something against their wishes. But this is not the case; what is needed for many people who are thinking of fundraising from individuals is a mind switch, a new way of thinking, a paradigm shift in their approach.

Actually what they are doing is offering individuals a chance to be involved in something worthwhile. They are offering people a chance to get involved in their organization's mission – and the tactic is to offer that chance to people who are likely to be interested in it. Most people in the world are concerned about the plight of people who are worse off than themselves. To a greater or lesser extent they worry about such people, and they would like to help them. Many people do not know how best to help them, and, under pressure of their own problems and their own working lives, their concern is shelved or forgotten.

Your organization then approaches them and says: 'We are offering you a chance to express your concerns practically. We think you are as worried as we are about street children (or AIDS orphans, or battered women, or landless peasants – or whatever is your particular cause). We know that you cannot do a great deal yourself because of your other work, but we have decided to work on this full time, and we would like to offer you a chance of helping street children through helping our organization.' You are not begging someone to do something they do not want to do, but are offering people a chance to support something that they would like to support, but do not know how to.

KNOWING HOW AND WHOM TO ASK

Now, of course soliciting funds from individual philanthropists will only make sense if you are able to get donations from considerable numbers of people. Thus the skills involved in accessing individual philanthropy lie in:

- Knowing how to identify likely potential donors.
- Knowing how to ask them for their donations in ways that unlock their desire to help.
- Knowing how to organize the solicitation process.
- Knowing how to present your request for funds in a persuasive way.
- Knowing how to get both one-off and long-term commitment from people.

NGOs that have been used to writing project proposals to foreign donors will not be accustomed to the very different ways of soliciting funds from the man or woman in the street, or the man or woman on the footpath. We need some practice.

A very useful exercise for NGO people to get such practice is to think how they would explain their organization to the man/woman on the street/footpath, and how they would ask for funds, using a basic pro forma kind of fundraising brochure whose outlines appear below. CSO staff can use this format (or something like it) to try to write a sample fundraising brochure. They should try to be persuasive and informative. Other staff members can then look at the brochure and see what they feel about the brochure's power to persuade them to give.

1 Name of Organization	2 About the Organization	3 A Case Study	4 How You Can Help
Photo	....	....	1 ....
	....	....	2 ....
	....	....	3 ....
	....	....	4 ....
Mission Statement .... Slogan	5 Facts explaining why the organization is needed: 1 .... 2 .... 3 .... 4 .... 5	Photo Endorsements/Quotes about your work...........	Address ....

This exercise really reveals the differences between appealing to a foreign donor, and appealing to the man or woman in the street. Once you have tried out this exercise, and seen which approach at this kind of brochure seems most convincing, you need to think about how such a fundraising brochure could be targeted, and how you can identify likely donors.

Some suggestions for writing this sample fundraising brochure may come from the answers to the following questions.

What Sorts of People are Likely to Support our Mission?

You need to think whether there is a particular group of people within the public who are likely to be enthusiastic about an organization that is working on the particular problem or issue that we are concerned about. If it is anti-corruption, perhaps students and churches would be most enthusiastic; if it is women's emancipation, then women and women's organizations are likely to be concerned.

Who Should Support our Mission?

Here you need to think of the kind of people who are likely to be enthusiastic about your mission, but have not yet been made aware of what can be done, and of what you are doing. This implies some public education and social mobilization before they are ready to be approached for a donation. If your organization is working with people living with AIDS, it is likely that relatives would be interested in your mission, but need to be educated that organizations like yours exist and that anything can be done.

Who Do We Want to Support our Mission?

Here you are talking strategy – what groups within society are important for you to convince of the value of your work? Probably high on many CSOs' list would come the business sector, and perhaps the organizations of organized religion, and political parties.

You need to be aware of the cultural traditions in your society, but you need not be bound by them. Certain societies are keener to support education, while others are more interested in promoting the arts, but all of them can be made aware of the current problems of society, and the work that your CSO is doing to help with them.

Do not think that your fundraising must be directed only towards the rich people in your country. In most countries the poor give proportionately more than the rich, usually because they can identify with the problems you are describing better than the rich can. Fundraising from individuals works best when there are lots of small contributions that together make a significant amount. It is possible, of course, to dream of a single huge benefactor, but that hope often stays at the level of dreams.

While of course it is the money that primarily interests your organization when you are mounting a fundraising effort targeted at individuals or the public, there are also important non-monetary reasons for this kind of resource mobilization.

NON-MONETARY REASONS FOR SUPPORTING INDIVIDUAL PHILANTHROPY

There are many reasons, apart from the actual money that is collected, for involving your organization in individual philanthropy:

- Many hundreds (perhaps thousands) of supporters give your organization stability, particularly if you are clever enough to make sure that they move from a one-off to a regular contribution.
- Individual philanthropy supplements and balances unstable funding from foreign donors or governments.
- Individual donations give the CSO untied funds that it can programme as it wants (within, of course, the fiduciary responsibility it has to the donors). Such funding is typically not tied to particular expenses as is funding from foreign donors.
- Individual donations do not require elaborate proposals. As we saw from the fundraising brochure, we are persuading people on the basis of our mission, our reputation and our experience – not on the basis of an elaborate proposal, as with foreign donors.

- Following the same track, our financial reports are simply the reports of any responsible CSO – they do not need to follow the sometimes tortuous and complicated reporting conditions of some foreign donors.
- Individual donations mean that the NGO is now responsible and accountable to a large constituency of local people who have voted, in effect, for the NGO by their donations, and are your supporters for the future (unless you disappoint them).
- Individual donations mean that people have made a personal decision to help – not to leave it to the government or foreign donors or someone else – and this is beneficial for your society as a whole.

THE ENABLING ENVIRONMENT

There are other issues that determine the likely success of attempts to raise funds from the public.

The Economy

In times of boom, or at least in relative prosperity, people are likely to be able to give more. In hard times, people will probably give less.

The Culture

As we have mentioned before, there are likely to be cultural traditions about giving. However, few cultures remain static – they are changing, and changing dramatically. There is likely to be a new middle class in your country with money to spend, and they will be open to new influences. There are people exposed to foreign influences (like people returning after studying overseas) who will be open to new ideas. A smart fundraiser is a close observer of new cultural patterns.

Public Awareness of Society's Needs

If the public is unaware of some of the things that are happening in your country that need to be reformed, then part of your job will be the kind of public education which will create, in effect, your market for fundraising. If it is revealed, for instance, that most prostitutes in your country are actually debt slaves who have been bought from overseas, you may find a different pattern of interest from people who previously thought that prostitutes in your country had chosen that life for themselves.

The CSO's Credibility

However good your idea is, and however sincere your commitment, this will not result in donations from the public if there is some serious problem with your organization's credibility. If scandal has hit your CSO, if it is too closely linked to a political party, if it is seen as a vehicle for one person's glory, people will not put their hands in their pockets. Another point to consider is the 'standard of living' of your organization and its staff. If your organization is conspicuous by its expensive four-wheel drive vehicles and computers (what has been called 'the Pajero and PC syndrome'), the public may not want to respond to appeals. Similarly if your staff are seen to be rather wealthy, this may not attract public donations.

The Helpful Context

Simply asking people face to face to give money to your organization is the simplest form of fundraising; however, that requires large numbers of people to go out and do the asking. A society that allows people to pay by cheque, a society that does not condone stealing collection-boxes, a society that allows tax concessions for those who give to CSOs, are all societies which enable CSOs to collect from the public more easily. Part of this is a legal and fiscal environment in which people who pay tax can expect tax relief on their donations to non-profit organizations. Limit your expectations of reforms in this field producing great bonuses for CSOs, however, by looking at the number of people who actually pay tax in your country. In many countries the tax base is very small.

METHODS OF INDIVIDUAL FUNDRAISING

After this discussion about the nature of individual fundraising, how do you go about it? There are eight different methods discussed below, all of which will be possible in different ways in your country, and all of which need to be put through your own country's cultural filters. A ninth possibility is Internet fundraising, which is a new and growing field, and is treated separately in Chapter 15.

In Person

Here, people, usually volunteers working to help your organization, ask members of the public for donations. There are traditions of collection-boxes, or envelopes left to be collected later, of static collection-boxes left in shops, at airports, in public places. The principles are to try to collect in small amounts, but to collect many small amounts. Obviously, it is also very important to have honest people collecting for your organization, and some countries provide identification certificates for their collectors.

At the Workplace

While individual collecting drives can be mounted in factories or other workplaces, an important strategy for collecting at the workplace involves persuading the whole workplace to make a regular donation by agreeing a certain cut from their salaries every month. To achieve this the NGO needs to persuade both the management (who will be responsible for the deductions from the payroll) and the workers (perhaps through the Trade Union) to allow a small deduction from their pay. Experience shows that workers are more inclined to do this if they see that management is making an equal or at least a substantial donation to the same cause. While this practice is common in the North, few organizations in the South have tried it. The UK-headquartered Charities Aid Foundation is encouraging its use in the South (see 'Resource Organizations', pp 222–223).

At Events

Most countries have a tradition of fundraising events – dinners, concerts, sponsored sports events, sponsored walks, fairs, etc. Other countries find it useful to 'piggyback' their fundraising on existing events (like religious festivals) when people are inclined to be charitable. Most people with experience of organizing events comment on the huge amount of organizing time that is required – sometimes a disproportionate amount of time given the income finally received. There are possibilities of film premieres, pop concerts, art exhibitions – the possibilities are endless. It requires a creative mind to think up some new gimmick or new idea that people will have fun doing, and that they are prepared to pay you for the pleasure of doing – one recent innovation is sponsored bungee jumping!

Many events will become more attractive if a celebrity is involved – like a film star, a musician, or a sports personality. People may come to see the personality, but will stay for the event, learn about your organization and spend their money.

Through Direct Mail

Direct mail means sending a letter to someone asking for a contribution to your CSO. In some countries it is quite common; in other countries it is unknown. Fifteen years ago an Indian organization, Lok Kalyan Samity, which runs eye hospitals, decided to raise money through direct mail and worked to build up a mailing list of good 'prospects', ie people who had shown an interest in the work and who had made donations. It cultivated its supporters, sent them a birthday card annually, asked them to find other donors – and it received so much support that it was not only able to pay for the costs of its own eye hospital, but it started to raise funds for other eye hospitals. Building up a responsive mailing list takes time, but provides for steady income without too much extra work. This method has become a whole science in the North, with linked computer programmes and specialized training. The Resource Alliance (previously the International Fund Raising Group) can provide a lot of experience in the management of direct mail solicitation.

Through the Telephone

Just as it is possible to make a solicitation through the mail, it is also possible to make a solicitation through the telephone, but it is much more difficult. The person telephoning has to be able to capture the interest of the person being called and sustain it through their speech, as well as to pass on important information like the address that the cheque should be sent to. It is possible, but difficult.

Through the Media

Many CSOs have had success by advertising their organization in the media (newspapers and television or radio), and through such advertisements asking for contributions. Sometimes this is a way to gain names that subsequently can be put on to a mailing list as regular contributors. Sometimes descriptive articles about the organization written by a journalist can have an appeal for funds attached. It is wise to get advice from those who are experienced in journalism or advertising before you do this (which is another opportunity for non-financial assistance from supporters) since an advertisement which gives the wrong impression can set back your organization many years.

Through Imaginative Ideas

People who are fundraising from the public must think of creative ways in which large numbers of members of the public can be separated from small amounts of money that they will not notice, and can be persuaded to send them to your CSO. Often this will involve collaboration with a business or another institution. As examples to get you thinking, here are three examples from Japan, British Airways and the ITT Sheraton, all of which involve small gifts of money at no great sacrifice, which have aggregated to very large amounts of money for different organizations:

- In Japan a scheme was set up to raise funds for Japanese overseas aid through Japanese CSOs. It involved the postal savings bank – 20 per cent of the interest earned on the ordinary deposit accounts of individuals who have a postal savings account are automatically deducted for Japanese CSOs working overseas (and account holders can choose to have a greater percentage deducted).
- The ITT Sheraton Hotel chain, in agreement with UNICEF, invite all their customers to round up their bills to the nearest US$10 when they settle their accounts and Sheraton gives the extra money to UNICEF.
- UNICEF have also persuaded British Airways to issue envelopes to all their customers (which come with their head-sets as they take their seats on aeroplanes), inviting them to give their spare change from the last country they were in. Other airlines have also taken up this idea for other causes and organizations.

Legacies

When people are making their wills, and deciding how their estate or their income should be divided, it is often possible to suggest to them that they leave a certain proportion of their estate to worthwhile causes. In some countries this is quite common, while in other countries it is unheard of and very surprising. It requires tact on the part of the soliciting organization to make such a suggestion without seeming to encourage the person to die soon! Of course, the most impressive way of doing this is for a rich person to set up an indigenous foundation from his/her estate (see p 47).

All these ideas receive many small contributions, and do not require a sacrifice from the donor. Other important ways of getting help from individuals, of course, are not financial, but require people to give their time, their expertise, and their skills. This has been discussed on p 15.

BEST PRACTICES

Lessons from professional fundraisers suggest the following best practices:

- See your fundraising as a way of offering people an opportunity to do something worthwhile; go for the heart – the purse will follow.
- Wherever possible, listen to donors and get feedback from them – they will advise you, through their reaction to your appeal, about the strengths and weaknesses of your fundraising efforts.
- Tell them about the people who are being helped by your organization – again an appeal to the heart.
- Sincerely thank donors many times for their contributions.
- All donors – big as well as small – are valuable. Small donors can be cultivated to become large donors over time.

The case studies that illustrate fundraising from individuals and the public are HelpAge India and the Al-Amal Centre for Cancer Care, Jordan.

CASE STUDY 6.1 *HelpAge, India*

HelpAge India Is the largest secular voluntary organization working at the national level in India for the welfare of elderly individuals. Projects supported by the group include old age homes, rehabilitation programmes, day care centres, and medical outreach programmes. Funding for these projects has been possibly only through the generosity of the public.

Direct mail is one of the fundraising techniques used by HelpAge India. The organization is constantly looking out for and acquiring addresses of potential donors through such means as newspaper advertisements. Relevant data are computerized and updated regularly. Potential donors are kept on the mailing list for up to 5 years. Since direct mail involves only written communication, a good appeal letter is critically important. The appeal letter is sent first to a small segment of the target audience to test both its effectiveness and the mailing list being used. If the response rate is over 2%, a large-scale mailing follows.

A first time donor is a 'hot prospect' who must be nurtured. He or she is sent newsletters, annual reports, birthday greetings, brochures, project lists, and personal letters. The aim is to develop a close relationship with each donor and keep the person as informed about HelpAge India as possible. The budget for direct mail is closely monitored: HelpAge India has been able to keep the cost/benefit ratio at 1:5 – that is, for every dollar spent on a mailing, five dollars is generated in donations. Each direct mail campaign is coded so that the response rate can be measured and analysed. Donors are then assigned a priority according to their income, frequency of giving, and the size of each donation: a donor profile is compiled based on these varying factors, and subsequent mailings are targeted so as to increase the donation revenue per mailing.

HelpAge India now provides 15% of HelpAge India's funding. The donor base has increased from approximately 3000 donors in 1990 when direct mail started, to more than 50,000 donors in 1997. The organizers attribute much of this success to careful planning, constant testing, and evaluation of the mailing lists, and increased public awareness of the organization's objectives.

Source: Sustaining Civil Society: Strategies for Resource Mobilisation, CIVICUS (1997)

CASE STUDY 6.2 *AL-AMAL CENTRE FOR CANCER CARE, JORDAN*

The Al Amal Centre for Cancer Care provides comprehensive cancer care to the people of Jordan and the surrounding region, including early detection, treatment and rehabilitation of cancer patients, public awareness and education and research.

The General Union of Voluntary Societies, under the guidance of its president, Dr Abdullah Al-Khatib, formed a national task force for the establishment of Al-Amal Centre in 1984. Following the death of his daughter, Dalia, from leukemia at the age of 13, Dr El-Khatib recognized the urgent need for a cancer centre to provide effective cancer treatment then available only in industrial countries and at high cost.

Dr Al-Khatib and the Task Force developed a capital campaign to raise the estimated US$30 million needed for the Centre. With the help of the media and word of mouth, Jordanians became aware of the Centre's goal. Many wealthy individuals began to donate generously, and other contributions flooded into the General Union of Voluntary Societies, which also contributed a great deal. About 25,000 students joined a nationwide 'Knock on the Door' fundraising campaign. Construction began in 1989, after some US$2 million had been collected.

An Al-Amal Centre Support Week held in 1992 under the patronage of His Late Majesty King Hussein and Her Majesty Queen Noor was one of the largest fundraising efforts ever. It included another 'Knock on the Door' campaign, as well as a charity march of thousands of people from Al-Hussein Sports City to Al-Amal Centre. The week ended with a 16-hour live telethon, in which Jordanians donated more than US$10 million, the largest amount in the nation's history.

Almost 26,000 donors contributed to the Al-Amal Centre, 6500 of whom did so in the memory of a loved one lost to cancer. Obviously important to the success of the capital campaign was the commitment to the cause and the excellent preparation and planning by all involved. A clearly defined goal gave potential donors something to aim for, and the fact that so many people had friends and loved ones with cancer helped create a special sense of national sympathy and unity.

Source: Sustaining Civil Society: Strategies for Resource Mobilisation, CIVICUS, (1997)

Chapter 7

Building Grass-roots Organizations

WHAT ARE GRASS-ROOTS ORGANIZATIONS?

Grass-roots organizations are village (or urban-neighbourhood) level membership organizations formed for self-help and self-improvement purposes. The premise of this section is that third-party CSOs have frequently tried to raise the funds they think are required to carry out activities at the grass-roots level, and have often found this difficult. CSOs often operate by trying to form (or encourage) grass-roots organizations (GROs), also called community-based organizations (CBOs), and, all too often, they feel that they have to raise the funds necessary for the activities of such GROs/CBOs. Many resources, however, can be mobilized at the grass-roots level by grass-roots organizations themselves – resources that an outside organization would not be able to access. Grass-roots organizations are also often indigenous and traditional organizations. As they are encouraged by CSOs to take on new tasks for development purposes, they sometimes have access to indigenous and local resources. Not only are these indigenous resources inaccessible by outside CSOs, but it means that CSOs do not have to try to raise those funds if the GROs are raising them themselves. GROs can also generate funds for themselves, and depending on the activity, CSOs can help them to do this, and by doing so:

- save themselves the need to try to mobilize such resources for GROs;
- empower GROs to mobilize their own resources, and control these resources themselves.

The first task in this section is to identify what grass-roots organizations exist in your country that have evolved into having new functions. It is likely that in every country there are mutual assistance associations of some kind or another, and in some countries there are more specialized traditional organizations. Try to make a list of all the organizations that you know, together with their original functions and any new functions that they may have taken on.

GROs and CBOs were originally formed to address concrete problems of their members in social (eg ritual, dispute resolution), economic (eg production, marketing), or natural resource (eg water, fodder, trees, fish conservation) fields, and to address these problems within the circumscribed world of that community.

Now, as communities open up to the influences of the outside world, they are able to ensure that their members' interests and problems are represented to power holders and representative bodies outside the community. As they take on such new roles they can mobilize resources for themselves – both raising funds from sources that are available to them, and generating their own resources.

The following are some examples of GROs that interact with agencies beyond the original community – often national government departments, but also CSOs, donors, and local government:

Social
- PTAs (Parent-Teachers Associations)
- Village pharmacies
- Mothers' clubs and women's groups
- Nutrition clubs
- Drinking-water committees
- Neighbourhood watch groups
- Village health management committees
- Peace and conflict resolution committees
- Early childhood development groups

Economic
- Producers' groups
- Cooperatives
- Credit unions
- Savings and credit clubs
- Women's income-generating groups

Natural Resource Management
- Irrigation users' groups
- Grazing associations
- Community forestry associations
- Fisherfolk associations

Originally GROs mobilized resources that were needed for production and marketing, and the maintenance of livelihoods. Now increasingly they are being asked to mobilize resources for various social safety-net functions as the state reduces its ability to provide, or indeed fails to provide, services in the field of education, health, and welfare. Indeed, in many places the state, rhetoric to the contrary, has never provided education, health, and welfare services, and it has been left to the community to handle such matters themselves.

As GROs evolve from traditional tasks to ones that interface with the more modern world and outside forces, they often change. Community groups in the past were often managed autocratically by traditional leadership (which was predominantly male), and they were directed to very local problems. Such groups are now more likely to be democratic, to involve women more in leadership roles, and to involve the community in larger social and economic problems.

GROs are, above all, membership organizations in which the membership provides the governance of the organization, and the members are the beneficiaries of whatever improvements or benefits the GRO brings. Usually they are formed locally to address a locally identified problem, although sometimes their formation is induced by outsiders (like government community development workers, or CSO animators), and the problem is identified by outsiders. In whatever way they have been formed, however, the problem around which they associate has to be one that is recognized and accepted by them. They need to accept and indigenize the problem as one that they recognize as important (for instance child spacing and birth control), and not simply associate around something that others have introduced to them.

Because they are voluntarily formed to address a local problem that requires the provision of a local good or service, they have strengths that an outside body, be it a government agency or a CSO, does not have. They are able to:

- charge fees from their members;
- mobilize and earn income from the resources that they control;
- get voluntary donations in cash and kind;
- lobby for and attract resources that are available to local groups from local government.

Moreover, such GROs are unlikely to have expensive overheads – they are likely to operate at a modest level of administration and management.

Moving into the political sphere, such GROs (particularly if they federate with other GROs into groupings that are larger than the village or urban-neighbourhood community) can:

- confront powerful interests from the state or the market which impinge on their lives;
- through their use of collective power and numbers overcome outside influences that are harming them;
- make sure that influences helpful to them are supported.

In many places in the world, as the power of central government shrinks, there is a de facto or de jure increase in the power and activities of local government. Foreign aid is being directed increasingly at local, municipal, and city governments, and such governance structures are looking for organizations to work with. Local governments' natural partners are GROs, representing a logical counterpart to decentralized government, rather than CSOs that are not usually so local. CSOs, however, can build up GROs to take on that role, and help them to command the new resources that will be available.

How Can GROs Mobilize Resources?

GROs can mobilize resources in the following ways:

- They can map and analyse community resources, and discover what they as a community own and can utilize. Techniques such as Participatory Rural Appraisal/Participatory Urban Appraisal (and their successor, Participatory Learning and Action (PLA)) have shown the ability to help communities to realize their own resources (both physical and skills).
- They can set up membership structures that can institute savings procedures and mobilize fees, subscriptions, and special levies (in cash and in kind).
- They can generate resources by offering the following services to their members for a fee:
  - administering credit;
  - adding value through crop processing or marketing;
  - providing social services (eg school or clinic).
- They can access resources from:
  - local government;
  - from members of the community who have left and are in good jobs;
  - local businesses that operate in their areas (eg seed and fertilizer companies, timber extraction firms, fish-processing plants) either as donations or levies.

Federations

All resource possibilities mentioned above can be multiplied many times through federations of GROs. Very large amounts of money can be generated by federations of GROs that have thousands of subscriptions, savings deposits, fees and levies. Such organizations can own their own banks, their own processing companies, and/ or their own heavy equipment. Such federations can organize, as credit unions do, cross-subsidies to help poorer areas with funds from more prosperous areas. They can also make available venture capital for new enterprises, and, perhaps most importantly of all, can put pressure on elected officials, councillors, and other kinds of local representatives to make sure that government services are relevant and useful rather than irrelevant and harmful.

This section – on GROs and their ability to mobilize resources for themselves – is predicated upon the view of CSOs as intermediary organizations that work to build citizens' membership organizations, and thus does not view CSOs as organizations that themselves implement work at the grass-roots. If a CSO is seeking to implement the work itself, usually it has to find the funds itself; if a CSO helps to create and build up a GRO, it is likely that the GRO can mobilize substantial amounts of its own funds.

CASE STUDY 7.1 *JARDIM SHANGRI-LA, BRAZIL*

The shanty town of Jardim Shangri-La is a haphazard cluster of small-scale shacks made of scrap lumber and cardboard, with no running water or sewage, perched alongside a putrid, garbage-strewn river. Taking advantage of the headway generated by a local branch of the Citizens' Campaign against Hunger and Poverty and for Life (the Acao da Cidadania Contra a Fome, Miseria e Pela Vida) from a nearby shanty town, 16 families in Jardim Shangri-La banded together to tackle long-standing community problems. For years they had waited for government help, now they realized that with limited outside help and their own sweat and ingenuity, they could take effective action. They established the Cooperativa Habitacional Jardim Shangri-La to upgrade their housing and generate much-needed income.

Cooperative members began by holding bingos and raffles and pooling their money to buy land for a brick-making factory. Next, they received a US$7000 grant from the Fundo Inter-Religioso, a small projects fund operated by an ecumenical coalition of Church groups and NGOs, to purchase a simple motor-run press to produce cement blocks and concrete slabs. Eight local residents were hired to work at the factory, which would cover their salaries from the profits of brick sales. Soon the factory was turning out 600 bricks a day. Other members of the community, including women and children, volunteered their labour on weekends to boost production and construct houses in the community.

The Coop has also used its bricks to renovate the community centre where meetings, sewing courses, and catechism classes are held, and residents built a 7000 litre storage tank that supplies potable water to the community for the first time. Now the cooperative plans to pool profits from its brick-making with a small donation from the Catholic archdiocese's social service centre to start a restaurant to feed poorer members of the shanty-town and to earn extra, steady income by selling prepared meals to workers of nearby factories.

The experience of Jardim Shangri-La vividly portrays the remarkable accomplishments and potential of the Citizens' Campaign. With only limited outside cash donations, and a good deal of volunteer support, complementary institutional partnerships, and a newfound sense of purpose, 16 families are vitally improving their community.

Source: Sustaining Civil Society: Strategies for Resource Mobilisation, CIVICUS (1997)

But apart from the matter of funds, by building the GRO, the CSO is also building:

- citizens' ability to organize themselves;
- citizens' ability to access resources from government;
- citizens' ability to negotiate with government;
- social capital (trust, conflict resolution, tolerance, collaboration);

and: if possible,

CASE STUDY 7.2   *CREDIT UNIONS IN LESOTHO*

In an attempt to increase local investment in agriculture in Lesotho, the National University of Lesotho Extension programme – a partnership between the National University of Lesotho and the Canadian-based St Francis Xavier University, CIDA and Misereor – suggested that credit unions be formed. Village leaders organized community meetings at which the extension service explained how a credit union worked. After this orientation the community members were responsible for deciding whether they wanted a credit union, and, if so, they had to take the initiative to invite the extension service back to provide training. The commitment of time, effort, and resources on the part of the community firmly rooted the project at the local level.

Once the decision to form a credit union is made, villagers form study groups and commit a year of study to become thoroughly knowledgeable about the concepts and operations. Then several members are selected to participate in an intensive course on book-keeping and financial management. They are required to pass qualifying examinations in order for the credit union to be formally established and officially registered with the Ministry of Agriculture and Cooperatives. Each credit union is managed and administered entirely by its members, who are responsible for all decision-making. The members also elect a nine-member Board of Directors, an Auditing Committee, and an Education Committee. Once the credit unions are established, it is government's responsibility to conduct an annual financial audit.

The World Council of Credit Unions and the Canadian-based Caisse Populaire provided training materials and assistance in establishing an umbrella organi- zation – the Lesotho Cooperative Credit Union League (LCCUL). At one point, when the government announced its intention to take over the credit unions and use them as a base for a national bank, the cooperation of the communities with LCCUL proved a formidable force in fighting this government initiative.

The movement eventually led to the formation of more than 70 credit unions throughout the region. Membership has increased steadily over the years: given the extended families of the average member, the credit unions reach more than 250,000 direct beneficiaries. Their programme has diversified to include a number of income-generating activities such as communal gardens and craft cooperatives, and some unions have even constructed their own facilities, which can be rented out to earn income. Due to its success, Lesotho has been selected as the site for the African Cooperative Savings and Credit Association training centre for Southern and Eastern Africa.

Establishing a credit union gives members an opportunity to save regularly, borrow in times of need, learn how to manage their own finances, and develop habits of thrift and honesty. They use the skills they acquire and their access to capital to start their own small enterprises. Approximately 30% of credit union members hold leadership positions throughout the village in develop- ment committees, churches and political parties. In addition, at least 45% of the credit union members have learned how to read and write. And since many of the men are absent from the village for long periods working in South Africa, women have played a dominant role within the credit unions, which helped to give them visibility as capable and responsible leaders.

Source: Sustaining Civil Society: Strategies for Resource Mobilisation, CIVICUS (1997)

- the citizens' ability to federate and form larger groupings.

The case studies that illustrate resource and grass-roots organizations are Jardim Shangri-La, Brazil, and Credit Unions in Lesotho (Case Studies 7.1 and 7.2).

Chapter 8

Resources from Government

COMPLICATED RELATIONS

The relationship between CSOs and governments is complicated and sometimes bitter. In many countries there is a history of governments regarding civil society organizations as potentially subversive and as organizations whose actual purpose is to discredit the government. In such places there are often extensive bureaucratic rules and regulations to control CSOs. In other places there is a recognized niche for CSOs, provided they restrict themselves to charitable activities and show no desire to move beyond that. In yet other places they are valued as supplementary agencies to the government which can be subcontracted to carry out government programmes.

The relationship has been complicated further by the supporters of the so-called Neo-Liberal Economic Policies or the 'Washington Consensus' (meaning the combination of free trade, floating exchange rates, and smaller government). This has urged the rolling back of the state and the promotion of the private sector and civil society within which civil society organizations operate. These new policies unfortunately have posed Southern governments and CSOs as competitors for foreign aid. This is further complicated when specific foreign aid projects have insisted that governments work with CSOs in the implementation of development programmes with the donors' money. Governments start to see CSOs as the darlings of the foreign aid agencies, funded and kept in place by them, and lacking local accountability.

All this does not suggest smooth sailing for CSOs that want to access public resources that are controlled by government. Just as governments have a spectrum of complicated attitudes towards CSOs, so also do CSOs in turn have a spectrum of attitudes towards government. It is important for CSOs to clarify for themselves how they regard government before they start negotiating for access to government resources. The attitudes of civil society organizations cover the range of the following positions:

- CSOs are by definition not government; their strength is that they have an alternative view of development from government and a different way of working, and they should stay that way. They should have as little to do with government as possible, and rarely use their resources.

- CSOs should be free to choose which aspects of government they consider admirable and with which they want to work, and also those with which they do not wish to associate.
- Government does not own the resources it controls; it merely holds them in trust for the public. CSOs, as organizations of the public, have the right to demand government resources. In particular, CSOs have the right to demand resources that the government holds, but is either not using, or using ineffectually.
- Government has the power. If CSOs want to access government resources, they have to accept that the government does control the resources, and learn pragmatically to engage the government on its own terms since they cannot successfully challenge it.

WAYS OF WORKING TOGETHER

In a situation where resources for CSOs are limited, and the sources of such resources are also limited, it is definitely in the CSOs' own interests to recognize that government holds resources which the CSOs, under certain circumstances, can access. Such access, however, depends on CSOs and governments clarifying their relations with each other and seeing how each can be useful to the other. The whole subject of government funding of civil society organizations is one that will benefit from a national level consultation between government and CSOs, perhaps brokered by bilateral and multilateral development agencies, since so often the government resources that are potentially available to CSOs originate with such agencies.

In some cases foreign donors provide funding to government on condition that they work with national level CSOs on the particular programme or project in question. In such a case the CSO does not need to persuade the government to fund it, but it certainly has to negotiate closely with the government to set up mutually agreeable modalities for such funding. If the funding from government to CSOs is a condition of foreign donor funding, but has neither been requested nor desired by the government, it is likely that the government will impose difficult operating procedures, often structuring things for the CSOs' failure. This is well documented in the World Bank's evaluation of its work with NGOs, nearly all of which is channelled via governments (see 'Further Reading').

If, on the other hand, a CSO does not have a foreign donor that is trying to channel funds to it through the government, it is likely that it has two ways to access government resources:

1   By persuading the government that its interests will be served by funding the CSOs to do what they themselves want to do – in other words for the funding

to be driven by the CSOs' mission, and for this to be accepted as valuable by the government.

2   By accepting government contracts – ie for the CSOs to do what the government wants to be done. In such a case the funding is driven by the CSOs' desire for income, although, of course, it is possible that the government's mission and the CSOs' mission coincide.

There will be many shades and gradations between these two positions, and the CSO will certainly be required to compromise when working with government. Where the CSO is unable to persuade the government to fund its programmes, the clever CSO will exploit the possible compromises to carry out its own mission-driven activities under the cover of activities that have been contracted by the government. Contractually the CSO will have to deliver what it has agreed, but it can do other things over and beyond what it has contracted to do.

A good example of this is Gram Vikas, a CSO in Orissa, India. Gram Vikas wanted to work on land and human rights issues with tribal people in the interior of Orissa, but found it difficult to get funding for this, particularly from the Indian or state government. The federal government was offering funds for NGOs that were interested in developing, extending, and popularizing biogas digesters, however, as part of the government's strategies to conserve fuel wood from forests. Gram Vikas' mission was not in the energy conservation field, but it was not averse to the concept of biogas digesters, and it saw the opportunity to get public funds to mount programmes in the remoter areas of Orissa where the tribal people lived. Gram Vikas has become the leading exponent of biogas technology in Orissa, delivering all that the government required of it, but it has also 'piggy-backed' advocacy and adult education work with tribals on this programme.

Before getting deeper into the subject of CSO/government collaboration, it is important for CSOs to try to be as objective as possible about the strengths and weaknesses that the two parties bring to the table. Since CSOs are frequently vocal on their strengths and the shortcomings of governments, a valuable exercise is for people who work with CSOs to brainstorm the reverse – the strengths of government and the weaknesses of CSOs. This will help to illuminate the difficulties and possibilities each has in working with the other.

CONSTRAINTS TO WORKING TOGETHER

Having listed these strengths and weaknesses (and recapitulated their own strengths and governments' weaknesses), it is worthwhile to consider the constraints to successful CSO/government collaboration.

A Lack of Understanding of Each Other's Goals

Often government's goals are quantitative – to increase production, or decrease morbidity, for instance – whereas CSOs' goals are more qualitative – for instance, to build self-reliance and community involvement.

The Inability of Government to Identify the Types of CSOs that Might Become Reliable Working Partners

Depending on which government we have in mind, the government may be more aware of welfare types of CSOs, or more aware of CSOs that are publicity conscious, or more aware of those that work in the capital city. They may choose these as working partners, rather than look further for the CSOs that are creating an impact in their chosen field. Governments also have a concern about working with CSOs that may be too critical of the government, or may show up government inefficiencies – and yet these may be the most effective CSOs.

Restrictive Government Procedures

Government tendering and reporting demands, and procedures for advances and liquidating imprests, are often very burdensome if they are applied in their entirety. Because of the inherent distrust that government frequently has of CSOs, they are often applied in their entirety, and CSOs find these conditions very difficult to comply with.

Problems of Attitude (Distrust) on Both Sides

This has been mentioned earlier. CSOs are suspicious that government ministries and departments are venal, corrupt, inefficient, and interested only in reaching numerical targets in order to please their political bosses. Governments are suspicious that CSOs are hazy, ineffective, ready to elevate process above demonstrable impact, and possibly subversive of government.

Lack of Clear Government Policy and Guidelines on CSOs

In many countries there are no clear government guidelines on working with CSOs. In cases where government has been 'forced' by donor conditionality to work through CSOs, but where there has not been any government policy to work with them, guidelines are usually set by the local government functionaries, often to the disadvantage of the CSO.

Poor Communications Among CSOs, and Between CSOs and Government

It is often valuable and necessary for CSOs working on a government programme in a particular area to liaise with other CSOs working in complementary programmes in the same area. Frequently CSOs do not have local fora for such liaison, preferring competition to consultation. In the same way, locally based programmes require good coordination with complementary government departments, but channels and fora for this are often missing.

Sharp Contrasts between the 'Top-down' Working Methods of Government and the More Participatory Approaches of CSOs

As mentioned before, governments' working methods are often directive (even autocratic), seeing citizens as the objects of development programmes that are being done to them, whereas CSOs are more participative, seeing citizens as the subject and the driving force of their own development. Where government programmes are based on nationally designed plans that demand that the government functionary who is responsible must deliver quantifiable results to fulfil his or her part in that plan, this can and will lead to difficulties with CSOs who do not necessarily subscribe to such ways of working.

Poor Understanding of the Relative Weaknesses and Strengths of Both Sides

CSOs do not appreciate the difficulties that well-motivated government officials work within, particularly their shrinking budgets and exposure to political interventions. CSOs do not appreciate either the wealth of experience of government officials, or the technical expertise available to them. In the same way governments do not understand the problems of managing an organization on the basis of serial projects, and the problems that come to an organization that is concerned to make sure that the people are committed to a project rather than ordered to participate in a project.

Lack of CSO Accountability to Their Constituency, and to the Public at Large, for the Ways in Which Resources are Used

Government officials will contrast the way in which they work, and their checks and balances, with those of the CSO. The government's position is that a government is tested by the people's faith in them through periodic elections, by the people's ability to complain about a recognized hierarchy, and by the complaints institutions like the Auditor General's Office. They contrast this with the autonomous nature of a CSO that can do whatever it can to get funding and its board's agreement to do so. As long as CSOs take foreign funds, their accountability is to foreign funders, not to the government, their constituency or the national public. This is an important point of vulnerability for the whole citizen sector, and it is still vulnerable to such accusations even when the government's own governance machinery does not work.

CSOs can probably give many examples, from their own experience, of these different constraints. While the emphasis has been on relations with national governments, much of this holds true with local government, particularly when local government has been very much an arm of national government. There are, however, increasing instances of very local and democratic municipal governments that are well suited to partnerships with CSOs. A very good example is Bolivia, where in 1994 a Popular Participation law was passed in which local municipalities became the focus for civil society organizations and local government. The more that local government has a participatory and democratic governance, the more that opportunities exist for civil society organizations and government to work together.

BENEFITS AND DISADVANTAGES OF GOVERNMENT–CSO COLLABORATION

CSOs must recognize the realpolitik that government will only fund CSOs if they see some benefit to themselves in doing so, and if they consider that these benefits will outweigh any possible disadvantages. CSOs have also to accept that there may be disadvantages to them in collaborating with government that will outweigh the value of the income they might receive.

Let us look at these in order. Table 8.1 comes from the fine quartet of books produced by the Overseas Development Institute (see 'Further Reading') on government/CSO relations. It lets us look at this from the perspective of both sides.

Table 8.1 *Benefits and Risks from the Government's Perspective*

Benefits	Risks
Better delivery for government services	Government services shown to be inefficient by the CSOs' presence and actions
More information available to the government from the grass roots	CSOs' mobilization work may promote social instability
More interaction with the target groups of the programme/project	The demand for government services may increase beyond the capacity of the government to meet it
Enhanced cost-effectiveness	CSOs may compete with the government for funds
Greater coordination of CSOs' activities	Greater control of the CSOs

contd p76

Table 8.1 (contd) *Benefits and Risks from the CSOs' Perspective*

Benefits	Risks
Improved access by the CSO to policy formulation	Cooption by the government and greater government controls
Access to specialist research facilities and expertise	The CSOs grow to assume a more bureaucratic character
An opportunity to improve and reform government services from within	The loss of CSO autonomy and independence
Access to new technologies	Relegation to mere service provision, to the detriment of the CSOs' wider programmes
	Loss of credibility among CSO clients
	Tendency to maintain existing social and political conditions
	The substitution of the CSO for government services perpetuates government inefficiency and absolves them of responsibility
	The government takes credit for the CSOs' achievements

GETTING TO KNOW THE GOVERNMENT

If the CSO has decided that on balance it wants to try to access government resources, it has to realize that it needs to do a lot of homework to acquaint itself with the way that government operates. It needs to learn much more about government budgeting and regulations.

What is the Source of the Government's Revenue? How Does this Affect Developmental Decisions?

To illustrate this, an anti-smoking lobbying organization in Bangladesh had no difficulty in persuading the Ministry of Health of the harmful effects of smoking and the costs to the country in health care and days off work. The Minister of Health, however, informed the CSO that the income to the Bangladesh exchequer from taxes on cigarettes was simply so important that it was non-negotiable.

What Government Funds Have Been Budgeted For What Projects?

Can the CSO get access to the national budget? Is the budget as stated likely to be realistic? Are the planned funds likely to be actually disbursed?

How Does the CSO Get Invited to Bid?

In each case of government programming that seems attractive to the CSO, will the government invite bids for its execution, or will it carry out the work itself? Is there scope for the CSO to lobby for one or the other?

What Are the Government Procedures?

What are the government rules about bidding procedures, allowable overheads, administrative costs, etc? How does the CSO find out about these?

Does Government Have a 'Niche' for CSOs?

Are there specific programmes that government has 'reserved' for CSOs? If so, how does any CSO find out about these?

If the CSO is prepared to get into the murky world of government procurement and contracting, they may become involved in:

- Extensive time spent lobbying and arguing their case.
- Competition from other for-profit contractors.
- Inefficient payment systems which may require the CSO to front some costs and be reimbursed, with all the dangers of delays in such reimbursements.
- Cumbersome bureaucracies that may take a long time to process funding or procurement requests.
- Design faults in government programmes that may not be renegotiable.
- Collaboration with an inefficient government system.

In South Africa, CSOs have been introduced recently to the complicated tendering and procurement procedures of the South African government. What they hoped would be an opportunity for them to get sustainable funding from government has proved very troublesome for most CSOs there.

In Indonesia, a CSO which was successful in a microfinance programme was asked by the government to extend this service to all acceptors of a family planning programme. The government wanted to make sure that all acceptors received loans; the CSO wanted to offer loans only to those who understood, accepted and wanted loans.

In Zambia, CSOs were collaborating with government on a range of basic health measures, which depended on certain government contributions for transport. The government vehicles were badly maintained and frequently broken, which prevented the CSO from doing its part of the work.

Legitimate Questions by Government of CSOs

If a government is prepared either to fund or contract a CSO, it has a perfectly legitimate right to have certain information about the organization – information which sometimes CSOs feel is invasive. The government needs to know:

- What does the CSO stand for? What has it done in the past and what is it doing now? Where is it operating? What objective evaluations and audits can the organization show?
- Who is in charge of the CSO? Do they effectively govern the activities of the organization? Do they observe the law?
- Do the CSOs' activities have the intended impact? Are they for the public benefit, or the benefit of a restricted clientele?
- Does the CSO demonstrate an ability to deliver on its promises, and manage/account for resources?
- Does the CSO work within the policy framework of the government?

CSOs should be just as ready to answer such questions as they are when they are asked by foreign donors. Because government openness and accountability are often seen as lacking by the CSOs, they sometimes resent such questioning from governments, but it is quite legitimate. It is, after all, the government's money that is to be spent.

What is Government Responsibility with the People's Money?

As Structural Adjustment Programmes (SAPs) operate in many countries of the South, governments in many places are being encouraged and/or forced to cut back on the services they have traditionally offered to their citizens in the fields of health, education and social welfare. In some cases they look to CSOs to take over this work, and this raises problems.

Firstly, CSOs are rarely placed to take over comprehensive services, like primary schooling. CSOs exist in places where their governing body wants them to exist – they rarely have regional, let alone national coverage. CSOs, almost by definition, are spotty in their coverage, and are thus not well placed to take over comprehensive government services.

Secondly, many thinking CSOs are worried about governments' seeming readiness/willingness to give up their responsibilities to their citizens. It is one thing for a government to contract at a time of financial crisis, but it is another for a government to rethink its responsibilities to its citizens, and decide to give up some of them. Should CSOs, even if they are offered grants and contracts, take on such work that lets governments out of their responsibilities? Some would say that contracting such work to CSOs is not abdicating responsibility, merely identifying and using the comparative advantages of CSOs, but others see this as the start of government divesting itself of difficult tasks.

NON-FINANCIAL RESOURCES FROM GOVERNMENT

There are a number of in-kind resources that a CSO could access from government, resources that a government is perhaps uniquely placed to have, such as land, buildings, skilled personnel (particularly artisans). As governments cut back due to SAPs, it is quite possible that governments have all these resources underemployed. Will the CSO ask for them and lobby government to 'reward' it by letting it have such resources? Or will the CSO demand these resources as of right since the government is not using them? Does the CSO think that government will offer such resources to the CSO on their terms, and, if so, what terms are acceptable to the CSO?

The other set of resources that it is within government's power to provide are the elements of an enabling environment that will allow your CSO and the citizen sector to be more effective. Again, you have to decide what your posture is going to be vis-à-vis government – will you lobby for these policies and practices, will you demand them as of right, or will you negotiate for them? They are such issues as:

- Governance: policies in place which will allow public debate and consultation between government and CSOs, along with the clear implementation of the right to associate and to form interest groups.
- NGO policy: recognizing the worth of CSOs as partners in development:
  - facilitating and streamlining registration, reporting, auditing and accounting procedures;
  - involving CSOs in policy-making and providing fora in which their views can be given;
  - accepting CSOs as potential implementers of government programmes and projects.
- Taxation policy – supportive legal and fiscal measures on local income, local fundraising, duty on goods used for philanthropic purposes, duty on imports for similar purposes.
- Access to information – providing CSOs with public information so that they can carry it to the people, and bring the people's opinions to the government.

CASE STUDY 8.1 *LOCAL COOPERATION IN GDYNIA, POLAND*

The successful collaboration between CSOs and the Gdynia local government was the result of a well designed strategy of the Civil Society Development Foundation (CSDF), and an international NGO working to enhance the sustainable growth of the non-profit sector in Central and Eastern Europe. In 1994 CSDF promoted the cooperation of the municipality and the CSOs in Gdynia, stimulated by the need for more financial resources and more efficient service delivery for local governments in Poland. The strategy CSDF prepared elaborated the benefits of collaboration for the city: a deeper understanding of the needs of the communities, deeper evaluation of social problems, access to more knowledgeable and less expensive service providers than local government agencies, and promotion of citizen participation. For the CSOs the collaboration aimed at ensuring a new source of funds through grants and subsidies from the local government.

The strategy included a step-by-step programme on how to persuade the local government to 'buy into' the cooperation – showing that CSOs are important partners, creating clear procedures for cooperation between CSOs and the city, and creating a model of cooperation that can be replicated in other municipalities.

In January 1995, the city accepted the plan, and appointed a consultant to the Mayor on CSO issues. The main turning point in the launching of the project took place in April 1995, when CSDF, together with the CSO coalition and the city, held a meeting with city council representatives as well as representatives of over 100 non-profit organizations. The CSOs elected a coordination committee to support activities in Gydnia and a Consultation Commission to evaluate the cooperation project. In June 1995 the programme of Cooperation between the local Government of Gydnia and CSOs was born. It was enacted into law by the City Council in September, and since then a wide range of projects has emerged.

In October 1995, the first grant-making session took place, awarding US$70,000 to 20 CSOs. Groups were invited to Council meetings and gained a consultative position in policy decisions. One of the CSOs received a building free of charge from the Municipality to establish a day care centre. In April 1996, the Gydnia Centre of CSOs opened its doors, serving as a meeting place for over 40 grass-roots organizations and providing access to computers and a library. The office was donated by the municipality, and two of the employees are paid by the City. CSOs contributed ten volunteers, and CSDF supports the maintenance of the centre.

CSDF learned that the success of the programme was based on identifying the common interests of the CSOs and the Municipality. In the process of programme development, the most important step was to gather representatives of both parties and engage them in discussions. The only significant obstacle to the development was the unclear legal regulatory system regarding local government-CSO partnerships. According to the leader of the programme, if he could start over again, he would prepare himself much more carefully to answer legal challenges.

Source: Sustaining Civil Society: Strategies for Resource Mobilisation, CIVICUS (1997)

CASE STUDY 8.2 *YMCA MEDICAL ASSISTANCE PROGRAMME, LEBANON*

The YMCA Medical Assistance Programme in Lebanon was initiated in 1988 to provide chronically ill low-income patients with free medication. Local communities, national and foreign CSOs and governments contributed to the programme. Medication was distributed through local dispensaries managed by local CSOs. In 1993 after the end of the civil war in Lebanon, soliciting funds for the programme became increasingly difficult. The YMCA finally asked the Ministry of Public Health to take over the programme. The Ministry responded by asking the YMCA to take over the programme, pledging to provide significant financial support in the amount of US$1.5 million a year. YMCA still solicits cash and in-kind contributions from foreign governments and CSOs, and clients also pay a nominal fee. But most client expenses are covered by the government contract.

The YMCA's decision to approach the government resulted from both internal and external factors. Many donors were not interested in continuing funding for the programme. The YMCA also believed that financing such a programme was the responsibility of the government, and that CSOs could not continue to shoulder this burden alone.

The YMCA had solid previous experience with the government, which encouraged them to pursue state funding. Despite this experience, however, the YMCA needed both technical and financial assistance to help solicit the grant. Staff needed to learn how to lobby for the programme in Parliament, and new staff had to be hired with public administration and public finance expertise. YMCA members, a network of more than 310 dispensaries, and about 75,000 patients, were involved in advocating the programme.

Overall the YMCA's experience with government is positive. The organization learned that in the long run, satisfying seemingly bureaucratic government requirements is worthwhile. The government's commitment serves as an excellent example to donors of its support for CSO activities, and it helps raise contributions to other programmes. To solicit the grant, YMCA had to demonstrate that it was the only organization that could deliver such a service with high quality standards. Also the continuation of external support was essential because it encouraged the Ministry to maintain its support.

But the collaboration also had some negative impacts. It pushed the YMCA into political debates, required the adoption of bureaucratic financial and administrative procedures to meet government requirements, and induced hostility from other CSOs who believed they should have received a 'share of the pie'.

Source: Sustaining Civil Society – Strategies for Resource Mobilisation, CIVICUS (1997)

Getting access to the policy-making fora where CSOs can lobby for such measures (and hopefully get them adopted) may be actually more effective than funding from government, but CSOs have to prepare themselves with clear demands for the policies and practices they want to be implemented.

The case studies that illustrate government–CSO collaboration are Local Cooperation in Gdynia, Poland, and the YMCA Medical Assistance Programme in Lebanon.

Chapter 9

Resources for Sustainability from Foreign Development Agencies

FOREIGN FUNDING FOR ORGANIZATIONAL SELF-RELIANCE

As discussed in the Introduction, many CSOs have been heavily dependent on the resources of foreign development agencies, and this has made them dangerously vulnerable to changes in such agencies' policies and practice, as well as separating them from the support that they might have received from their own countrymen/women and their country's institutions.

There is definitely a place for foreign donor support to CSOs, but it has become dangerously unbalanced, and moreover it has not tended to support the long-term sustainability of CSOs. Foreign donors' insistence on project funding has not helped to build independent and sustainable CSOs, nor an independent citizen sector. There is a place for programme funding from foreign sources, but as a supplement to core financing which has been found from other sources, and for which the CSO is not dependent on a foreign donor.

This section, therefore, focuses on the kinds of foreign financing that support organizational self-reliance and leads towards organizational financial autonomy.

The different methods of financing that are available to foreign agencies are basically the following:

- Emergency relief and welfare grants.
- Small grants tied to specific development projects, time limited and with specific budgets.
- Programme grants that allow the CSO to take its own decisions within agreed programme areas, and to adapt its plans as necessary.
- Grants for revolving loans, specifically for CSOs working in the microcredit business.
- Unearmarked organizational grants – ie contributions towards the CSO's whole work for them to use as they see fit.

What is being suggested here is expanding the methods of financing to include those that are specifically designed for organizational sustainability, like building reserve funds (sometimes called corpus funds), providing venture capital funding, financing fundraising strategies, and endowments. The locus for making decisions on grants to CSOs has in the past varied greatly, depending on the nature of the foreign donor (NGO, bilateral, multilateral), and the kind of grant. In some cases the decision was in the hands of local country offices of the foreign donor; in some cases it had to be referred to head office, and in some cases there would be 'graduated' decision-making processes, depending on the size of the grant being considered. A smart CSO manager would research the way that each foreign funder worked and be prepared to submit proposals that fitted the requirements of each donor. These change over time, and CSO managers are often adept at packaging their proposals to fit the language that is attractive to donors.

In some cases foreign donors have introduced a range of new procedures that invite the participation of CSOs in defining and deciding on how they should be funded in different countries. In some cases foreign donors (like the European Union) introduce new 'windows' that have been identified for CSO funding.

The fields that we are talking about here, however, are not likely to be 'supply driven'. There are few foreign donors that have policies on financing CSO sustainability. It requires the CSOs to make the case (either individually or through a federation) to educate the prospective donor about the relevance and value of such financing, and to be well informed about the parameters of such funding, as well as the experience of different donors in its use. In many cases CSOs will have to be the driving force in getting such concepts discussed by their potential foreign donor.

FINANCING FUNDRAISING STRATEGIES

A frequent response from CSOs that are responsive to the idea of moving from project funding through foreign grants to local resource mobilization, is that they need to have some funds up-front before they can employ new resource mobilization strategies, and they do not see where such funds are likely to come from. Where will they get the funds to build up, for instance, a mailing database, finance a fundraising event, or place the initial advertisement?

There is very little experience of foreign donors providing the start-up capital for a CSO's resource mobilization strategy, but, at the same time, there is very little experience of CSOs asking for such funds, mostly because very few of them have seriously considered such strategies.

This is a chicken-and-egg situation. CSOs have not thought much about alternative resource mobilization; as a result they have not committed themselves to learn more about it; as a result they have not devised strategies that can be turned into funding proposals; and, as a result, few foreign donors have been faced with such proposals, and do not have in-house expertise in assessing any such proposals that are made to them.

The expansion of interest in CSO financial self-reliance (of which this book is an example) means that more CSO staff are likely to get training in this field, and, following this, to make proposals to donors about the financing of self-reliance strategies. As is often the case, the foundations and international NGOs have been the pioneers in this field; organizations such as the Inter-American Foundation, the Ford Foundation, Ashoka: Innovators for the Public, and Oxfam all have some institutional experience and memory of funding resource mobilization strategies. A book of case studies of such experiences would be very valuable.

We need to take a sceptical (even a cynical) look, however, at the fact that very few foreign donors have initiated or promoted financial self-reliance financing. The 'aid trade', including the aid trade to CSOs, has mushroomed since the '60s. Large numbers of people from metropolitan countries are employed in the management of CSO funding, and large numbers of Northern development agencies have their basis in the supposed continuing need that CSOs have for their services. If foreign donors were successful in making CSOs self-reliant and independent of them, many jobs might no longer be needed, and much rhetoric might need to be changed. A possible point of view might be that foreign donors have a definite interest in preserving a way of working that requires regular project proposals, together with the allied practices of proposal assessment, grant making, monitoring, and evaluation. If this was changed, they might be out of work!

CSOs need to challenge this. They need to point out the huge disparity between the rhetoric of self-reliance and the practice of serial dependency through project grants. They also need to point out the simple logic of foreign donors helping CSOs to practise doing without them. They could also point out that their services will be required to create self-reliance just as much as they were required to create dependency.

PROVIDING VENTURE CAPITAL FUNDING

In this case a CSO has identified an enterprise that it would like to run and is looking for the capital to start it up. Foreign donors are sometimes approached for such funds. Look back to the problems identified in Chapter 4 for some of the likely responses to such requests. Foreign donors are probably most concerned about the CSOs' business competence – ie their ability to identify a viable business opportunity, their ability to make a viable business plan, and their ability to run the business efficiently, make money, and make sufficient money for the enterprise to provide sustainable income for the civil society organization.

A CSO that requests funding from a foreign donor for a business venture whose profits will be used to sustain the CSO's operating costs must expect their proposal to receive very tight scrutiny from the donor. Few CSOs have a reputation for commercial entrepreneurship, and donors will be very anxious (and rightly so) that the business will absorb the time and energy of the CSO management that should be going into the main mission of the organization. CSOs should think of separating, where possible, the management of the business from the management of the main work of the organization. Donors may also respond to a proposal for a grant by saying that a business should be prepared to take a loan, rather than a grant, and they may even say that a good business idea should be able to persuade local banks to lend them the money.

Apart from concerns about the viability of a business proposal, a donor is only likely to respond to a proposal for venture capital from an organization that the donor knows well, trusts, and believes in. It is not a viable strategy for a CSO that has not built up a long-term relationship with a donor. Donors are concerned that once a CSO has an independent source of income, it is free from donor oversight, and there is the danger that it may be taken over by a board or managers who will use that income for other purposes. When CSOs have to come to donors every three years for a further grant, the donor can serially satisfy itself that the organization is still doing the work that it says it is doing. Once it has an independent source of funds, the donor loses that control.

The argument may well be made that handing over control is part of the essence of development, but this argument is countered by donors saying that they have fiduciary responsibility to their government to minimize the risk of their funds being misused.

It is true that a good business proposition should be viable using local commercial finance, but since the purpose of the enterprise is to make money to sustain the CSO's main work, the requirement for a commercial bank loan to be repaid will simply prolong the period before the CSO is able to realize this original aim. There are examples of both ways of working in Zambia. The Zambian Red Cross and the NGO Coordinating Committee, for instance, were both given the funds to put up buildings from which they could receive rent (by respectively the Norwegian Red Cross and NORAD), whereas MultiMedia Zambia borrowed money at commercial rates from Zambian banks to put up housing for rent. MultiMedia Zambia had to wait a long time – until the bank loan was paid off – before the income from rent provided substantial income to the organization, whereas the other two were making money from their property as soon as it was rented.

The examples from Zambia have all been of property that provides income to CSOs through rent. This is often seen by donors as the most attractive way of providing for an income to CSOs since it requires much less business expertise than, for instance, running a business. Often donors have combined the idea of providing a building for the offices of the CSO with the idea of providing rentable properties as an income stream. In such a case a donor helps the CSO to acquire a large enough building for both the organization's headquarters (thus saving expenditure on rented property) and for renting out to commercial paying tenants. There are good examples of this in the experience of the donors themselves – Oxfam UK, for instance, rents out the ground floor of its headquarters in Oxford to a variety of businesses, defraying its operational costs by so doing.

Donors have shown a variety of responses to proposals for venture capital, which suggests that they have not worked out a policy for themselves. Responses are ad hoc and often based on individual preferences. Two examples from Bangladesh (one mentioned on p 41) illustrate this: the Canadian International Development Agency (CIDA) was asked by the CSO Proshika to underwrite the costs incurred by Proshika to acquire a bus company there. CIDA provided an expert to do a feasibility study, and on his recommendation agreed the grant. The bus company not only failed to make sufficient money for Proshika, but also sucked management time away from the main work of the organization. It was sold off. Proshika's revenue generation is now based on income from a service fee on its large loan programme, by renting out a floor of its office building, and by running an Internet service provider. Another organization, Proshika Comilla, received funding from CIDA for an export-clothing factory, again after an expert feasibility study. Again it was a disaster for the organization, and eventually was sold. For ten years CIDA in Bangladesh never tried anything like that again. Many years later CIDA provided venture capital at a very much smaller scale for smaller CSOs that were handling small-scale credit. The Canada Fund helped them to acquire, for example, a number of rickshaws or a boat as a way of gaining the income to pay for their running costs. In nearly all cases the CSO rented out the asset to existing entrepreneurs. These initiatives worked well, but were regarded as a pilot operation by CIDA and not repeated.

Another organization in Bangladesh, the Bangladesh Rural Advancement Committee (BRAC), however, has consistently managed to persuade its donor consortium to fund asset creation for the organization. Donors have paid for a potato cold-storage plant, a printing press, a craft production business for both local and export sales, a silk export business, a computer training and contract accounting operation, and a local building firm. All are running well, making money for BRAC and contributing to BRAC's financial sustainability. Some, like the silk business, are intimately connected with the main work of BRAC because very poor rural women raise the mulberry trees and the silk worms, but others, like the printing press, are intended purely to produce income for BRAC. One of the strengths of BRAC's enterprises is that they are run as independent cost and profit centres within the organization, each with its own management. The undoubted business acumen of BRAC has been a strong factor in their getting such funding. BRAC knew what it wanted, and successfully lobbied its donor consortium to provide it.

Non-financial Resources

Foreign funders can be immensely useful to CSOs, not just as suppliers of funds, but also in the information and advice they can give, which can help CSOs to become more self-reliant. The Ford Foundation, for instance, as well as being a funder of CSOs, has also organized a large number of exposure and training visits for them to the USA to see how community foundations, and other forms of sustainable citizen sector organizations, work.

Another way in which Northern NGOs or foundations can help is to lend Southern CSOs some of the expertise that they have in fundraising in the North. Oxfam, for instance, is very experienced at both fundraising (in a variety of creative ways) and revenue generation (especially through their trading arm, Oxfam Trading). From time to time, they have lent people from their fundraising department to work with CSOs in the South.

The case study that illustrates ways in which foreign development agencies can contribute to the sustainability of CSOs or the CSO sector is Organisation of Rural Associations for Progress (ORAP), Zimbabwe.

CASE STUDY 9.1   *ORGANISATION OF RURAL ASSOCIATIONS FOR PROGRESS (ORAP), ZIMBABWE*

The Organisation of Rural Associations for Progress (ORAP) is a social movement created in southern Zimbabwe in 1980 that currently links some 50,000 families grouped into peasant associations and federations of associations. It has become one of the most important rural social movements in Africa with an annual budget of some US$2 million. The promotion of local economic activities such as farming, traditional crafts, and social activities clearly demonstrates the movement's impact, although there is still much to be done in terms of acquiring technological know-how and boosting output.

Aware of the implications and dangers of becoming over-reliant on the aid system, and of the system's inability to generate local capital, the director of ORAP recently drew up a long-term autonomy policy:

- *Stage One: Self-Help.* ORAP is well organized and its members have received sufficient training to realize that future success depends on self-help and members' savings. A savings and credit scheme is therefore being promoted at the village, regional, and national levels.
- *Stage Two: Flexible and Unearmarked Financing.* ORAP's negotiations with its donors ensure that external financing is elastic and flexible. About 80% of this aid is not earmarked for specific projects.
- *Stage Three: Creation of Enterprises.* With the RAFAD Foundation's help, a study of possible financial activities was conducted. It found that, thanks to good management, it had assets that would enable it to launch three activities. Firstly, ORAP purchased a garage/petrol station in the regional capital: profit is made from petrol sales and the garage is used as a depot for ORAP's eight large trucks, donated for the transportation of food to regions in which there is a shortage. Secondly, a warehouse was built in the regional capital to help supply the villages and urban areas with building materials and other much needed products: it is managed by an ORAP team. Finally, a farm has been purchased that permits modern livestock breeding and technology transfer to groups of peasants in the surrounding area.

- *Stage Four: Creation of a Capital Fund.* The main aim of ORAP's strategy is to use its reserves, already invested in economic activities, to increase its capital so that it can create businesses and grant credit to its members.
- *Stage Five: Partnership with the Business Sector.* In 1993, ORAP actively sought ways to establish a source of sustainable income through the business sector. On the advice of the local business sector, ORAP enlisted the help of OXFAM Canada and Christian Aid UK as well as RAFAD. Several business ventures have since resulted, some successful and others less so.
- *Stage Six: Creation of a local investment company.* To reduce the number of economic activities and create new businesses, ORAP decided to create a local investment company using the central campaign fund. Contributions are requested from certain investors for specific projects. This company is also open to investors from other Zimbabwean development organizations with the same objectives.
- *Stage Seven: Creation of the ORAP Foundation.* All these tools and financial mechanisms require a legal structure to assure coordination and the integration of each tool into a global strategy. ORAP felt that the best way to manage this fund was to create the ORAP Foundation that will provide a legal, fiscal, and financial framework.

Source: Sustaining Civil Society – Strategies for Resource Mobilisation, CIVICUS (1997)

Chapter 10

Resources from the Corporate Sector

WHY DO BUSINESSES GIVE TO CSOS?

Businesses aspire to generate profits for their owners and their shareholders. It does not seem obvious for them to be interested in helping civil society organizations, or the causes that such organizations stand for. Civil society organizations seem to be a diversion from their main purpose of making money, and yet businesses are increasingly helping CSOs. The following seem to be the reasons.

Because They Want to be Seen by the Public, by the Government, and by Their Shareholders as Good 'Corporate Citizens'

If they are identified with causes that people think are worthwhile and worth supporting, people who are important to them will think well of the company. They will then make decisions at the margin that are advantageous to the company, either in purchasing, or contracting, or contacts, or in some other way in which the company benefits.

Because They Want to be Associated with Specific Causes that Enhance Their Image and Focus Attention on Their Product or Service

If a company is identified with a particular service which society considers worthwhile, and which reflects the specific product or service of that company, the identity of the company as a good citizen is deepened. Thus printers can gain greater image recognition as printers, as well as more general approbation as good citizens, if they support, for instance, literacy work; similarly, drug companies with health programmes, and mining companies with environmental programmes, etc. Such work would build a conducive environment for the operations of the business, as well as reminding people that they are the brand leader in a particular field.

Because Their Competitors are Supporting Good Causes

Businesses are notoriously keen on watching their competition. If it appears that their competitors are involved in the support of good causes, it is likely that they will look for opportunities to do so too.

Because Senior Staff are Interested in a Particular Issue

In times gone by it would probably be the wife of the chairman who would take responsibility for the welfare involvement of the company. Now, with a greater company interest in social responsibility, the senior staff of a company, particularly the board members or the managing director, are encouraged to take a corporate interest in good causes. This will often be expressed through the particular interests of those people.

Because They are Asked, and are Given Compelling Reasons for So Doing

Businesses do not change overnight, even under the pressure of fashion, to become less interested in maximizing profits. They are amenable to arguments, however, which demonstrate that they will gain long-term advantages in the market-place by being identified with good causes, and by being identified with CSOs which are credible and experienced operators in the particular field in which they are interested. They need to be convinced that their assistance to a CSO is a long-term investment that will lead to an increase in new markets in the future.

Because They are Interested in Having a Good Reputation with Their Staff

A number of businesses consider that a well-motivated workforce, including one that respects the business' social commitment, will be both more productive and less susceptible to work disruption. Many businesses are prepared to link their corporate giving to their staff's interests, perhaps matching the contributions raised by staff, or by accepting a workplace-giving scheme for the whole firm, or by allowing their staff time off for specific causes agreed with the firm.

Because They Get Some Tax Benefits

This is often advanced as the argument for corporate social investment. It is more likely to be an added incentive at the margin when other factors persuade a company into programmes of social responsibility.

What's In It For Me?

Companies in business to maximize profits are inclined, not surprisingly, to ask this question (often abbreviated to WIIFM?) when they are approached by CSOs. CSOs that are interested in accessing resources from business must therefore do their research well, and be able to put forward proposals to potential corporate funders that emphasize the advantages that their support to the CSO will bring them. CSOs need to know more about the companies that they wish to target, think about the valuable information, exposure, contacts, services, and experience that they can bring to the company, and consider the cultural differences between the ways in which they work as CSOs and the ways in which companies work. Pioneering work in this field has been done more by international NGOs than by Southern CSOs. Save the Children USA was successful, for example, in allying itself with Castrol in Vietnam. Castrol underwrote important work that Save the Children USA was doing with malnourished children there, while the company saw this as a way of positioning itself in a growing oil extraction and production market, and hopefully improving its image vis-à-vis its competitors.

Sadly, many CSOs do not operate like this: they make proposals to businesses with the attitude that it is the duty of business to support their work, and that they are, in effect, doing businesses a favour by offering them a chance to fund their work. A much more sensible and effective approach is to accept that the major motivation for businesses to help CSOs is enlightened self-interest – and help them to see the WIIFM? ('What's in it for me?') angle. Look for ways that the mission of your CSO can be furthered in some way that also provides an advantage to the company.

CSOs should not be naive in their relations with business, however. There are risks of doing business with the corporate sector. It would be possible for a CSO to get involved with a company promoting a technology or a product that is not of real benefit to the community with which the CSO is working. Examples might be a particular kind of seed or fertilizer, or an inappropriate drug or luxury consumer item. CSOs must think carefully about which company they should collaborate with, and which they should avoid. It is even possible that the CSO's proper role with some companies should be to campaign against them.

If, however, a CSO has done its research properly and has decided that a particular company has good potential as a collaborator, it must approach the company prepared to think like a business. It needs to learn what businesses are looking for. Two likely goals from the business perspective are:

To build employee morale:

- through the development of employees' living area;
- through offering volunteering possibilities;
- through offering donation-matching programmes.

To develop the company's business image and its market development:

- through linking the company to a respected topic;
- through increasing its name recognition;
- through involving the company in recognized critical social problems.

As an example of the latter, it has been relatively easy for CSOs that are involved in youth development to get funding for literacy, remedial education, and vocational training in post-apartheid South Africa. The whole nation is very aware that a generation of young people has not been educated, and that everyone (including every company) has a duty to remedy the situation.

A very interesting initiative has been started in India by ActionAid, an international development support agency that has been working there since 1972. Within its organizational framework of promoting corporate partnership, it has started an organization called 'Partners in Change'. This organization acts as a broker between corporate bodies that are interested in getting involved in social development and the kinds of organizations that need their support. Partners in Change suggests all the different ways that businesses might want to contribute to social development, and helps them to manage their corporate social investment. The need for 'Partners in Change' suggests that there are potential partners from the business and CSO worlds who are trying to find each other, but that each does not know enough about the other to make the connection.

RESEARCH IN THE SOUTH[*]

There has been a lot of research on company giving behaviour in the North, but very little on that in the South. In 1997, however, the NGO Resource Centre in Pakistan undertook an interview survey study to document and analyse the current trends of corporate philanthropy in Pakistan. Interviews were conducted with senior officials in 120 companies. The questions focused on the role of development NGOs as perceived by the country's business community, and explored the underlying factors governing the volume and direction of corporate giving.

The survey found strong evidence of a definite willingness among corporate leaders to 'play their part' in social development. It is widely asserted among corporate leaders that the government of Pakistan has been unable to keep pace in providing social services to the growing population. Although this has created a forbidding social backlog, business recognizes that there is a promising potential to tackle the backlog through organized voluntary citizen initiative. At the same time, the most common form of corporate philanthropy is directed towards needy individuals and families. Business leaders expressed an 'in principle' openness to a more developmental approach, but do not yet have the confidence in or experience with CSOs to invest in working through and with them.

---

[*] 'The Dimensions of Corporate Giving in Pakistan' in *Philanthropy in Pakistan*, Aga Khan Development Network (1999)

The survey result details indicated the following:

- **Low levels of professionalization in giving**
  Only a fifth of the companies surveyed have written corporate giving policies. Another 30 per cent claim to have a formal policy that is followed but not recorded. The remaining half identifies 'policy' as informal, broad and flexible. Only 7 per cent of the companies have a department/staff who are dedicated to grant-making activities. Where written policies were maintained, the companies' chief executive officers and directors were identified as the critical influence in adopting a more formalized and professional approach. In line with practice elsewhere, however, those corporations with a more formal and professional approach were far more likely to provide support to intermediary development agencies than to give directly to needy individuals and families.

- **Encouraging patterns of participation**
  93 per cent of participating companies reportedly engaged in social development activities in one form or another. These activities ranged from small one-time cash donations directly to beneficiaries, to undertaking large projects engaging company personnel.

  Of the companies that were actively involved in social development, the study found that:

  - 75 per cent were interacting directly with the ultimate target groups or individuals rather than working exclusively through intermediary CSOs;
  - 7 per cent were acting through the company's own trust;
  - another 7 per cent donated to professional societies; and
  - 33 per cent were supporting both intermediaries and target groups.

- **Corporate policy on involvement in social activities**
  The companies commonly understood their 'corporate social responsibility' as made up of four components:

  - paying taxes;
  - looking after employee welfare;
  - making donations to CSOs, charities, and/or target groups and needy individuals; and
  - seconding staff to charitable projects.

- **Social fields supported**
  The survey found that health (at 37 per cent) and education (at 25 per cent) received the highest levels of corporate philanthropic support. Environment protection and pollution control (at 20 per cent) ranked third, ahead of child welfare (at 16 per cent). The relatively high level of support for environmental work may reflect the combination of global awareness of the issue (a high proportion of companies that were active in this area were multinationals), an effective national policy and regulatory framework, and a vigorous set of citizens' groups who were pressing the issue.

- **The deciding factor**

  While respondents to the survey were hesitant to assign a high level of significance to personal affiliations between the company and social project sponsors/managers, more often than not such personal relationships were the most important and, in some cases, even the deciding factor. This result is unsurprising as, in approximately one-third of the companies, the chief executive was actively involved in social development decisions.

- **The credibility of CSOs**

  About one-third of the companies felt that if their support was to be extended through CSOs, a process of careful screening would have to be adopted, and only organizations that were well known and credible should be considered. The most important consideration when evaluating a CSO was the track record of the organization in respect of the achievement of targets, the transparency of operations and utilization of funds. A company's previous experience with a CSO was often cited as a deciding factor. In assessing the strengths of CSOs, transparent reporting and effective resource utilization were given the greatest importance by the corporate sector. The quality of personnel employed by the potential grant recipient was regarded as the next most important indicator.

- **Realization of expected benefits**

  The majority of the companies reported satisfaction with the extent to which the benefits of their interventions had been derived. Those that did not appear to be satisfied felt that more time was needed to evaluate their interventions.

- **Expected benefits from involvement in social development**

  The majority of respondents to the survey claimed that development activities were undertaken for purely altruistic reasons. Building the image of the company and enhancing public goodwill were generally considered to be closely linked, and were rated after altruism. None of the respondents volunteered tax benefits as an incentive.

CORPORATE SOCIAL RESPONSIBILITY

Those who have studied the corporate sector's behaviour in relation to the non-profit world often refer to the subject as Corporate Social Responsibility (CSR). This terminology is becoming increasingly the acceptable way through which CSOs can approach the corporate sector. Not all businesses are at the same stage in their approach to CSR, however, and not all businesspeople see their role in the same way. It is likely that the CSO approach to a business will be targeted at one of the following three stages in business thinking:

1   Corporate philanthropy.
2   Business/community partnerships.
3   Strategic business interest.

Corporate Philanthropy

This is usually in response to requests that come to the company from CSOs for a huge variety of help. Depending on the company, there may be a special section that deals with such proposals, or they may be handled by the company director (or the spouse, or the secretary of the company director), or they may be passed to the public relations or marketing departments.

Some companies like to handle their corporate philanthropy through contributing to a business foundation which then takes on the responsibility for identifying which proposal to respond to, some larger businesses set up a corporate foundation of their own which becomes the agency for their philanthropy. The attitude of the business is that they ought to help 'deserving causes' and that they are interested in identifying the most competent organizations and proposals to respond to. They may have particular causes that they are most interested in – eg drug rehabilitation, disability, conservation – but they are, in the main, responsive to community initiatives.

Business/Community Partnerships

This is usually based on a collaborative decision-making process whereby both the community (often represented through a CSO) and the business see an opportunity for a mutually satisfactory programme of collaborative work. The idea may come from either side, but both partners are involved in the decision-making process, both sides are committing something, and both sides are assuming some of the risks. An example in Harare, Zimbabwe, was the desire of a soft drinks bottling company to get its product better distributed in the slum townships. It was prepared to invest in bicycle-powered sales outlets, but it needed bicyclists-cum-salesmen to operate them. A CSO dealing with street kids and out-of-school youth wanted to find employment for their older youth. Both sides came to an arrangement whereby the CSO supplied and trained the youth to be salespersons, and the bottling company set them up to sell soft drinks on commission.

Medium and small companies and business/trading associations have immense potential to support local causes in imaginative ways. Their strength lies in easy access, understanding local needs, and non-financial resources. One example of the last is secondments, whereby local businesses lend staff (like accountants) to local CSOs in order to help them become better organized (see p117).

Strategic Business Interests

This is usually based on an initiative of the business, and the decision is made in the company to invest in some aspect of social development that will provide tangible benefits to the company. CSOs may help to develop the ideas, or may be implementers of them, but the company is in the driving seat. For instance, the operations of many businesses in Africa are hampered by the HIV/AIDS epidemic. Businesses are concerned to limit the spread of the epidemic and reduce the lost days in an AIDS-affected workforce. CSOs can be hired to provide AIDS testing and counselling.

Another kind of example can be seen through computer firms, like Apple Computer, that are enthusiastic to donate computer equipment to CSOs and, through them, to communities. While the CSOs benefit, the computer firm is trying to establish brand loyalty. Other examples reflect companies in the agricultural inputs field. They offer free or subsidized seeds, fertilizer, and pesticides through CSOs that are involved in the rural development field, in the hope of eventually selling more products.

Because most CSOs are unfamiliar with businesses, businesspeople and the business culture, they are shy of initiating business contacts, not knowing the language they should use and the concerns that should be addressed. The Concern India Foundation produced a very useful primer for CSOs engaged in addressing businesses for the first time, produced in the form of likely questions from business, and useful answers from CSOs. A CSO intending to approach a business would do well to learn some of these responses by heart (see Box 10.1 on p98).

OVERTURES FROM THE CORPORATE SECTOR

While it is obviously important for CSOs to learn how to approach businesses, and to know how to put their case for support, it is also true that businesses are increasingly looking for CSOs to help them with their social investment. Sometimes companies themselves decide the cause that they would like to support, and look for CSOs to help them to implement programmes; sometimes companies (either on their own or, increasingly, in collaboration with other businesses) set up grant-making foundations with the mandate to fund professionally good development work. In some cases the companies pass over the responsibility for the funding criteria to the board and management of the foundation; in other cases companies define the funding criteria to fit in with their own interests; and in yet other cases they combine the two, with a certain percentage going to the foundation for funding decisions, and a certain percentage being left to the discretion of the company (see Case Study 10.3 on p 103).

Box 10.1 Concern India: Questions and Answers

Why is giving relevant to my company?
- Business cannot operate in isolation from society.
- Having a social vision is integral to the success of the business mission.
- A social investment strategy is a must for any progressive company.
- Qualified professionals increasingly prefer to work for a company with a social commitment.
- Customers show preference for doing business with companies that are environmentally conscious and socially driven.
- Communities and governments expect companies to be good corporate citizens.

Why should I be asked to do this? I pay taxes, shouldn't the government be doing this?
- Government does not always have the capability or resources to do everything.
- There are some things that are best done by NGOs and local communities.
- There are some sorts of support and expertise that only companies can provide.

How do I make sure that my money will be well spent?
- Select a project that meets your criteria, has clearly identified objectives and the right development approach.
- Route your support through a credible development agency.
- Insist on the NGOs providing you with the feedback you require.
- Visit the project.

I don't have any spare funds, so how can I contribute?
- You can give material resources, such as old furniture and equipment, or company products.
- You can provide technical know-how, financial and management skills, media links.
- You can help implement schemes through your company's operations – like constructing low-cost housing or toilets.

Source: The World Wide Fundraiser's Handbook – a Guide to Fundraising for Southern NGOs and Voluntary Organisations, by Michael Norton, DSC and Resource Alliance, London (1997)

LIMITATIONS AND BARRIERS

The following are the possible limitations and barriers to good corporate social investment through CSOs.

Many Requests, Limited Resources

Businesses will tell CSOs how many requests they receive for funds. Usually they will say that most are consigned straight to the wastepaper basket since such proposals are photocopied letters without any attempt to identify the interest of the business except as a writer of cheques. Businesses will tell CSOs that while they recognize the need and value of corporate social investment, CSOs expect them to underwrite the costs of so many activities that they would have to be professional donors to meet the requests. They may well say that the business of business is business, and that no assistance at all will be forthcoming unless the business itself makes a profit.

Corporate Structures and Responsibilities

CSOs do not necessarily know whom they should approach with their proposals. Unless a business has set up a business foundation, the marketing and publicity departments, the director's office, or even others may make their funding decisions. CSOs do not know to whom they must make their pitch, and they may target the wrong person who does not have either the budget or the mandate to support the CSO.

Business Unfamiliarity with CSOs and Community Issues

It is important for CSOs to present themselves to business as fellow professionals. Business people know about their world, and CSOs know about their world. If businesses are interested in social investment, it is important for them to realize that their best guide to this world is a civil society organization.

Time

It is a cliché to say that 'time is money' for a business person, but business people will not give a CSO a great deal of time to 'sell' them an idea. CSOs need to rehearse their presentation and be ready with a short, hard-hitting, and persuasive approach.

Personnel Changes

It may well be that the responsibility for corporate social investment resides with one person in the business, and that the CSO invests a lot of time and energy in educating that person about what should be done and what can be done – then the person is transferred. CSOs should aim, wherever possible, to get an organizational commitment to helping your agency rather than just the interest of an individual. This can be done by providing reports and encouraging visits from a range of people in the company.

Stereotypes

Do not try to involve a business in your CSO's work unless you are prepared and ready to involve a business in your work and receive their funds (or other kinds of support). If you believe that all businesses are exploitative and corrupt, it is hypocritical to invite them to get involved in your programmes. If you believe that a particular business is unethical – for instance, the tobacco industry – do not approach them for funds, or respond to their solicitations. The request for, and the acceptance of, corporate social investment is a two-way process. It should be entered into by people who respect each other, and respect the value of what each other is doing.

It is likely that CSOs have strong stereotypes of the business world, and it is also likely that the business world has strong stereotypes about the CSO world. The first exchanges between the two are likely to need time for these respective prejudices to be aired and dealt with. The Prince of Wales' Business Leaders Forum, an international organization committed to building more and better business/ community partnerships, deals with the problem by convening a one-day workshop between business and CSO leaders. At this workshop, each group is asked to brainstorm and list all the worst things about the other side, and all the best things about their side. Then the two sides show their respective lists to each other. A poignant silence ensues. Slowly each side, through facilitated discussion, sees strengths in the other side to which they can relate, and agrees limitations on their own side. Once this period is over, working relations are built on solid and not prejudiced foundations.

The three case studies in this chapter correspond to corporate philanthropy, business/community partnerships, and strategic business interests: the Red Cross in Botswana; Citicorp's Banking on Enterprise in Bangladesh, and the Philippine Business for Social Progress, the Philippines.

CASE STUDY 10.1 *HOW THE RED CROSS IN BOTSWANA RAISES MONEY FROM COMPANIES (RECOUNTED BY LADY RUTH KHAMA, PRESIDENT, BOTSWANA RED CROSS)*

We started off by writing to larger businesses appealing to them to donate to us on an annual basis. We suggested Pula 5000 for the larger companies, and reduced this amount where we felt it necessary. We did not expect any of them to give at this level, but if you suggest a smaller amount, they offer an even smaller sum. But it did give them an idea of what we were looking for. Some actually did come up with the amount suggested. Overall the response was very pleasing. And most who made a commitment did actually pay up. We enjoy popular support in the community as the Red Cross Movement, which makes it easier to persuade people to part with their money. It really is essential to have their confidence and for them to be aware of what you are doing; and also to keep proper accounts, and to supply audited accounts on request if anyone wants to see them.

It is not just enough just to write letters to General Managers or Managing Directors. The personal approach has far more impact. It is more difficult to refuse if someone is sitting across the table from you. It also helps to invite people home and share a meal or a drink whilst discussing the issue.

The Managing Director of one of our leading companies has always been a dedicated Red Cross fan. He decided not to give to us in response to our appeal, but instead to organize once a year a fundraising evening for our benefit, meeting the cost of this himself. He put on fantastic shows that were hugely popular and charged enormous amounts for the tickets! He has now left Botswana, but the man who has taken over has continued with a similar idea – not putting on shows, because he says he has no talent for it, but, as he is a keen golfer, once a year he organizes a golf championship as a charity event to benefit the Red Cross.

A corporate appeal can snowball if you have the right people receiving your requests. We raise about Pula 70,000 annually, but some companies give to us in kind – for example, one wholesale company donates bags of mealie meal each month for our disabled training centre. The cost of running the appeal is almost nothing, as it consists mostly of stationery and stamps to remind companies if they happen to forget. Most companies take advantage of giving to us by promoting themselves in the media when they hand over cheques. We do not mind this: in fact we welcome it, as it also advertises what we do. Other competitor companies, in order not to be outdone, decide also to give. More snowballing.

The main lesson learnt is the need to build the donor's confidence – making people aware of our rehabilitation and relief programmes, our training centre for the disabled, the work of our volunteers, and most importantly to convince them that the money they give us will be well spent, that we are working with the most needy and doing the best work. In Botswana we have far too many organizations appealing to too few donors. It is therefore our job to persuade people that they could do no better than support our cause because we will use the money the way that they would want it to be used.

Source: The World Wide Fundraiser's Handbook – a Guide to Fundraising for Southern NGOs and Voluntary Organisations, Michael Norton, DSC and Resource Alliance, London, (1997)

CASE STUDY 10.2   *CITICORP'S BANKING ON ENTERPRISE*

Citicorp does not normally offer loans secured against a one-woman hair braiding business. But in the last few years it has started to do just that, as part of a corporate policy to support 'microcredit' schemes. The idea is that such small businesses are promising but are so small and speculative that they would fail to appear on the radar of Citicorp or any other mainstream commercial bank.

The policy also forms part of a changed attitude to development in emerging economies and in the poorest inner-city areas of the USA. Rather than attempt to build the economy through big infrastructure projects, or through persuading large companies to re-locate there, the idea is now to stimulate small businesses to grow. According to Paul Ostergard, president of the Citicorp Foundation: 'Most corporations look in their philanthropy for an obvious connection, something that will make obvious sense. Micro-lending fits that criterion.'

Citicorp, the largest bank in the USA when judged by deposits, still does not make the loans directly. Through the Citicorp Foundation its money funds a variety of non-profit, independent charitable or religious foundations that administer the schemes on the ground. Geographically the spread of small business matches Citicorp's global presence. It offers loans in a range of developing nations, particularly in Latin America and the Indian sub-continent.

Citicorp's involvement has, so far, been solely philanthropic but there are clear opportunities for the scheme to create direct advantage for the bank. In Bangladesh, where the schemes were first launched by the Grameen Foundation, there is evidence that the repayment rates on small loans (around $50) is between 95 and 100% and borrowers are returning for second and third loans – steadily becoming 'economic citizens'.

Like most corporate community involvement schemes, micro-lending is, ultimately, in Citibank's indirect or 'enlightened' self-interest. Citibank has set a goal for the organization to build its retail customers globally, aiming for a billion customers by 2010. Any programme which increases the number of people who could benefit from a current account is likely to help the bank reach this goal. It could also produce direct, positive results for the company. Some micro-lending institutions themselves are not large enough to need the services of an international bank, such as Citicorp. They are not being targeted by the bank's financial institutions group as offering potential for expansion.

Source: Responsible Business – A Financial Times Survey, 1998

CASE STUDY 10.3 *PHILIPPINE BUSINESS FOR SOCIAL PROGRESS*

Several collaborative efforts in the Philippines provide corporate support for the highly active NGO sector. The Philippine Business for Social Progress (PBSP) was founded in 1970 by 49 companies to engage corporate commitment to social development and to support programmes promoting self-reliance and the sustainable development that is critical to the Philippines' economic growth and development. The intent was to pool resources in a multi-business effort to address critical issues facing the nation ranging from economic stagnation to natural disasters. The businesses pledged 1% of the preceding year's profits to support an organization that would have professional staff act on their behalf to address social issues in a significant way. Later it was agreed that 20% of that 1% would be given to PBSP to spend, while 80% of the 1% would be spent by the donating company in ways that they decided – usually on projects to help the areas where their employees lived.

Today PBSP has 179 members including local and multinational companies such as San Miguel Corporation, Shell, IBM Philippines, Nestlé Philippines and Jardine Davies. Its 1994 budget was US$6.5 million. It is not a philanthropic organization. Its primary mission is to develop economically self-reliant communities. Even assistance given to disaster victims is designed to focus on crisis preparedness and income generation.

PBSP has four programme areas in which it works on its own account, through local NGOs, and through local governments. These are community organizing, enterprise development, institution building and technology transfer. It also works to improve the effectiveness of local government management of services; provides access to credit for small- and medium-sized enterprises, particularly in rural areas; supports agrarian reform; promotes environmental protection and conservation; and offers a venue for corporate CEOs to consider business responses to important social issues such as education and the environment. In 1994 PBSP undertook 179 projects in its four priority areas. The organization has also adopted the Area Resource Programme approach which integrates the four areas in single projects to bring comprehensive socio-economic development to targeted poverty areas.

Source: Sustaining Civil Society – Strategies for Resource Mobilisation, CIVICUS, Washington DC, 1997

Chapter 11

Building Reserve Funds and Endowments

BUILDING RESERVE FUNDS

A reserve fund is a fund that a CSO sets up from savings that it has been able to make on its main work, and which then can be used either to generate more money through investments, or for venture capital for new ideas that the CSO may have. The main point about a reserve fund is that it is untied – ie it consists of money owned by the CSO that does not have to satisfy any donor conditionalities.

Reserve funds can be built up from the following sources:

- Money raised from the general public (or other fundraising ventures) that is not needed for immediate operating expenses, usually because the programme operating costs are being provided from another source.
- Money that the CSO has saved on contracts that it may have undertaken for donors or government.
- Money that CSOs have received from fees for service.
- Money that the CSOs has saved from financial dealings (income from exchange rate fluctuations, or from short-term investments of funds received from foreign donors).
- Money received from management fees or a management overhead as part of a foreign-funded project.
- Contributions to the reserve fund (sometimes called a corpus fund).

Any money that is surplus to the CSO's immediate needs can be put into a reserve fund, which is then invested to attract interest and increase in size. CSOs have the option of using these funds in a variety of ways. They can invest the funds in financial instruments locally or, depending on the banking rules in their country, offshore. They can use the funds to invest in their own (or others') businesses. As was mentioned previously, however, CSO people are not usually very good business-people, and lack experience and expertise in such fields. They would be well advised to get professional help in how and where spare funds can be invested. In some cases they will need legal advice as to how such funds should be owned since, in some countries, CSO reserve funds will attract tax. Figure 11.1 shows how this might be achieved.

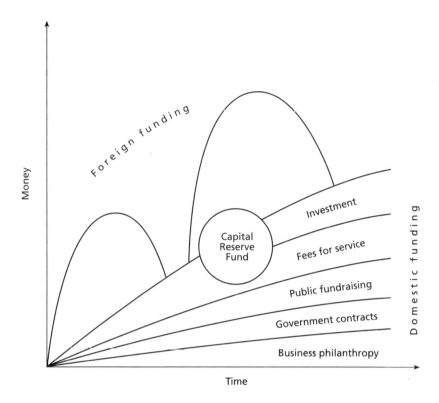

Figure 11.1 *The Use of a Reserve Fund*

The practices of many donors, however, prevent such capital accumulation by CSOs. In many cases foreign donor funds are so tightly controlled that they do not allow CSOs to carry out any of the activities mentioned above. United States Agency for International Development (USAID), for instance, only provides funding on a one-month or three-month advance system such that there is no possibility of investing this money short-term, and indeed such investments are expressly forbidden. Any interest on money deposited in banks has to be returned to USAID if it is over US$250 per annum. With USAID, allowed overhead costs are very tightly controlled so that they reflect real costs and allow nothing for organizational income beyond actuals, and USAID expressly forbids management fees to be charged by CSOs.

This is defended as wise stewardship of and fiduciary responsibility for USAID's funds, but this clashes with the larger picture of trying to help CSOs to become self-reliant. There is confused thinking in USAID (and many other donors) about the real objective of their CSO funding; whether it is to be used to achieve USAID's sectoral development objectives with CSOs as the delivery mechanism, or whether it is to be used to build a viable CSO sector to be able to achieve USAID's ultimate development objectives in the long run.

At the same time, and on the plus side, USAID has pioneered some very innovative ways of encouraging CSO self-reliance by allowing CSOs to build up their reserve funds. They have done this by helping them to set up a system of fees-for-service which produces income for the CSO, but then continuing to fund their operating and programme costs for a period of 5 to 10 years, which allows the income from their fees-for-service to build up into a sizeable reserve fund which can then be invested. This is how PROCOSI in Bolivia, an innovative primary health care organization, has been funded.

CSOs need to put the case to donors that there are a variety of ways in which long-term organizational sustainability can be encouraged, but that in many cases their existing systems prevent this from happening. The foreign donors have to reflect on their own thinking as to whether they are using CSOs as their own development project delivery mechanism, or whether they are interested in building up a viable and sustainable citizen sector to be able to deliver development benefits into the future.

ENDOWMENTS

As we have seen in the previous section, reserve funds can be invested to create an income stream for the CSO into the future. In this sense they become endowments. This section looks at funds that are used to set up an endowment as a deliberate policy of sustainable financing. While we usually think of endowments as money in the bank or in stocks and shares, endowments can equally be in property, land or equipment.

Foreign donor funds for endowments can be directed either at a particular CSO (in which case it is likely to be a large organization to have the financial management skills to handle an endowment), or, more often, directed at a purpose-built foundation which then acts as a source of funding for smaller CSOs. Whether the endowment is for the former or the latter, however, the requirements are similar.

Trust by the Foreign Donor in the CSO's (or Foundation's) Long-term Future

A donor has to be convinced that the governance of the CSO or foundation will not modify the aims and mission of the organization once an independent income stream is acquired. This requires either a long-term relationship between CSO and donor, or very tightly crafted legal articles of association for the CSO or foundation, or both.

Very Competent Financial Management Skills by the CSO or Foundation

The CSO or foundation has to know how to plan and manage investments that will maximize income, but at the same time provide an income flow of the size and at the time that it is needed. It has to know the respective advantages of investing locally or offshore and of complying with all local laws and regulations, and it has to be able to deal with very volatile money markets and rates of inflation in many countries.

A Supportive Legal and Fiscal Environment

This basically means a situation where the governance of the CSO or foundation is inviolate from invasion, and where the CSO or foundation will be free from taxes.

Enabling Donor Rules and Regulations

At the time of writing, for instance, CIDA is unable to use its funds to set up endowments for CSOs because its Treasury Board rules do not allow it. USAID did not allow it originally, but changed their rules by Act of Congress in 1988.

Time

Setting up an endowment is not in any way a quick fix for a CSO's funding problems. It requires a lot of preparation and training of staff for new roles, or hiring of new staff. In the case of a foundation that is intended to deal with the civil society sector as a whole, even more time is required because the CSOs as a whole need to agree to its setting up and a long participatory process of consensus-building needs to be undertaken.

COMPARISON BETWEEN GRANT FUNDING AND ENDOWMENT FUNDING

A donor who is asked for an endowment has to consider not only the priority it places on building financial self-sufficiency for the CSO or the citizen sector, but also the alternative uses of its funds.

Endowments are extremely expensive. A large amount of money is granted to an organization to invest in order to get a percentage of that money as interest for the organization to spend on its ongoing work. An organization can look to an endowment to supply the funds for all its operating expenses, or it can look to it to supply a portion of this, with the rest being made up from other resource mobilization strategies. Whichever way it intends to operate, it needs to start from what it needs in operating revenue, and then to work back to what investment is needed to supply that revenue.

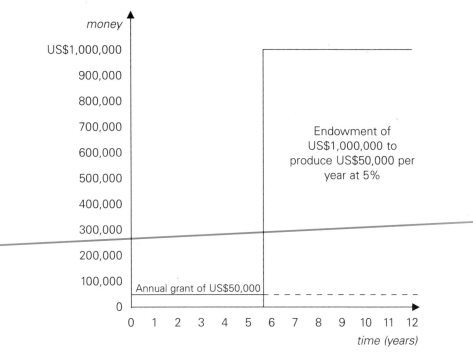

Figure 11.2 *The Difference between an Annual Grant and an Endowment*

Figure 11.2 illustrates the difference from the donor's perspective of making an annual grant of US$50,000 to a CSO, or making an endowment that will result in the CSO receiving interest of US$50,000 based on a 5 per cent rate of interest. A conservative rule of thumb is that a CSO might get 5 per cent real interest on its investment after allowing for inflation and the cost of managing the money. This may seem surprising given the high rates of interest being offered for term deposits in many banks in the South, but inflation can undercut these advantages.

As can be seen, a donor has to think about tying up US$1,000,000 in one organization, as opposed to funding 20 organizations at US$50,000 per year. On the other hand, an endowment strategy will result (if it is well managed over a 20-year time-frame) in 20 autonomous and self-reliant organizations at the end of that time. A grant-making strategy will only result in the same 20 organizations being as donor dependent at the end of 20 years as they were at the start.

The case study that illustrates building reserve funds and endowments is the Foundation for the Philippines Environment.

CASE STUDY 11.1 *THE FOUNDATION FOR THE PHILIPPINES ENVIRONMENT*

The Foundation for the Philippines Environment (FPE) was legally established in January 1992 through the efforts of environmental and development NGOs in the Philippines and the United States, and the Governments in each country (principally USAID and the Philippine Department of Environment and Natural Resources). The process included extensive civil society consultations in the Philippines, eight formal regional consultations, and national conferences of eight major NGO networks. In total, more than 300 NGOs and 24 academic institutions were engaged in the process.

The founders of FPE also consulted widely with international actors and conducted a study tour on philanthropy, funded by the Ford Foundation, to expose the new organization's initial governing board to US organizations with expertise in foundation formation, governance and grants management.

It took more than three years to create the endowment – from the beginnings of negotiations between governments in 1991 to the 1994 completed debt swap issued to the World Wildlife Fund (now the Worldwide Fund for Nature) and the Philippine Business for Social Progress, which in turn led to the creation of the FPE. Foreign assistance of about US$18 million (mostly from USAID) was used to purchase debt valued at about US$29 million. Currently FPE's endowment is worth US$23 million.

FPE has been careful not to compete for funds with Philippine NGOs, viewing itself as a fund facilitator. It turned down an opportunity for funds from Switzerland that it felt might better go to other organizations.

In 1993 FPE disbursed more than US$1.5 million in grants through a variety of mechanisms that include responses to proposals and pro-active grants on issues that the Foundation deems of importance. FPE also acts as a fund facilitator, generating additional financial resources and providing financial linkages between donors, Philippine NGOs, and Philippine people's organizations.

Source: Sustaining Civil Society: Strategies for Resource Mobilisation, CIVICUS (1997)

Chapter 12

Conversion of Debt

Many Southern countries' governments are heavily in debt. The servicing of that debt eats up a huge amount of the countries' income, and there is very little hope that the principal will ever be repaid. In many countries, North and South, there is a growing determination to get such debt cancelled to different degrees; one campaign is called Jubilee 2000 and has been started by churches (but spread far beyond them), and another initiative is called the Highly Indebted Poor Countries (HIPC) Initiative and was designed by the World Bank.

Apart from these macro-level efforts to resolve the problems of poor countries' indebtedness, there are other ways of converting foreign debt into funds that are available for CSOs. This creates new money by working a procedure that allows organizations to 'buy debt' in foreign currency at a discount, and to make available a multiple of that in local currency for development purposes. The procedure is complicated and time-consuming, but has been successfully implemented in many countries of the world.

BACKGROUND TO NATIONAL DEBT

Many countries in the South have borrowed hard currency from sources in the north. These sources may have been commercial banks, countries – ie bilateral aid organizations – or multilateral institutions, and the money borrowed has to be repaid in the same hard currency in which it was borrowed. Many countries are now unable to repay those loans, and are unlikely ever to be able to repay them. The most that they can do (and that with difficulty) is to pay the interest on the loans.

Faced with such a situation, countries in the South have the following options:

1 They can ask for the rescheduling of the debt.
2 They can negotiate for total debt forgiveness (the Jubilee 2000 approach), or partial debt forgiveness (the HIPC approach).
3 They can negotiate for repayment of the debt in local currency, not hard currency.
4 They can refuse to repay the debt.

Very few opt for the last option since that would prejudice their chances of future borrowing.

Repaying Hard Currency Debt in Local Currency at a Discount

Since the creditors know how unlikely it is that they will ever be repaid in full in hard currency, a secondary market has grown up in which buyers offer to purchase the hard currency debt at a discount – ie at a fraction of its worth in hard currency, but to receive the full amount of the original debt converted into local currency. This system allows the country concerned to convert hard currency debt into local currency debt which it can pay, and thus to cancel the hard currency debt.

Because this idea is attractive to a Southern country (which is thus freed from the problem of finding hard currency to pay its debt), it is possible to negotiate some conditions along with the debt conversion. These conditions usually involve a development agency (often an international NGO) that wants to:

- persuade the creditor to allow the local currency that has been generated to be used for development purposes;
- persuade the Ministry of Finance in the Southern country to allow the local currency funds that have been generated to be used for some agreed development purpose.

There are thus three or possibly four actors in a debt conversion:

1   The creditor (a Northern commercial bank, bilateral aid agency, or a multilateral agency).
2   The Southern country's Ministry of Finance that has legally engaged in the borrowing and the promise to repay.
3   A Northern NGO that offers to negotiate a debt conversion provided that a developmental use of the local currency that has been generated can be agreed (usually, but not essentially).
4   A Southern civil society organization or foundation that will act as the custodian and manager of the local currency fund generated.

The transactions involve the following steps:

1   A Northern NGO persuades the Northern creditor to accept that it is not going to be repaid in hard currency, and either to cancel its demand for repayment in hard currency and accept local currency, or to sell its debt at a discounted amount of hard currency.

2   If the Northern creditor is prepared to cancel its debt in hard currency and to accept the local currency, the Northern NGO persuades the debtor to donate the local currency amount to a development purpose in the Southern country to be managed by a Northern NGO.

3   If the Northern creditor is prepared to sell its debt for a discount, to persuade it to do so, making it a condition of such a sale that the local currency that has been generated should be used for a development purpose to be managed by a Northern or Southern NGO – typically an endowment to generate sustainable income into the future. A further possibility is that the northern creditor would accept repayment in some other form – eg land or a building – linked to a development purpose.

4   To persuade the Ministry of Finance of the Southern country that it is in their interests to get their hard currency debt either cancelled or converted on these terms, and to get their agreement to set up a structure by which the development purposes can be fulfilled.

An example of how this might work is:

1   A Northern NGO persuades a Northern donor to give it US$200,000 to purchase US$500,000 worth of a Southern country's hard currency debt on condition that the Southern country makes available to the Northern NGO the equivalent of US$500,000 in local currency or some assets worth US$500,000, to be used for a specified development purpose.

2   The Northern NGO persuades the Southern Ministry of Finance to convert its debt thus and to set up the legal and fiscal structures for US$500,000 worth of local currency (or its equivalent in other kinds of assets) to be managed in the Southern country by the Northern NGO or a Southern NGO identified as part of the negotiations.

Examples of how this has worked have been:

1   UNICEF bought discounted debt from the government of Zambia on condition that it made available the agreed local currency equivalent to UNICEF in Zambia (and the NGOs with which UNICEF works) for children's programmes.

2   Conservation International bought discounted debt from the government of Bolivia on condition that it agreed to set up a national park and allow the local currency generated to be used for the funds required to manage it.

3   The World Wildlife Fund/USA with funds from USAID bought discounted debt from the government of the Philippines in order to set up an endowed foundation for grant-making to civil society organizations in the Philippines that were involved in environmental protection (see Case Study 12.1 on p114).

Funds generated by this strategy can also be augmented by funds that have been created in the South from money that has been generated from in-kind gifts from Northern donors – typically food aid. The USA, the European Union (EU), Canada, and several other countries, that have provided food aid, have usually made it a condition that funds generated from sales of such food aid should be kept as a separate fund for development purposes.

It can be seen that Northern NGOs can act as catalysts to leverage more local currency from a given amount of Northern aid – typically twice as much. Such local currency can be used for the work of a Southern CSO, or it can create, through an endowment, a sustainable source of funding for Southern CSOs for the future.

DIFFICULTIES AND COMPLEXITIES

As can be seen, however, there are considerable difficulties and complexities involved in the process of debt conversion. Some of these are:

1   Decisions to allow such discounted debt sales and put the local currency generated into the hands of NGOs are intensely political both in the North and in the South. The NGO that wants to work as the catalyst for this process must be ready with strong arguments and good negotiating skills.
2   The final decisions are made between governments – usually the respective Ministries of Finance – and these are not usually ministries that NGOs, North or South, are familiar with.
3   The negotiations, the agreements, and the processing of the paperwork take a long time – perhaps two years – during which time the Northern NGO has to keep pressing its case, and possibly keep dealing with changes in government, and certainly changes in personnel.
4   If the funds are used to set up an endowed foundation for making grants to NGOs, it is likely that the structure for this must be set up with the participatory agreement of the citizen sector. Negotiations on the governance and management of such a structure are likely to be a long-drawn out process.

However, these difficulties should not obscure the fact that many funds for civil society organizations have been generated in this way, involving converting debt to Germany, Canada, Switzerland, France, and Belgium, and creating new funds for citizens' organizations in the Philippines, Bolivia, Zambia, and Jamaica. Much of the pioneering work has been done by environmental NGOs who have popularized 'debt for nature' swaps, and a specialized NGO to advise other NGOs in this field was created in the USA called the 'Debt for Development Coalition'.

The case studies to illustrate the strategy of debt conversion are the Foundation for a Sustainable Society Inc., Philippines, and the Environmental Foundation of Jamaica.

Case Study 12.1 *Foundation for a Sustainable Society Inc., Philippines*

In August 1995, the Governments of the Philippines and Switzerland signed an agreement on the reduction of Philippines' external debt. Under this accord, 50% of the Philippine Government's outstanding export credit debt to Switzerland, amounting to 42 million Swiss Francs (approximately US$35 million), was cancelled. The remainder was converted into Philippine pesos. These were then provided by the Philippines Treasury as an endowment to the Foundation for a Sustainable Society Inc., Philippines (FSSI), a foundation formed to manage the counterpart funds.

FSSI supports productive activities of NGOs, people's organizations, co-operatives and similar private organizations in the field of agriculture and fisheries, as well as in the urban and rural small industries sector. The foundation is, in the first place, a loan-making institution, but it also provides grants for activities such as technical assistance, feasibility studies, and market research. FSSI has three interesting features:

- it is exclusively managed by NGOs, and its resources are exclusively being allocated to civil society organizations;
- it is structured as a long-term capital fund – that is, only the interest, or the return on investment, and part of the loan re-flows are used to fund projects and programmes;
- the process that led to the forging of the agreement was marked from the start by a close and intensive collaboration between Philippine and Swiss NGOs.

Several important lessons were learnt from this experience. Firstly, it is clear that close coordination and permanent communication between organized NGO constituencies in the debtor and creditor countries are crucial to the success of negotiations between governments.

Secondly, official debt conversion involving the establishment of an autonomous management structure such as a foundation consume a lot of time (2 years in this case) and energy, because there were many actors involved (two governments and two NGO communities) with sometimes differing interests. Thus transaction costs tend to be rather high, and the donor government or NGO must be prepared to pay for the major part of these.

Thirdly, a participatory approach is very important for the ownership of the process and the funding mechanism to be created. The Southern NGOs should be involved right from the beginning in designing and preparing the scheme, otherwise there is a risk that they will not stay involved if major difficulties or delays occur.

Fourthly, it is crucial to have good working contacts with relevant govern-ment officials on both sides in order to get access to important information. For instance, the Northern NGO may get some important information from its government on the Southern government's negotiating position that it can pass on to its NGO counterpart to use in its lobbying work, or vice versa.

There should be no illusions about the outcome of the official debt conversions: these are negotiated between two governments, and the final decisions will be taken by these parties. So the results may be different from the scheme initially proposed by the NGOs. Thus it is all the more important to have strong NGO networks on both sides with a high capacity to advocate their positions in order to reach the best result possible.

One of the most positive aspects of this process was the excellent collaboration between the two NGO communities, which were both very motivated and committed to the common cause. Another positive point was the broad and inclusive consultation process amongst the Philippine CSOs, including those who are critical of debt swaps and cooperation with the Government. This inclusive process allowed broad participation in FSSI's Board of Trustees, and especially in its membership.

One negative aspect was the pressure of time during the negotiation period that did not allow for sufficient consultation of the participating NGO representatives, since decisions had to be taken very quickly. This is a major drawback of this type of official debt conversion, where as a rule NGO representatives are not permitted to sit at the negotiating table.

Source: Sustaining Civil Society—Strategies for Resource Mobilisation, CIVICUS (1997)

Case Study 12.2 *Environmental Foundation of Jamaica*

The Environmental Foundation of Jamaica (EFJ) was the result of debt reduction agreements in August 1991 and January 1993 between the Governments of Jamaica and the United States. Under these, and follow-up agreements, 77% of Jamaica's debt originating from Food Aid (PL480 debt) and its USAID debt was cancelled – a total of US$405 million. The remaining 23% was re-structured for quarterly payments by the Jamaican government into a fund controlled by the EFJ. Over 20 years, this will amount to US$21.5 million

The debt conversion came about through the efforts of US environmental NGOs. It was included in the 1990 Enterprise for the Americas Initiative of President Bush that was designed to promote hemispheric trade and investment, to which the burden of debt servicing was seen as an obstacle.

The EFJ Board of Directors has nine members – six seats for NGOs, two for the two governments, and one for a representative of the University of the West Indies. An interesting feature of the EFJ is its membership – some 59 NGOs and community based organizations. More than half participate actively in selecting a slate of Board representatives (from which the Minister of the Environment appoints the Board), guiding policy, advising on project selection, and monitoring the work of the Board and the Secretariat.

This collaboration between NGOs works well in spite of its novelty and initial differences in age, size, and degrees of organization. The older development agencies were fairly well organized, while the newer, smaller environmental groups that were just trying to get their act together took the lead on debt conversion. More difficult and challenging was the collaboration with the governments. NGOs in Jamaica, in the absence of any legal, regulatory, or policy restraints, learned that it had to be done and could be very useful, but also that collaboration had to be approached carefully and critically.

The object of the EFJ is to provide grants towards the conservation and sustainable management of Jamaica's natural resources. Priority is given to projects involving local community management and capacity building of NGOs and community groups. A set amount of funds also goes to child development and child survival projects that have an environmental dimension.

From August 1993 to July 1996 the Foundation approved 219 projects for an average annual total of US$1.5 million, a figure that was expected to top US$2 million in 1996–7. At the same time, effective management of income by professional investment firms has brought the EFJ's resources to more than US$12 million. This has gone into an endowment fund established in 1997 to ensure the continuity of the foundation after the debt conversion payments cease. EFJ is also seeking to diversify the sources of funding in order to build up the endowment.

For the NGO community and their umbrella organizations, the EFJ has been a valuable experience. Grasping the opportunity for collaboration on several fronts and showing patience and persistence, the NGOs have asserted control of the foundation, put it onto a sound footing and kept it faithful to its mandate. Yet its leaders remain aware of the need to establish sustainable funding, and of the difficulty – with limited funds – of having significant impact on massive environmental and development needs.

Source: Sustaining Civil Society – Strategies for Resource Mobilisation, CIVICUS (1997)

Chapter 13

Microcredit Programmes

CREDIT FOR THE BORROWER, INCOME FOR THE CSO

More and more CSOs are running microcredit programmes, often inspired by the example of the Grameen Bank in Bangladesh, and the publicity generated by the Micro-Credit Summit of 1997. The objectives of such programmes are to build microenterprises (possibly moving into small enterprises) and to help poor people to build a sustainable income for themselves. They do this by helping the borrowers to work together in groups to mobilize capital from among the group and take collective action. The group of borrowers, in many programmes, is also urged to address social issues.

The attractive feature of well-run microcredit programmes is that they are financially sustainable since they rely on money being loaned out and repaid with interest, and thus being available to be loaned again, or loaned to others. Microcredit programmes, however, can be a source of income to the CSO beyond the cost of the microcredit programme, and thus microcredit programmes become a special kind of 'revenue from earned income' (see Chapter 4).

The thinking behind this is that microcredit programmes can have two outcomes:

- Benefits to the microentrepreneurs, who are enabled:
  - to be self-employed;
  - to create and sell goods and services;
  - to gain income which they did not have before;
  - to escape from crippling debt.
- Benefits to the CSO running the microcredit programme that can:
  - get the original loan repaid;
  - get income through a service fee charged to the borrower for running the microcredit scheme;
  - use any surplus funds generated by the microcredit scheme for other work of the CSO.

A good microcredit programme also produces benefits to the community in that it reduces the power of local money-lenders, generates social capital, mobilizes the financial power of many small savers, and builds social capital.

Usually CSOs running microcredit programmes receive an original grant from a donor to set up a microcredit programme, and to start the revolving lending system. Sometimes a CSO can set up a savings programme initially, and from the savings can start to make loans. The latter is the model of the credit unions. If the interest rate for the loans is well calculated, and any other charges for the administration of the programme are factored in, then the income received from the borrowers should be enough to cover the cost of administering the credit, as well as programmes linked to the credit system, such as training.

If the CSO designs the repayment structure slightly differently, it is able to generate enough money to cover all the costs of the savings and credit operations, as well as make a small surplus which the CSO can use for other programmes or to pay for its overhead costs.

It might be argued that a CSO should not charge more than the bare minimum that is needed to cover the costs of the savings and credit programme; since the target is the very poor, anything beyond that is exploitation. We need to return to the arguments made in Chapter 4 (p34) that poor people are prepared to pay the costs that a CSO charges for a service, provided the service (in this case, credit) is available where and when they want it, is flexible, professionally run, in the amounts they need, and within their power to repay.

The advantages of a well-run savings and credit programme are that:

- Loans given to the poor under a well-managed system show excellent repayment rates (higher than those lending to the middle class or the rich).
- It is possible to cover costs and make a small surplus if the interest and repayment conditions are soundly calculated and efficiently administered.
- The poor are prepared to pay market rates, and even higher, if the service they receive is good, efficient, and they have some voice in its management.

The disadvantages to a CSO of operating a savings and credit scheme are:

- It only succeeds if the CSO is very professional about the way it designs and administers the scheme.
- The law in any particular country may, or may not, be helpful to the CSO that wishes to undertake a savings and microcredit operation. Sometimes existing statutes restrict such work to legally set up banks.
- There is a danger that the CSO may lose sight of its mission in the business of becoming a money-lender and deposit-taker.

Many civil society organizations find that operating a small and cost-covering savings and credit scheme is quite enough work, and they do not want to go beyond this. They usually receive savings from the people to whom they lend money as part of the general package of assistance, and the whole process is targeted to people who are limited by both geography and income level.

Going Beyond Linked Savings and Credit

If, on the other hand, the CSO wants to become a microfinance institution (MFI) and optimize its income from operating as a financial institution so that it can bring income into the organization to use in the furtherance of its mission, it will need to expand its range of customers both geographically and by income level. It will also need to offer a range of services beyond linked savings and credit.

The CSO very probably will need to receive deposits from people who are not necessarily borrowers to increase the amount of capital it can mobilize. It will also need to acquire new capital for expansion, and this money will probably be 'bought' from banks or finance institutions at market rates, rather than received as a grant from a donor. It will also probably have to design and sell a variety of financial services (like house loans, cattle loans, agricultural loans) to meet customers' requirements. It will have to continue, of course, to be very professional in its original operations, and to become very competent at a range of more complex financial services, particularly since many of its new customers will not come from its old and well-known client base.

Many countries have legal statutes that set out standards for those institutions that are allowed to receive deposits. This usually requires a minimum level of capitalization that is beyond most CSOs. In many cases microfinance institutions are protesting these rules and seeking changes in government laws and policies that will allow the expanding number of CSOs entering this field to take deposits, and earn income from this. The legal statutes were originally designed, however, to prevent crooks from taking customers' money and running off with it. CSOs that want to take deposits will have to prove that they are competent enough to be able to pay out customers' deposits on request.

Key Issues

If a small savings and credit CSO wants to move from simple operations to the full range of services of a financial intermediary – which is where the income is to be made – it must think about the following key issues:

Savings

Whose savings will you take? Anyone's? What protection will you offer big depositors?

Interest Rates

Will you keep them at existing market rates? Or will you go higher if the market will bear it? Will you exclude your poorest customers by doing so?

Group or Individual Lending

Most CSOs have initiated their savings and lending operations through group lending backed by peer group pressure. Will you continue like this? Or will you lend to individuals? If you lend to individuals, how will you handle the question of collateral, or establish creditworthiness?

Legal Identity

Will you set up a separate financial intermediary organization, with the status of a bank, and offer a range of financial services?

Acquiring Capital

Will you be able to finance your operations by borrowing money at the market rate? Or will your scheme require start-up capital in the form of a grant? If you want to borrow money from a local bank either for capitalization or for working capital, will you be able to do so? Are you seen as creditworthy?

Mission

Is there a danger that your original mission (of helping poor people to employ themselves) will be lost in pursuing the making of money through banking services, or will you be able to separate the money-making from the mission-linked services?

BANK GUARANTEES

One of the most interesting services offered by foreign donor agencies that are enthusiastic about helping CSOs to sustain themselves through providing financial services is the idea of bank guarantees. Donor agencies (local or foreign) can agree with a local bank that loans taken out from it by CSOs (or MFIs) will be guaranteed.

RAFAD in Switzerland has pioneered a further extension of this work. The first step is to link the bank used by a microfinance institution in the South to a bank in the North. The second step is for the donor agency to guarantee the bank in the North that borrowings up to a certain level by the specified bank in the

South will be honoured. The third step is for the bank in the South to offer credit to the CSO/MFI up to a certain level, knowing that its loans will be guaranteed by the Northern bank. The beauty of this scheme is that Northern money is not tied up, and indeed will never be employed if the CSO/MFI carries out its work competently. It will only be required if there is the problem that the CSO/MFI cannot repay the bank from which it borrowed money.

IRED (Innovations et Reseaux pour le Développement), which gave birth to RAFAD, has produced an interesting 13-stage process for a CSO that wants to take on the role of an MFI; this ties in very closely with Chapter 4.

Box 13.1 RAFAD's 13 Stages Leading to Greater Financial Autonomy

1 Creation of the NGO and development of its links to grass-roots or community-based organizations (GRO/CBOs).
2 Development of the GR/CBOs' resources with the NGO helping them to do this.
3 Initial sales of products and services by the NGO.
4 Establishment of a capital reserve fund, using profits from sales and services.
5 Local fundraising.
6 External fundraising based on projects.
7 Institutional development – building up management capacity, strategic planning, financial management.
8 Development of the capital reserve fund, and making more investments.
9 Negotiation of flexible programme grants from donors.
10 Negotiation of a grant for a revolving loan fund that the NGO administers.
11 Increases in sales and services, increases in deposits in the reserve fund, and in investments.
12 Negotiations with local banks for credit for your NGO with, if necessary, bank guarantees from international finance institutions (eg RAFAD, Women's World Banking).
13 Direct access to credit from local banks.

The case studies for the section on microcredit programmes are Shri Mahila Sewa Sahakari Bank, India, and the Kenya Rural Enterprise Programme.

CASE STUDY 13.1 *SHRI MAHILA SEWA SAHAKARI BANK, INDIA*

The Self-Employed Women's Association (SEWA) is a trade union formed in 1972 to improve the lives of poor informal sector women workers. Any self-employed woman in India can become a member of SEWA by paying a membership fee of at least 5 rupees a year. As a membership based organization, SEWA has spawned numerous self-help initiatives, including a cooperative bank.

The clients of SEWA bank are all self-employed women. SEWA clients have low incomes, little or no savings, no assets, and no direct access to raw materials. Access to financial services is a major problem for poor self-employed women such as hawkers, vendors, home based workers, manual labourers and service providers. Because they do not save, emergencies and obligations often force women to borrow heavily from informal money lenders. However – they are unlikely to have the experience or self-confidence to obtain credit from a formal financial institution.

At the same time, the institution's regulations and procedures rarely meet the needs of a woman seeking a loan. Therefore poor self-employed women often depend on informal money-lenders, contractors and wholesalers who charge exorbitant interest rates. This often starts a downward spiral of increased indebtedness, perpetuating poverty.

In response to this constraint, in 1974 some 4000 SEWA members established a cooperative bank owned by shareholding members to provide credit to self-employed women and reduce their dependence on money-lenders. SEWA bank borrowers are required to buy 5% of the loan amount in bank shares when receiving a loan and in order to open a savings account. The women are therefore the Bank's shareholders, and they hold annual shareholders' meetings. The bank is supervised by the Reserve Bank of India, which determines the interest rates on loans and savings deposits, the proportion of deposits that can be loaned, and the areas of operations.

The members of the Bank elect the Board of Directors. The Board consists of 15 members, 10 of whom are trade leaders. All major decisions are made by the board, including sanctioning all loans advanced. The sources of capital for SEWA bank are savings deposits, share capital, and profits that are ploughed back into the institution. SEWA Bank has currently approximately 60,000 depositors and 6000 borrowers.

Between 1974 and 1977 SEWA Bank concentrated on attracting deposits from self-employed women and served as a guarantor to enable depositors to obtain loans from nationalized banks that are required to lend to the poor. In 1976 SEWA Bank started to extend loans to its own depositors from its own funds and gradually withdrew from the credit arrangement with the nationalized banks.

Source: Sustaining Civil Society – Strategies for Resource Mobilisation, CIVICUS (1997)

CASE STUDY 13.2 *KENYA RURAL ENTERPRISE PROGRAMME*

The Kenya Rural Enterprise Programme (K-REP) is a private microfinance institution registered as an NGO. Its mission is to facilitate poverty alleviation by developing systems and institutions that will enable poor people to organise their lives financially. K-REP's activities include micro-financial services, research and evaluation, information dissemination, and consulting services. K-REP has one of the most extensive resource centres for microfinance in Africa.

Recently K-REP has established a commercial bank that will assume its microfinance operations. This will be owned by K-REP, the International Finance Corporation, Shorebank Corporation, Triodos Bank, and possibly the African Development Bank. The decision to create a bank was based on the realization that NGOs lack the capacity to serve as effective financial intermediaries. In part this is because the corporate image of NGOs elicits scepticism in the minds of the community, clients, the government, and particularly other institutions in the financial markets.

Second, NGOs have limited legal capacity to explore other financial instruments and products such as savings mobilization. K-REP commissioned a study in 1994 to determine the best institutional form to support its continued expansion. The study looked at different types of institutions, such as credit unions, non-bank financial institutions, and commercial banks under the banking act. It recommended the commercial bank as the best form, given its capacity to provide a wide range of financial services.

The Government of Kenya's bank supervision division had limited exposure to microfinance, and no experience with an NGO owning a bank. And the banking industry in Kenya had been badly hit by a significant number of bank collapses, which made the bank supervisor even more wary of new ideas. So K-REP worked with highly placed and respected individuals to secure the attention of decision makers, and to garner political and media support for the idea of establishing a bank. Once this was established, it embarked on an education process for the bank supervisors, providing them with information about successful regulated microfinance institutions elsewhere in the world.

Finally K-REP organized an exposure visit for the Deputy Governor and the Director of Bank Supervision of the Central Bank of Kenya to see BancoSol in Bolivia. This visit was instrumental in shaping their understanding of the vast potential as well as the inherent risks of microfinance.

In discussing the K-REP Bank with the bank supervision division, some of the key issues raised were ownership (with K-REP allowed to be a shareholder of the bank as long as it did not hold more than 25% of the shares), governance (with K-REP required to have at least three bankers on its management team), security, lending methodology, and the overall relationship between the NGO and the Bank.

During the course of these negotiations, the bank supervisor agreed to consider special legislation for microfinance institutions to create a new regulatory category. K-REP intends to become a full commercial bank, in part because it wants to challenge the thinking of the financial sector regarding the acceptance of low-income communities as a legitimate market. K-REP's efforts appear to be opening the door for other microfinance institutions in Kenya.

Source: Sustaining Civil Society – Strategies for Resource Mobilisation, CIVICUS (1997)

Chapter 14

Social Investment

WHAT IS SOCIAL INVESTMENT?

When a CSO has a project that it would like to implement that has a chance of being financially viable and able to produce an adequate return on capital invested, it is possible that it will go to a bank to try to get the finance required. It might go to a foreign donor and be told that its idea is a viable business proposition and that therefore it should be able to access commercial credit.

Unfortunately many CSO project ideas may well be viable, but they may not be bankable given the existing rules and regulations of the banks, together with their conservatism regarding new ideas. CSOs need a source of investment finance that is flexible enough to meet their needs, to be interested in the social aspects of their work (rather than considering the optimal returns on capital) and prepared to deal with them.

This is the field of social investment (known in the USA as 'Programme Related Investment') – ie organizations that have set up funds to lend money to CSOs that prioritize social and environmental considerations through business-like activities. Such funding organizations broadly share two characteristics:

1   They tend to serve social organizations and small or microenterprises that have social or environmental objectives.
2   They finance sections of the population, projects, sectors, or regions that have been abandoned by the traditional banks or financial institutions.

The funds are not grants – they are social investment funds from organizations that want to support viable and socially responsible work, want to have their investment returned with interest, but that are not investing their money with the prime purpose of maximizing their income from the interest to be earned. They are usually satisfied, therefore, with a below-market rate of return on their investment.

The organizations that are involved in social investment are often of the opinion that investment in a project is healthier than making grants to a project, and that encouraging organizations to become financially self-reliant is better than allowing them to become dependent on grant funding.

Social Investment Organizations

There are presently over 40 social finance organizations from 21 countries (both North and South) who have identified themselves as such actors. They have a coordinating body called INAISE (International Association of Investors in the Social Economy) based in Belgium. Examples of the kinds of work they support are:

- Housing for people with no collateral.
- Venture capital for small businesses that cannot get bank loans.
- Insurance for poor people who cannot comply with the conditions of the usual insurance companies.
- Bridging loans for marketing.
- Loan guarantees.

Information on INAISE can be found from the website www.inaise.org, but a list of these organizations comprises:

Bangladesh	BURO Tangail
Belgium	Credal
	Netwerk Vlandeeren
	Reseau de Financement Alternatif
	Soficatra
	Triodos Bank (Belgium)
Congo	Crédit Populaire
Costa Rica	Fondo Latinamericano de Desarrollo (FOLADE)
Denmark	Jord-Arbejde-Kapital (JAK)
	Merkur – den Almennyttige Andelskasse
Finland	Osuuskunta Eko Osuusraha
France	Association pour le Droit à l'Initiative Économique (ADIE)
	Banque Populaire du Haut Rhin
	Entreprendre de France
	Fédération des Cigales
	Institut de Développement de l'Économie Sociale (IDES)
	Société de l'Invest et de Développement Internationale (SIDI)
	Société d'Investissement France Active (SIFA)
	Société Financiére de la NEF
	Socoden
Germany	GLS Gemeinschaftsbank
	Oekobank

Ireland	Clann Credo Ltd
	Tallagh Trust Fund Ltd
Italy	Banca Etica
	Compagnia Finanziaria Industriale (CFI)
	MAG 2 Finance
Japan	Citizen Bank
Luxembourg	Appui au Developpement Autonome (ADA)
	Alterfinanz
Netherlands	DOEN Foundation
	Triodos Bank
New Zealand	Prometheus Foundation
Poland	Foundation for Social Policy Development (FRPS)
South Africa	Get Ahead Foundation
Sweden	Ekosparkassan Sola
	Jorde-Arbete-Kapital (JAK)
	Nordiska Sparlan
Switzerland	Alternative Bank ABS
	Freie Gemeinschaftsbank BSL
	RAFAD
Tanzania	Coopec Kalundu
UK	Aston Re-investment Trust
	Charities Aid Foundation
	Ecology Building Society
	Full Circle Fund
	Industrial Common Ownership Finance
	Shared Interest
	Triodos Bank (UK)
USA	South Shore Bank
	Women's World Banking

The case studies for social investment are Tabora Beekeepers, Tanzania, and Shared Interest, UK, and the Triodos Bank (UK, Belgium, the Netherlands)

CASE STUDY 14.1 *TABORA BEEKEEPERS, TANZANIA, AND SHARED INTEREST, UK*

Tabora Beekeepers is a cooperative of 2500 beekeepers in Tanzania. They needed hard currency to buy the imported drums to ship their honey to Traidcraft, a fair trade organization based in the United Kingdom. Traidcraft had already paid them the maximum advance possible so Shared Interest stepped in to help with a direct loan to Tabora of GBP20,000, to be repaid when the honey reaches Traidcraft.

Source: Sustaining Civil Society – Strategies for Resource Mobilisation, CIVICUS (1997)

CASE STUDY 14.2 *THE HIVOS-TRIODOS FUND FOUNDATION*

The Hivos Foundation is a Dutch humanistic development NGO co-financed by the Dutch Ministry of Development Cooperation. The Triodos Bank was established in the Netherlands in 1980 and now also has offices in Belgium and the UK. The bank lends only to organizations and businesses with social and environmental objectives. Triodos is an independent bank owned by public shareholders. Shares are held through a trust that protects the social and environmental aims of the bank.

Dialogue between Hivos and the Triodos Bank began in the early 1990s with a view to establishing a joint fund for financing projects in developing countries. Triodos was motivated to look for projects in developing countries by its need for growth and new funds. Triodos was also interested to involve itself in the trend to establish microcredit programmes. Hivos was already involved in microcredit and had contacts with potential clients in the South because of its decentralized structure.

The Hivos-Triodos Fund Foundation was established in December 1994. Its purpose is to provide guarantees and loans to, as well as to bear the risk of participating in, projects, enterprises and institutions in the area of development cooperation. It is not intended that the foundation shall earn a profit.

The Board of Management consists of two members of the Board of Directors of Triodos Bank and is appointed by the Supervisory Board, which also supervises the Fund's policy and approves the annual accounts. The Supervisory Board is appointed by the Hivos Foundation.

A request for finance is a two-step process. First, Hivos evaluates the request on the basis of its content. It is processed further by the Fund only after Hivos makes a positive recommendation. Second, Triodos Bank evaluates the request from a financial point of view. If this evaluation is also positive then a proposal is made to the credit committee of the Fund, which consists of representatives of both Hivos and Triodos Bank. Hivos has the right of veto in the credit committee if, in its opinion, the request does not fulfil the social development and environmental criteria and policies of the Fund. Triodos Bank can advise against making an investment from a financial point of view. The final responsibility rests with the Board of Management.

After finance has been provided, its management is overseen by the Hivos-Triodos Fund Foundation. Each borrower is subject to an annual review that is discussed in the credit committee. The follow-up also takes place in consultation with Hivos, usually through its regional offices in Zimbabwe, India and Costa Rica.

The fund gives priority to microcredit institutions and small banks since this makes best use of the expertise and experience of Triodos Bank and best fulfils the desire of Hivos to support economic activity in developing countries. Fair trade and trade finance are also considered important areas deserving attention.

In the process to establish the joint fund there were a number of challenges arising from differences in the organizations' cultures. For example, the minimum level of finance request considered acceptable by Triodos fund managers was 100,000 fl (US$47,775) but many development projects require a far smaller sum. Hivos initially placed insufficient emphasis on training staff members that were to be involved in the joint fund. Only recently did staff benefit from more comprehensive training.

It has been a challenge of the partnership to maintain recognition of the two cultures and different roles in the partnership. This has been achieved through mutual investment in time and resources for the partnership and a genuine dialogue that has resulted in increased trust and respect for each other's expertise over time.

The original expectation of the partnership was to generate a self-financing joint fund of 35 million fl (US$16.7 million). In fact only 10 million fl (US$4.7 million) has been generated to date and Hivos is continuing to subsidize the programme.

Source: INTRAC Workshop Report – NGOs and the Private Sector, (1998)

Chapter 15

Use of the Internet

The Internet provides a different way of handling resource mobilization ideas that have been described in the preceding chapters. In some cases it is simply an extension of work that could otherwise have been done through letters, telephone calls, advertisements, articles, etc. In other cases the astonishing range of the Internet, and the way that it allows you to access information that you would otherwise be unlikely to obtain, suggests a different way of working. Many of the possibilities for Internet resource mobilization are being developed as you read, and will be spread with astonishing rapidity. Many of the innovations are based on Northern experience, but have great possibilities of Southern application. They all depend on a certain level of technological sophistication – access to computers, reliable electricity, local maintenance engineers, local service providers – which may be a problem in certain parts of the world.

THE RANGE OF THE INTERNET

The Internet provides CSOs with a host of new opportunities, many of which have the potential to mobilize resources. 'Potential' is a word that is used a lot in this context since many of the approaches are still being developed. The Internet at present, however, enables you to:

- Publish information about your organization and make it available 24 hours a day to anyone with access to the Internet.
- Communicate with actual and potential volunteers in your organization in large numbers at very low cost, and allow them to communicate with each other.
- Publicize products and services that your CSO offers for sale.
- Make available (to anyone with access to a computer) research, studies, surveys, interviews from the field, local information of strategic interest, etc.
- Build networks of people interested in the same subject.
- Access an incredible variety of information on topics that are pertinent to the work of your CSO, and make this available to anyone you want.
- Identify new information that is valuable to the work that you are doing.
- File, archive, store, process and retrieve information as and when you want it.

If you think about any of the other 11 approaches to resource mobilization that have been presented in this handbook, there are likely to be Internet implications. Lists of donors and subscribers, promotion and sales of goods and services, publishing of newsletters for volunteers, accessing the regulations of foundations, governments, businesses, keeping records of microcredit borrowers – these are only a few of the possibilities.

ANNOUNCING YOUR CSO ON THE WEB AND ATTRACTING PEOPLE TO IT

Perhaps the biggest opportunity offered by the Internet is simply to inform the world about your CSO and what it does. A CSO can establish a web page that clearly and competently provides information on its structure, its programmes, its plans, what it has done and what it would like to do. It will probably need professional help with this, particularly for some of the options discussed below. Once your CSO has established a website, it has set up the possibility of attracting interest from any member of the Internet-browsing public. If it goes further and specifically solicits funds or seeks volunteer support and informs people how they can help the organization, it is providing an electronic version of some of the fundraising approaches mentioned in the other chapters of this book. If you are seeking funds from the public, from business, from indigenous foundations, from the government, it is useful to have an accessible reference point where people can go to find out more about your CSO. You are using your website as a virtual point of contact, as a way in which you can inform those who are potentially interested in your organization, and consolidate information for those who definitely are interested in it.

This, however, presupposes that you are able to get close enough to someone (or some organization) to inform them that you have a website, and that the website, once visited, is found to be informative and communicative. In general, however, the Internet is not targeted: once a website is established, you hope that someone will visit it and read the contents, but you have to leave that up to them. There are ways, however, to tilt the odds in your favour, and this is part of the design of your website. This involves making sure that the name of your website is connected to 'search engines'. These are the devices that search the Internet for sites with names provided to them. Key word searches are also common among users of the Internet, and you can arrange to bring people to your website if they type in the key words that you have chosen that are pertinent to the work of your organization.

In Zambia, an organization called CHIN (Children in Need) acts as a coordination and liaison secretariat for 50+ organizations working with children affected by HIV/AIDS – children who either have AIDS, or are suffering from the effects of AIDS on others (parents, caregivers, members of the community). CHIN started a website to make easily available at one point all the information on the activities of its member organizations, and thus publicize their work. To its surprise it started receiving messages from foreigners who had visited the website, found out about the work of members' organizations, and were interested in making financial donations. The website was not set up for that purpose, but found itself accessible to anyone who keyed in 'Zambia' and 'children' and browsed the results. There are, it seems, people in the world – particularly in the North – who spend at least part of their time doing this.

Once a visitor has been attracted to the website, the CSO has a tremendous opportunity to educate and inform the visitor about the CSO's mission, programmes, activities, track record, and future plans. These are all very important aspects of the information that might persuade someone to support your CSO with funding or with a variety of non-financial resources, particularly volunteer time.

Just as with brochures (see Chapter 6), you will have to decide what language you want your website to be written in, and how to present the information. You will also have to decide if you are directing your website at fellow countrymen or foreigners. In this, the website is an advertisement for your organization, and you will have to think through who you want to read or see that advertisement. Case Study 15.3 at the end of this chapter has some useful advice regarding a Thai CSO that specifically targeted young people.

Websites can also be set up by organizations that are not trying to attract funds to their own organizations, but to persuade web browsers to give to some other worthy cause. An example is an Indian organization called Hughes Software Systems that traded as 'Partners in Building Global Communications Solutions'. They set up a part of their website www.hssworld.com as a fundraising device for the droughts in India in early 2000. Visitors to the website were encouraged to click on a button saying 'send H_2O', at which point they were offered an opportunity to send money for the relief of a variety of natural disasters in India by contacting the Charities Aid Foundation India that would receive and forward funds. The organization acted as a stimulus to get website visitors to give, suggested which organizations they could give to and how it could be done (see Case Study 15.1 on p144).

GETTING CONNECTED

This handbook assumes a certain level of expertise in electronic communication via the Internet. For those of you who need further instruction in order to understand and manage your connection to the Internet, there are very comprehensive materials available free on line at http://unganisha.idrc.ca/itrain/materials.php3 put together by an organization called the ITrain Collective connected to the International Development Resource Centre (IDRC) of Canada. These materials (also available in Spanish and Chinese) teach you how to navigate the web.

WHO WILL VISIT YOUR WEBSITE?

Obviously, only those with access to a computer will visit your website, and this breaks down into those who own a computer (or whose organization/employer owns a computer), and those who have access to a commercial 'Internet café', by which is meant those who sell Internet access from small shops/booths/kiosks. Increasing numbers of organizations have computers and Internet access, particularly schools and businesses.

Since computer ownership and use is greater in the North than in the South, it is likely that many visitors to your website will be from the North, provided that the language is one that is common in the North. If your website is written in Chinese or Thai or Indonesian, it is clear that you will only attract fellow countrymen or women (wherever in the world they may be), and the numbers are likely to be smaller. They may be, however, the most relevant people for you to contact from the point of view of resource mobilization.

Many people in the computer business are concerned about the huge disparity between computer use in the North and the South (this topic has been given the name 'the digital divide') and there are many attempts to increase Internet access in the South, but the truth at the moment is that people from the North are more likely to visit your site than your fellow countrymen/women, provided it is in a language they understand. The possibility of seeking charitable donations from people in the North directly (as opposed to seeking them via Northern NGOs) is thus a very real and expandable possibility. In essence this is not, however, very different from child sponsorship programmes or appeals to Northern donors – it does not lead to local support or the involvement of local citizens in your work since local people are unlikely to have computers. Computer use is changing so rapidly, however, particularly the institutional use of computers, that it may be sensible to add a local fundraising component to any work that you do to document your CSO on a website.

THE RANGE OF LOCAL RESOURCE MOBILIZATION OPTIONS VIA THE INTERNET

Save money on communication

Once your CSO owns a computer (and for many CSOs that is not a high priority unless someone gives them one), and provided that you have a competent local service provider who connects your country to the satellites, you may well find that you can communicate much more cheaply by email than by fax and telephone, and possibly letters. You need to do a cost/benefit analysis to be sure of this, but email is generally a very cheap means of communication, and it can be scaled up to go to a group of people very easily.

The communication will certainly be faster than letters, but, of course, it can only go to people who also have computers. As we have said, the number of these is growing fast and 'Internet cafés' are proliferating. In Eastern Europe email between CSOs is the standard method of communication. As CSOs were created in the aftermath of the fall of communism, they moved straight into the Internet. In many rural parts of the South, this is, however, all a pipe dream since there is no electricity, or telephone connection, let alone computer or Internet connection.

The use of email and the Internet to save money does require discipline, however. You usually pay the service provider by the time that you spend. It is easy to spend a lot of time on the Net because it is so interesting, and because there is such a wealth of information available there. Internet Service Providers (commonly known as ISPs) are now starting to provide a range of services that are not always based on the amount of time you spend on the Net. Do not forget, however, that the link between you and the Internet Service Provider is a telephone line, and the telephone bills may be prohibitive.

Network

A spin-off from bilateral email connection is coordinated email connection around a particular topic or issue shared between many people who have joined a 'listserv', ie a linked series of addresses that all receive the same information. It is also possible to participate in a 'chat room' where others are on line at the same time as you are, and you can send messages back and forth. Some resource mobilization implications of this are:

- Bringing together subscribers to your CSO to talk about important developments.
- Distributing newsletters or updates to interested parties.
- Learning from other people about subjects that are important to your fund-raising efforts, like new laws.

If you are interested to plan a joint activity, like an advocacy campaign, or merely to find out what other people have done when they are faced with a similar situation, email allows you to be in touch with many other people simultaneously.

Learn/Get Informed

The possibility of entering a structured learning experience (joining a 'virtual' training course), or simply gathering information that is pertinent to your CSO's work is greatly enhanced by the use of the Internet. It is likely that such means of learning will grow greatly in the future. The sections under 'Further Reading' and 'Resource Organizations' that are linked to this chapter provide many places on the Internet where you can learn more about Northern fundraising practices. The trainer manual connected to this handbook is available on the Internet – the first time that material on Southern resource mobilization is so available (see p14).

It is now common practice for conferences, workshops, forums, and other places where knowledge is exchanged to post the proceedings of their meetings on web pages. It is now policy for many development agencies to put their deliberations on their own websites in a new spirit of transparency and openness: huge amounts of information are available, for instance, from the World Bank's website – probably more information than you would be able to access in your own country. You can often find out information about what is happening in your country more easily from such sources than from 'official' channels within your country.

Campaign

If you put together a combination of networking and information, you have a very useful tool for campaigning. In any advocacy effort you need information, particularly information on existing policies and on new events that challenge existing policies, and you also need supporters and members of coalitions who are both informed and committed. The Internet provides a powerful tool for seeking, finding, and working with such people to campaign for a particular issue. Provided people regularly read their mail, the Internet can also work as an instrument for very topical information – for instance, which room to meet in at Parliament to lobby for the new bill, or which place to visit to see the effects of industrial effluent.

Members of the network or the campaign coalition can also post the information that they have on the topic – for example, reports on human rights abuse, documents on the corruption unearthed, suggestions for new laws. Apart from providing information for fellow campaigners, powerful information can be a means of energizing fellow citizens and getting them committed to campaigns to right wrongs. And if secrecy is needed, the democratic Internet provides for a people's encryption service called www.hushmail.com.

Market your Products

If you have decided that you want to generate revenue for your organization through running an enterprise, the Internet allows you the opportunity to advertise and possibly to sell your products (if there is credit card use in your countries). Particularly if your organization is involved in export trade (see Case Study 4.1 or 14.1), there are many ways in which the Internet can help you to produce a catalogue for customers to read on your website, and for them to order goods from you. Just as there are alternative marketing organizations (AMOs) that try to sell handicrafts from the South to the North, there are now 'virtual AMOs' (see www.peoplink.org for North America, for example). Another possibility is to sell books or other kinds of publications through the Internet – many CSOs have saleable research or extension publications, and could very well have a publications list with prices on their website. Many CSOs are also involved in training – there are many possibilities of virtual training courses that learners could access for a fee. It is true that credit cards are not yet in great use in Southern countries – and credit card numbers are required for buying on-line – but it is quite possible that their use will expand.

Make Proposals to Local Supporters

If you are making proposals to possible funders in your own country (governments, businesses, local foundations), it makes sense to do this formally by email, after you have had face-to-face discussions and considered that the time is ripe. Sending proposals by email allows the potential donor agency to follow up with further requests for more information or queries, and for you to answer these quickly and efficiently. It also allows for modifications and negotiations to be conducted transparently.

Seek Volunteers

If you need people to help you, put the word out on your website. For rallies, for building, for assistance in the office, for data gathering – the website offers a way for you to announce your needs 24 hours a day, 7 days a week. Once you have made the announcement, you do not need to spend further time soliciting help. The problem, as mentioned previously, is to try to make sure that the sort of people you are trying to attract visit your website. A website can match volunteers to needs; it is also possible to build up rosters of volunteers who are prepared to make their skills available for worthy causes – lists of musicians, painters, accountants, lawyers, etc.

Keep Records

If you are working in the microcredit field, for instance, you will need to keep detailed records on borrowings and repayments, and these will have to be sent from the field to head office. If you are in the election-monitoring business, data need to be assembled, kept, and transmitted. If you are part of a campaign documenting costs of raw materials or a daily shopping-basket, or water quality, if you are engaged in novel information-gathering on such topics as the number of hours teachers actually teach, the number of people arrested for a particular offence, the number of people with a particular disease, then the Internet provides a ready way both to keep your documentation and to pass it on to others.

If you decide that fundraising from the public is the approach that fits best with your CSO, then you will need to keep track of your donors, and have them accessible by area, past giving history, birthdays (so you can send them a card!), and many other aspects to make your fundraising as efficient as possible. Many software programs are now available to help CSOs to keep track of funders.

LIMITATIONS AND BARRIERS

Money

Computers cost a lot of money to buy, and a lot of money to repair if they fail. In addition to a computer, you also need to have a modem, a printer, and, very possibly in the South, a back-up battery called a UPS (uninterrupted power supply). Then there are the costs for the Internet Service Provider, which is sometimes linked to the telephone companies. A CSO has to balance whether the advantages that Internet access brings are balanced by the costs.

Quality of the Websites

A great deal of enthusiasm exists in designing and building web pages, but this enthusiasm often wanes subsequently. If you have decided to have a website it must be kept up to date, and a person or people have to be designated to do that. Visitors to a web page that has out-of-date information, or no information at all, are not impressed, and are not likely to support your CSO. Website design and maintenance is a new skill that needs to be learnt, but once learnt, it requires commitment to keep it at a high quality.

Informing People Where to Find You

If you have a website, make sure that you tell people about it. If possible, have a name that is memorable, and make sure that people can find their way around the website easily. It is useful to ask your service provider to tell you how many visitors you have had to your website. It is also useful to use the occasion of their visit to your website to try to develop a deeper relationship. Many websites have 'visitors' books' which they urge visitors to write in, and provide their addresses. The CSO must then follow up and cultivate the guest's interest. Just as in person-to-person fundraising, a one-off time event can be built up into a regular and deep interest in the cause of the CSO, so this can also be done via the Internet. The CSO, once it has invested in a website, must try to move beyond using it as a 'billboard' where people just come and look; they must try to interact with their visitors in order to develop their interest and to solicit their support. They must try to keep people's interest so they will stay on the website and learn more about your CSO's work.

Ready Arguments to Counter Retractors

It is possible that people in your country will accuse you of unnecessary luxury and irrelevant expenditures if you promote your organization through the Internet. You will be asked to defend yourself as an organization that is helping the poor and the powerless, and yet also using computer technology. There is enough suspicion about CSOs by the general public in your country for it to be likely that you will be accused of being a 'PC and Pajero NGO'. It is for you to think this through and decide for yourself the advantages for your organization's mission of working the Internet. Once you have worked this out, however, make sure that you have strong arguments ready to counter such people.

Wasting Time

There is an incredible amount of information on the Internet. You and your staff will be very tempted to over-indulge. The Internet can be very helpful to your organization in the ways described above, but it can also waste huge amounts of time, and incur considerable online costs, if users do not know how to navigate the web effectively.

It May Yet Come to You

This last section shows ways that the Internet is being used in the North for resource mobilization. Some of these options may be available for you in the South, in which case you should be ready to 'catch the wave' once it comes. Others may not be adaptable to your country, culture, and level of technology, or may not be yet. This section, written by Nadia Keshavjee, gives suggestions for the sorts of questions that you need to ask if you decide to enter this world and the kinds of services that are now available in the North. As you might expect, many of the references on how to get further information are themselves references to websites. The language of this section of the handbook is the language of Northern NGOs, particularly North American NGOs.

Your Fundraising Strategy

Specific technologies should never drive your online fundraising strategy. Your use of technology should be part of an overall fundraising plan based on a thorough assessment of your organization's fundraising strategy, including the use of digital technology. (See Chapter 16 for some guidelines on this.)

Here are some questions to ask, to which you will need answers as you consider the implications of digital technology:

- What are your current fundraising strategies?
- Do you have a website?
- How does your website support fundraising strategies?
- How can your website be a more effective solicitation, cultivation, or stewardship tool?
- If your site offered secure online transactions, would your web visitors use it? Why or why not?

- What is the potential for new revenue and/or new donors?
- Does your organization transact any other business on its website?
- How might e-commerce and online donations be integrated?

Source: Kanter, Beth *Exploring Online Fundraising for NonProfit Arts Organisations,* www.idealist.org/beth.html

The answers to some of these questions are given below.

Exploring Approaches to Online Fundraising Technologies

There are a number of different approaches to online fundraising. The options fall into four different types.

Donation/Charity Portals

A donation/charity portal website typically provides a directory of many different non-profit organizations. Web visitors can select their favourite charity and make a donation online using their credit card. The donation portal processes the transaction, acknowledges the gift and forwards the money along with a report, including donor information, to the non-profit organization.[1]

Donation portals do not typically have a set-up or monthly fee, although some retain a small percentage to cover credit card fees. These portals often make money from advertising on their site.[2] Examples include: www.helping.org; www.giveforchange.com; www.charitableway.com; www.allcharities.com.

The main advantage for non-profit organizations is that it requires a minimal investment in time, staff, or technology to experiment. Several of the donation portals are marketing their services to corporations to assist with employee giving via the company's intranet as well as heavily promoting their sites on other portal sites to drive visitor traffic. To evaluate vendors, visit their sites and read their materials.[3] In addition, here are some useful questions to ask when negotiating with a charity portal:

- What and how many other non-profit organizations are included on the site?
- What is the cost of registering?
- Are there any restrictions in terms of participating or working with other online fundraising vendors?
- Can the non-profit organizations provide a direct link to an organization's information page on the charity engine site?

---

[1] Kanter: www.idealist.org/beth.html; Stein: www.netaction.org
[2] Kanter: www.idealist.org/beth.html; Stein: www.netaction.org
[3] Kanter: www.idealist.org/beth.html

- What is the fee? Is it a flat fee, based on transactions, or a combination?
- Does the donation portal make its revenue from sources other than fees? Is it in business to sell services to the non-profit organization?
- How does the donation/charity portal promote its site?
- What is the traffic?
- What are the legal risks?

Source: Kanter, Beth *Exploring Online Fundraising for NonProfit Arts Organisations,* www.idealist.org/beth.html

Payment Service Providers

Some organizations are interested in setting up their own e-commerce system to accept credit card information, but would like to avoid the complications and costly strategies that may be involved. A Payment Service Provider (PSP) may be a solution. A PSP is a vendor who will manage the entire back-end of your donations and payments. PSPs specialize in setting up secure credit card systems for non-profit organizations and enable them to accept credit card donations by providing a link on the organization's website to a pledge or donation page that resides on the PSP's server. They make their money through a fee structure based on the contributions you receive.[4]

Most PSPs allow you to customize the look of your donation page, thank you message, and reports. Rates range from a flat monthly fee to a tiered per transaction or gift amount fee.[5] Examples include: www.entango.com; www.remit.net; www.donornet.com.

You can ask your payment service provider the following questions:

- Does the vendor offer secure transactions?
- What is the level of technical support?
- How reliable is the service?
- How much does it cost? What is the per transaction fee? What are the set-up costs?
- What is the length of the contract for services?
- How long does it take to set up an account?
- What does the organization need to provide/do for the set up?
- How much control/customization is available on the donation solicitation page, or is it simply a 'submit' link?
- Can the confirmation email/screen be customized?
- What type of customer support is provided to the donor should there be a problem?

---

[4] Kanter: www.idealist.org/beth.html; Stein: www.netaction.org
[5] Kanter: www.idealist.org/beth.html

- What type of reporting is available to the organization online or via email?
- Can it be customized? Can it be exported in my database?

Source: Kanter, Beth *Exploring Online Fundraising for NonProfit Arts Organisations,* www.idealist.org/beth.html

Charity Mall or E-commerce Commission Portals

In this case, your organization places a banner advertisement link to an online merchant or mall on your organization's website. Web donors (and/or members to the site) click on the link and are taken to an e-commerce site where they can purchase a variety of items, designate their favourite cause or charity, and the merchant or mall donates a percentage (usually 5 per cent) of the sales revenue back to your organization.[6]

For non-profit organizations, the main advantage is that it requires no investment in staff, time, or technology. Your organization simply collects a cheque. However, that cheque can take a long time to find its way into your organization's cash flow as charity malls set a minimum of collected contributions before they issue a cheque. And it might be a small one unless your organization can generate significant traffic and purchases at the online mall. If your site has many supporters and those supporters are comfortable with shopping online and purchase products, this may make sense.[7]

There are a growing number of charity malls. One of the more popular ones is GreaterGood (www.greatergood.com) which contributes between 5–15 per cent of the sale to an IRS-registered 501(c)(3) charitable organization. Shoppers can designate a specific non-profit organization, or select from a list of charities featured on the site. As a non-profit organization, you can register easily online.[8] Other examples include: www.igive.com; www.shop4charity.com; www.4charity.com; www.shop2give.com; www.shopforchange.com.

One of the best ways to compare vendors is to contact non-profit organizations that are listed already on the site, and ask if their experience has been positive. You will also want to do a bit of comparison shopping by reviewing the fine print and specifics for each vendor on their website before you sign on the electronic line.[9]

Questions to ask charity mall or e-commerce commission portals are as follows:

- How many merchants, non-profit organizations, and consumers participate?
- How does the charity mall promote its site?
- What is the monthly traffic?

---

[6] Kanter: www.idealist.org/beth.html
[7] Kanter: www.idealist.org/beth.html
[8] Kanter: www.idealist.org/beth.html
[9] Kanter: www.idealist.org/beth.html

- Are there any up-front or hidden costs?
- Does the mall restrict recipients to specific organizations (for example, in the US they may restrict recipients to 501-C organizations)?
- What is the retail mix? Are these products of interest to *your* donors?
- What is the percentage of each sale that is contributed to your organization?
- What are the rules in terms of banner/advertisement link placement on your website and other requirements for promoting the charity mall on your website or to your audiences?
- What is the minimum amount that needs to accrue before the mall issues a cheque?
- How is the cheque issued ('snail mail' or electronically)?
- Can you enter into relationships with more than one charity mall?
- What is the privacy policy of the site and how is it enforced?

Source: Kanter, Beth *Exploring Online Fundraising for NonProfit Arts Organisations,* www.idealist.org/beth.html

Click and Give

Another approach to online fundraising has been the 'click and give' or 'click and donate' sites. It offers web visitors a simple method of giving by simply clicking on a button. One example of this kind of site is the Hunger Site (www.thehungersite. com). The Hunger Site aims to help alleviate world poverty by raising funds for the United Nations anti-hunger work. When you click, the web server registers your action and adds your 'food donation' to the daily total. You then receive a page that names the corporate sponsor that paid the donation on your behalf. In this way, you can make one donation a day at no cost to you, and you do not have to hand over any details about yourself.

So how much is your donation worth? Every click on the button earns 3 cents, which is paid by the sponsors directly to the participating relief organization. This is worth about one and a half cups of food such as cooked rice or grain cereal. Of the 3 cents, 'approximately 2 cents pays for the serving of food itself, 0.3 cents pays for the relief organization's overhead, and 0.7 cents goes toward the transportation of the food'.

The simplicity of the site and the attraction of making a difference at no cost to the donor are a compelling combination. Not surprisingly, the site has received considerable media attention in the US, and elsewhere. Other examples: www. peaceforall.com; www.ecologyfund.com; www.endcancernow.com.

Frequently Asked Questions

How do I choose between the various services to find the right solution for my non-profit organization?

Size yourself up. Kurt Hansen, the chief executive officer and founder of www. CharityWeb.net, suggests that if you are a non-profit charity with less than a US$2 million annual budget, or with little traffic through your website, you should probably use www.helping.org or similar charity portals. It is probably not worth the investment of time and energy to do it any other way. If you get a surge of donations or you want to add a shopping cart, you can look for a more customary alternative.[10]

What questions should I ask an online fundraising service that wants me to sign up with them?

- Get all the information you can about how the service works.
- Examine their website in complete detail to see how they present their service, and how they feature the non-profit organizations that are signed up with them.
- Make sure that you have a very good understanding of what fees you might have to pay when you receive a donation, or any sign-up or monthly fees.
- Don't get forced into signing a multi-year contract if you are not comfortable with that (request a shorter contract so that you can evaluate the effectiveness of their service).
- Ask for referrals and find out how much money they have raised through the service.
- Make sure you understand what the service requires you to do as part of the deal. Some ask for buttons on your home page or announcements in your email newsletter.

Source: Stein, Michael, *Elementary E-Philanthropy*, www.netaction.org

Database/Fundraising Software

Purchasers are confronted with a multitude of options at every price level, from comprehensive proprietary packages with sophisticated add-on modules to introductory-level shareware or freeware programs available on the Internet. This section will not be able to recommend a particular software package to you or be able to distinguish for you 'the good, the bad and the ugly'. However, it will be able to guide you through the process of 'How do we evaluate and choose a fundraising

---

[10]   Stein: www.netaction.org

database program that best meets our needs?' and 'What are some of the things we should keep in mind during the process?'[11]

Begin your search with a thorough analysis of your current situation, including:

- Programme operations (What are the specific elements in your fundraising programme plan?)
- Computer equipment (How many computers are there in your office? With what chip, speed, RAM, and storage? And if you have a network, how many are on it, and what is your network software?)
- Expense budget (How much can you spend?)
- Staffing (What is your departmental structure? Who and how many currently use your database software and at what level of proficiency?)

Source: Batchelder, Duff, *How Do We Select Fundraising Software? Management Solutions for Non-profit Organisations*, www.allianceonline.org/faqs/frfaq7.html

Now make a determination of where you will be in three to five years in each of these same areas. These two steps will help to clarify the most basic features and performance priorities required of your future software.[12]

Preplanning also requires the successful integration of your existing data and a successful articulation of how the new software will function. One of the best ways to do this is to describe in detail what elements of your previous system you want to keep and what you want to discard, as well as what you need the new software to do.[13]

The kinds of questions that you should ask of a software provider are listed in Duff Batchelder's material: 'How Do We Select Fundraising Software? Management Solutions for Non-profit Organisations' which is available on www.allianceonline. org/faqs/frfaq7.html.

Keep in mind that prices for software packages can range from free to US$1500 to over US$6000. To make your investment worthwhile, consider a range of packages that match your current situation and current fundraising strategy, but that will also meet your needs as your situation and strategy grows and changes. Examples are as follows: ebase (www.ebase.org); Blackbaud/Raiser's Edge (www.blackbaud. com).

The first case study illustrates Internet use for philanthropy in India, the second is from the USA, and the last is from Thailand: Hughes Software Systems India; the Virtual Foundation USA; The Mirror Arts Group, Thailand.

---

[11] Batchelder: www.allianceonline.org/fags/frfaq7.html
[12] Batchelder: www.allianceonline.org/fags/frfaq7.html
[13] ArtsWire: www.nptoolkit.org/forum.html

CASE STUDY 15.1 *HUGHES SOFTWARE SYSTEMS, INDIA, CHARITIES AID FOUNDATION, INDIA, AND DROUGHT RELIEF*

Send H$_2$O

Parched earth, sweltering heat, nothing to eat, no water to quench the thirst, loss of cattle, and thus means of income, is a typical scene in the famine stricken areas of Rajasthan and Gujarat. This colourful land is the next victim of nature's fury after Orissa. Most of the areas in this region today are absolutely dry where the basic source of sustenance, water, has become a mere mirage for the millions of faceless villagers. The sordid tale of these villagers is one of parching human throats and singeing human souls and psyches. As a result thousands of people are forced to leave their home in search of a few drops of water for survival.

Think about them. . .

Kehem Singh of Sanawada, Pokhran, who worked in temperatures of 45 degrees for 10 days and was given Rs140 by the contractor as his dues. That's Rs14 a day to buy food and water for himself and his family.

Phool Devi, who toils for hours to feed her nine children.

Thousands of women across Rajasthan and Gujarat whose first chore of the morning is to spend hours trying to draw up clean water from drying village wells.

Unable to feed their cattle, the farmers are bidding them a tearful goodbye and abandoning them to die of hunger and thirst. There is hardly any village left in the area that is not strewn with carcasses of animals rotting in the scorching sun.

Human life is also going to meet the same fate if a timely help is not provided to tide over the situation. Five crore [50 million] people are already affected by this frightening catastrophe with casualties increasing every day.

In times of such crisis we all need to rise to the occasion and prove our character as corporate citizens by extending a helping hand.

Let's contribute generously to the cause of the drought victims. In an earnest effort to do their bit for the cause, HSS has started the send H$_2$O campaign wherein the employees on a personal level and the company on its account will be contributing to this fund, and all the proceeds that are collected from them would be utilized for the relief of the drought-hit villagers of Rajasthan and Gujarat.

Aid Delayed is Aid Denied
If you would like to contribute to Drought Relief, please click here.

If you click on the place mentioned, you see the following page

DRY – Disaster Relief and You

Disaster Relief and You – DRY is an initiative on disasters with information and details provided by persons on the spot. DRY is also your opportunity to help those facing disaster.

The country has seen a series of disasters – the present drought in parts of Andhra Pradesh, Madhya Pradesh, Rajasthan and Orissa, the cyclone in Orissa and Gujarat earthquakes and possibly even famine.

Those affected need your helping hand to recover and rebuild their lives. DRY and you in partnership, we do it. For further information contact CAF India.

CAF India Floods Droughts Earthquakes Famine Cyclone Response

This initiative is being promoted by CAF India on behalf of voluntary agencies. CAF India is a registered public charitable trust and donations made to CAF India are exempted under section 80(G) of the Income Tax Act.

This site is supported by Hughes Software Systems.
Copy of the website of HSSworld, *http://www.hssworld.com/peoplenet/working @hss/sendh20.htm*

Case Study 15.2 *The Virtual Foundation*

The Virtual Foundation is a unique online philanthropy program that supports grass-roots initiatives around the world. We post carefully screened, small-scale project proposals on our website where they are read and funded by online donors.

The Virtual Foundation was founded in 1996 by ECOLOGIA, an international non-profit organization that has supported environmental movements and groups across Eurasia since 1989. The mission of the Virtual Foundation is twofold: to support local projects initiated by non-governmental organizations in the field of environment, sustainable development, and health; and to encourage private philanthropy among citizens from all walks of life.

The Virtual Foundation works in cooperation with a network of organizations throughout the world to develop and support projects. The member groups of this network, called the Virtual Foundation Consortium, have offices and staff working 'in country' with local groups they know well. Consortium members work with these local groups to develop small-scale project proposals that are submitted to the Virtual Foundation. The proposals are then posted on the Virtual Foundation website. Individuals, families, and community groups visiting the website read the proposals, see pictures illustrating the project, evaluate the project's budget – and then make a donation to the project of their choice. In short the Virtual Foundation helps grass-roots organizations obtain vital support for their projects and allows individuals and groups to easily become international philanthropists!

To learn more about the Virtual Foundation, continue on to the How it Works section. Or, if you have questions, feel free to contact us by email or by phone.

If you click How it works, *then you get:*

How it Works

The following is a step-by-step look at how a project is funded through the Virtual Foundation

Step 1: A community group in a participating country (ie a country with a Virtual Foundation Consortium Member) wants to carry out a project that would, for example, clean up a polluted stream in their region. The group submits their project idea to a local Consortium member. The Consortium member works with the group to develop a detailed proposal describing the need for the project and how the project will be realized, as well as an itemized budget for project activities. The proposal and budget are then submitted to the Virtual Foundation.

Step 2: The proposal is evaluated by the Virtual Foundation's Grants Coordinator and Proposal Review Committee. When questions arise, the proposal is returned to the Consortium member for clarification. If the proposal meets the Virtual Foundation's criteria, and is approved by the Proposal Review Committee, it is posted on the Virtual Foundation website.

Step 3: Visitors to the Virtual Foundation website read the description of the project's goals and activities accompanied by a budget and photos that illustrate the proposal. These visitors select a project to support and may even make online donations directly through the Virtual Foundation's website.

Step 4: Following transmission of the donated funds and initiation of the project activities, reports on the project's progress are posted on the Virtual Foundation's website. Donors are encouraged to communicate with members of the project they funded, and follow the project's development. The goal of the Virtual Foundation is to foster lasting global partnerships between grassroots groups and our online donors.

From the website http://www.virtualfoundation.org

CASE STUDY 15.3 *THE MIRROR ARTS GROUP, CREATING A NEW TOOL FOR RESOURCE MOBILIZATION IN THAILAND*

Vision

The Mirror Arts Group (MAG), a community development organization in Northern Thailand, seeks to raise awareness of social problems and galvanize the resources and community support necessary to find solutions.

It considers the Internet to be a cost effective means of accomplishing this goal, given the recent dramatic interest in the number of Internet users in Thailand, both urban and rural. It is estimated that there are 800,000 Internet users in the country. For MAG, the cost of using the Internet to attract attention to and support for social problems is minimal: the cost of design and the cost of connection. And the return is large, as the size of the Internet audience is increasing every day.

Though the primary purpose of the website is educational, it has since demonstrated the added benefit of becoming a tool for resource mobilization. Said Sombot Boonngamanong, the MAG Founder and Ashoka Fellow: 'We needed to create a quick low cost means of mobilizing resources that enabled them to respond to community problems as they emerged.'

Strategies

- **Know how to build and revise your website in order to keep it regularly updated and geared towards members' interests**

MAG updates its site every two days keeping information current, a strategy that draws visitors back to the site. MAG's own self-sufficiency in computer technology, website design, and knowledge of the Internet language HTML are key factors in keeping its site timely and inexpensive.

Customizing information to visitors' interests is another key component. 'In Thailand, the Internet is a form of entertainment,' reports Sombat Boonngamanong, MAG Founder and Ashoka Fellow. 'Young people, students mostly, are the most active Internet users, and they use it for chat rooms.' MAG realized that this was its primary audience and designed the site to appeal to the 'entertainment interests' of this crowd, while simultaneously shifting their focus to social issues.

- **Advertise the website through multi-media to a variety of sectors**

To bring people to its site, MAG utilizes a variety of marketing channels, which not only vary by medium, but also vary by target audience. These channels include linking MAG's site with other sites, advertising on banners, and registering with portal pages. When advertising through links, MAG recommends not linking to the site, but linking to a specific project – this tailors the interests of a specific target audience to a corresponding project.

MAG also advertises its site through its own newsletter. 'It's a quick update on "What's New on the Internet",' says Boonngamanong. A factor in its success is that it is geared to a variety of sectors, and does not only focus on social issues. 'We invite new sites to submit a short profile for advertising and we discuss new Internet programs. In each edition we post five new items; only one is social. This is one of the reasons for success, we appeal to many types of web users.'

- **Build a membership and resource base through information, relationships, and interactivity.**

To obtain resources from its website visitors, MAG has created 'an on-line membership'. MAG successfully turns visitors into members by offering them information and personal relationships, and providing the opportunity to give back to the organization. Boonngamanong is adamant that a request for donations should not be the first contact that members have with the site. 'Make potential donors feel that they want to participate,' he advises. 'Make them feel, not simply know, about the issues and the need for resources. . . . And then offer a way to give back.'

Some respond by returning to the site; others respond by interacting with the site through bulletin boards and chat rooms. Still others find the need to give something tangible, which was what launched the site as a tool for resource mobilisation. MAG's website now offers members the chance to donate cash and books. It also offers a chance to volunteer in the community.

- **Track website visitors, building an electronic mailing list of email addresses**

MAG tracks the visitors to its site, keeping names and email addresses in an electronic mailing list. As a result of this system, MAG has a list of on-line members to whom it can regularly send announcements, new information, and emergency requests for donations.

Results

MAG receives about 600 hits a day to its site, yielding 7200 members for its mailing list. In 1999, through on-line recruiting, 400 people visited MAG's community development initiatives: about 100 of these volunteered to work in the community. In 1998, they received over 100,000 books. Today they are receiving one box of books every three days. Six months ago, they began soliciting financial donations through the Internet, and have since raised over 200,000 Baht (approx US$5406).

Source: www.changemakers.net/respources/0400mirror.cfm This is part of the Ashoka web page www.ashoka.org

Part Three

Deciding Which Way to Go

Chapter 16

Next Steps

_____

This handbook has illustrated 12 different ways by which a CSO can acquire resources or generate resources to support its work. The CSO that is interested to move from its present likely approach of dependence on foreign grants into one (or more) of these alternative approaches has to develop a strategy for the application of these approaches that is relevant and suitable. Experience in delivering training courses on this subject, however, suggests that the formulation of a strategy from a menu of options for action is difficult and requires considerable effort.

ADDICTION

Most CSOs are addicted to foreign funding; they cannot imagine a world without it, and they have difficulty in moving beyond a theoretical understanding of the value of financial self-reliance to its practical application. Various arguments for local resource mobilization presented in Part One will be convincing to them, but a gulf separates those organizations that are intellectually convinced and those that are prepared to commit themselves to trying out the new approaches practically. The new approaches illustrate a new paradigm, a different way of structuring experience, and different organizations, depending on their background and fields of interest, will embrace this new paradigm with different degrees of enthusiasm.

The situation is most stark (and easiest to deal with) in countries where the standard of living has increased, poverty has been reduced, and donors have consequently pulled out – eg Malaysia, Thailand, Botswana, and Chile. Not only are there very few donors willing to help CSOs in such countries any longer, but the disposable income of both individuals and organizations in those countries has increased, and thus a strategy of pursuing local resources seems both feasible and worth pursuing.

The situation is, however, soon likely to be stark everywhere. The amounts available from the traditional donors are diminishing everywhere, and, at the same time, the conditions and regulations laid on the funds that are available are becoming more and more donor-directed and burdensome. Once CSOs have been exposed to some of the possibilities other than foreign grants (and once there is a pool of experience among CSOs in using some of these other possibilities), the message of

Chapter 1 will be persuasive – 'existing patterns of resources will likely (a) not be available to your organization in the future, (b) will be felt to have disadvantages that outweigh their advantages, (c) will seem less attractive in relation to some other resources'.

A complicating factor is the 'inconsistency' of the patterns of foreign donor funding. Countries that are gradually evolving to a situation where foreign funding is less available and local resource mobilization is becoming an attractive option may suddenly become the focus for large new infusions of foreign donor funding for particular sectors that appeal to donors' agendas at that time. This is the situation in Indonesia, for example, where NGOs that are active in the field of democracy and governance have started to be wooed by foreign donors since the fall of Soeharto in 1998, and the transition to democracy. Existing donors have increased their funding and new donors have arrived. It is thus difficult to persuade Indonesian CSOs to look for alternatives to foreign funding when it is not only so easy to get, but is actually being promoted. Such promotion also has the effect, however, of encouraging new entries into the CSO sector simply to take advantage of the funding that is being offered. And yet the time to move on from foreign funding to local resource mobilization is precisely when the going is good and there is time to manoeuvre – not to wait until funding has dried up. Planning for a drought is easiest at the time of plenty.

STRATEGIC PLANNING

If a CSO has made the 'leap of faith' decision to embrace the new paradigm, it is important for it to remember that the taking up of any of these local resource mobilization approaches will require changes in the structure and management of the CSO if it has been dependent previously on foreign funding. The CSO will likely require new sections, departments, skills, staff, and even a new vision and mission. There will be a need to build new capacity in the CSO.

Because of the far-reaching and fundamental nature of the changes that are required in CSOs moving into some of these alternative approaches, it is sensible to link such a move with a strategic review of your CSO and a strategic planning exercise. Strategic planning is not a new field for many CSOs – it is likely that they have undertaken strategic planning exercises previously. These typically involve thinking about vision, mission, external and internal environments, alternative strategies, choice of programmes and projects. It is also likely, however, that previous strategic planning has considered expenditures rather than revenue.

An organization that is serious about local resource mobilization will appreciate that the changes to revenue planning are radical and will require the organization to re-examine many organizational concepts, and to include in its strategic review some attention to the benefits of local resource mobilization. Its vision will be one in which the organization's work is supported by the people of its country; its mission will be one in which the organization actively encourages local stakeholders and their support.

Some exercises can help you to identify the factors that will help or hinder your move to financial self-reliance. One such is a PEST analysis (political, economic, social and technological). This exercise helps an organization systematically to think through what aspects of your society (within these categories) will be helpful in a move to financial self-reliance. Another exercise is a SWOT analysis (strengths, weaknesses, opportunities, threats) of your organization. This helps you systematically to think through what aspects of your external and internal environment will help or hinder your moves to financial self-reliance.

It is very important that the CSO persuades all its stakeholders of the importance of the changes, and listens to any concerns they may have. For the organization to move forward convincingly with a new resource mobilization strategy, the CSO at all levels (governing body, senior and junior staff, volunteers) must be convinced of its need and viability.

Some members of staff may not be able to accept the new strategies (working with the corporate sector, for instance) and may decide to leave. Others may be delighted at the possibilities for creativity that the new work entails. Others still may need retraining.

What Aspects of the New Paradigm are Most Important to Your CSO?

Different organizations will give different degrees of emphasis to the opportunities and the constraints provided by the new paradigm. It is important for CSOs to think these through as part of the process of choosing the most suitable approach for them. Certain of the approaches will involve constraints of one kind, and opportunities of another. Looking back at Part One of this book, the following positive and negative issues in pursuing local resource mobilization have been noted. Once you discuss your own organization's position you may well come up with others:

Positive
- Links to your own society.
- Control over the use of resources.
- Variety of resources (thus reducing vulnerability).
- Ability to design your own programmes.
- Commitment to sustainability.
- (Please add your own ideas).

Negative
- Danger of distorting mission.
- Amount of work required.
- The likely return on effort.
- Distaste for certain partners (eg business or government).
- Difficulty of getting support for your particular cause.
- Lack of skills or experience in resource mobilization.
- (Please add your own ideas).

A useful exercise is to arrange a matrix of the positive factors on one axis and the kinds of resource mobilization options on the other axis, and to think through how important these features are to you in your choice of the different options. Then do the same exercise with the negative factors. This will help you systematically to think through the features of your organization that are most important to you, and which of the resource mobilization options thus seem most attractive. Look at the matrices on pp155 and 156.

Let us consider some examples of pursuing local resource mobilization:

- A CSO practising a service delivery strategy among very poor people in a very remote place may feel that accessing existing wealth is not a viable strategy since there is little wealth around, but that generating income has real possibilities. It then has to consider if it has the skills that are needed and whether it will be able to acquire them, and the start-up capital required.
- A CSO working with slum children in a big city may think that its best approach is to try to access existing wealth from individuals and businesses. It will probably need to learn a variety of fundraising techniques and consider where it can find the initial 'venture capital' to start up this process.
- A small CSO working with an advocacy strategy in the human rights field may be most constrained by the need to have reliable funds that will not be vulnerable to political pressures. It may consider that a membership drive to register a large number of sympathizers who will all provide steady, although small, contributions is the way to go. If one of its tactics is to expose injustices in the media, this could also be a means of attracting more sympathisers. Moreover, setting up such a list of subscribers will not take away time and energy from a very small staff, and can be linked to the Internet.

The balance of positive and negative factors for you to weigh up is far from fixed at any one moment in time, however. An alert and active CSO has to be opportunistic and see what existing and new possibilities there are, even though it had not thought of these originally. A change in tax law, for instance, might make it more attractive for businesses or individuals to support the work of CSOs; a particular event might allow a CSO to capitalize on the interest generated by its work; a new indigenous

	POSITIVE				
	Links to own society	Control over own resources	Variety of resources	Ability to control resources	Commitment to sustainability
Earned income					
Indigenous foundations					
Individual philanthropy					
Grass-roots organizations					
Government					
Foreign agencies					
Endowments/ reserve fund					
Corporate sector					
Debt conversion					
Microcredit					
Social investment					
Internet					

Figure 16.1 *Positive Factors in Pursuing Local Resource Mobilization*

	NEGATIVE					
	Danger of distorting mission	Amount of work required	Likely return on effort	Distaste for certain partners	Difficulty of getting support	Lack of experience in financing self-reliance
Earned income						
Indigenous foundations						
Individual philanthropy						
Grass-roots organizations						
Government						
Foreign agencies						
Endowments/ reserve fund						
Corporate sector						
Debt conversion						
Microcredit						
Social investment						
Internet						

Figure 16.2 *Negative Factors in Pursuing Local Resource Mobilization*

foundation might be set up, or a foreign donor might start a programme of venture capital for CSOs. A business person with entrepreneurial ideas might join the board and have many suggestions for income generation.

A sharp CSO will have thought through its own response to the variety of possibilities of resource mobilization, but will also be ready to respond to possibilities that arise. In every case the CSO will have to consider:

- Costs: what will be the expenses involved in setting up a local resource mobilization strategy?

- Capacity building: what skills does the organization have and what does it need? Where can such skills be acquired?
- Disruption: how can this new strategy be embraced by the organization with the least damage to its ongoing work?
- Energy and creativity: how can this new paradigm galvanize all stakeholders in the organization to be creative in finding ways to make it work?
- Sequencing: what needs to be done, in what order, to make sure of success?

In all cases it should factor in the possibilities that the use of the Internet may provide.

DONOR EDUCATION

Since the assumption of this book is that most CSOs are probably presently working with foreign funding, it is important, where possible, to keep on board the foreign donor that you have been working with for some time during the transition to local resource mobilization, because this donor is an important potential stakeholder in the process. It should be possible for the CSO to persuade its foreign donor of the rightness of its strategic change, and indeed to persuade them to help it in this change. Sadly, however, many foreign donors are stuck in a rut of serial project funding from foreign grants, and have not thought through how they can better support CSOs by other means. In this connection, rhetoric and reality are far apart. Richard Holloway's article 'The Unit of Development is the Organization not the Project' puts it this way (SAIS, 1999):

> *Where lies sustainability and self-reliance – two important concepts for Northern development agencies? The gap between rhetoric and reality is astonishingly wide. Northern donors are saying on the one hand that SNGDOs (Southern non-governmental development organizations) are important agents in development because of their unique characteristics, and their existence is important as representatives of the civil society, but they do little to help the organizations do anything more than implement Northern designed projects with Northern money. Northern donors are also saying that SNGDOs should be sustainable agents of effective development into the future, but they assist them in ways that not only do not build organizational continuity, but also isolate them from their own people. They do not, moreover, help them to build financial self-reliance.*

There is considerable need to educate donors, and not just civil society organizations, about the value of indigenous resource mobilization.

There may also be the possibility of keeping a funding relationship with a foreign donor for certain programmatic activities, while scaling down your organization's vulnerability to it. If a CSO has been convinced of the arguments for local resource mobilization, it can build towards it, gradually involving more and more citizens in its resource base, and decreasing its dependence on foreign sources.

CITIZENS' INITIATIVES

While educating foreign donors is undoubtedly important, the onus lies with the CSOs, the organizations of citizens in the South who care about social change and better development, to 'make the path by walking'. Most of the examples in the case studies of this book reflect strong civil society organizations that have pioneered ways of working (and ways of funding that work) that owe more to their own initiative and social entrepreneurship than to educating foreign donors. By constantly expanding the range of what is possible, they have created space for others to follow.

The Aga Khan Foundation has put the case well in its submission to the Department for International Development (DFID) (UK) when DFID asked for advice on how it could best support civil society:

> *Citizens' organizations will only become a permanent, stable part of the social order – will only become viable as a sector – when a stable resource base for the sector as a whole is secure. As it stands in most developing countries, the sector depends far too heavily and dangerously on foreign aid. Once citizens' organizations tap broad public support – through money, volunteer time, in-kind support, quasi business sales and/or information – they will have as steady a foundation as businesses, religions, unions, political movements, and all other groups that developed and set down their roots in earlier periods.*
>
> *Towards this end, one should work on both supply and demand side solutions. On the supply side, one should promote indigenous philanthropy, including through the creation and support of national philanthropy resource centres and through experimentation with new indigenous mechanisms of philanthropy. On the demand side, one should foster effective local resource mobilization.*

Civil society organizations convinced of the rightness of this approach need to start to make the road by walking – to create a path by making it. There are some pioneers from whom lessons can be learnt, it is true, but there are enormous spaces for social entrepreneurs to develop new ideas where there have been no such ideas previously. CSO staff who are aware of opportunities, who are prepared to take risks, who have competitive drive and determination, and who have imagination, can change the face of CSO resource mobilization. In the future it may well be that organizations that rely on foreign funding will be the exception rather than the rule.

An Introduction to the Commentaries

David Bonbright
Director, NGO Enhancement Programmes,
Aga Khan Foundation

The 20 commentaries that follow situate this handbook firmly within the particularities of place. They demonstrate that the handbook is relevant in settings as diverse as Thailand, Kenya, and Argentina. Whether we are in Indonesia or Zimbabwe or India, we hear a similar call to follow the steps indicated in the handbook to become more self-reliant.

These commentaries, all from recognized international authorities, also set out some additional challenges for those of us who seek to support the practice of resource mobilization. Several point to areas of needed research. Most highlight the obstacles that our own organizational cultures create for effective self-reliance, and the corresponding need to undertake resource mobilization within a process of holistic organizational development. Most also highlight the wider environmental factors that need to become more enabling – particularly the tax, legal, and policy frameworks. And all of them emphasize, often with telling illustrations, that every new supporter of our work brings new demands and new perspectives to our work. How we plan for and cope with these is a central theme through these fascinating commentaries.

With an expression of gratitude to the authors, I heartily commend these commentaries to you. They have significantly enhanced my understanding of the global ferment around indigenous philanthropy, while setting out some future markers for the Aga Khan Foundation's NGO Enhancement programmes. I am certain that their wisdom contains similar riches for you in this dynamic field.

Commentaries

QADEER BAIG, PAKISTAN
Acting Director, NGO Resource Centre,
Aga Khan Foundation (Pakistan)

Pakistan, a nation of about 140 million people, has a tradition of 'giving for charity'. Recent studies conducted by AKF on indigenous philanthropy have shown that most local charity goes to the religious institutions. Thousands of CSOs involved with development work, on the other hand, have yet to tap this rich vein of local support – which AKF-sponsored research estimates at US$1.5 billion in 1998 in cash, in kind and time giving – and rely predominantly on international foreign aid. By contrast, total foreign grant aid in 1998 was approximately US$120 million. In other words, the value of local giving – which runs in the main to religious activities – was more than ten times higher than international giving.

The majority of the community organizations working in rural areas and urban slums do not have access to external resources, however, and therefore typically become dormant for want of financial resources after an initial burst of voluntary effort. Their constituencies have limited capacity and a low inclination to pay for their services. The many intermediary CSOs depending on external funding sources are also constrained by its relative scarcity, the heavy administrative burdens that accompany it, and their lack of influence over the changing priorities of the international donors.

It is in the mandate of the NGO Resource Centre (NGORC) to work to strengthen CSOs in Pakistan, including building their capacity to mobilize resources for their work. The NGORC has found that few CSOs are familiar with the range of ways in which non-profit organizations may mobilize resources. In February 2000, I facilitated a five-day workshop on resource mobilization based on the Holloway handbook and the accompanying trainer manual. Both served admirably.

The handbook was informative and instructive. The one exception is the chapter on 'Conversion of Debt', which has not yet been introduced in Pakistan. We spiced up some of the sessions by introducing role-plays and improvised some of the approaches on the basis of our experience of working with Pakistan's CSOs. The handbook's case studies from different countries were pertinent and helped participants, mostly from intermediary CSOs, to understand the feasibility of various approaches.

Noting the effectiveness of resource mobilization strategies discussed in the handbook, the NGO Resource Centre has decided to include it into its organization development package, and actively work with its client citizens' organizations in developing and practising resource mobilization. The NGORC intends to enrich the course by developing local case histories.

Perhaps there is no better commentary than the written evaluations of our workshop participants:

- 'There is no doubt, the material that was presented during five days is really knowledgeable to the individual as well as my organization. I think the material will really be helpful in the future.'
- '. . . certain parts of the handbook were very enlightening and interesting. The new approaches to resource mobilization were certainly most applicable (especially business enterprise).'
- 'I feel that the course will help me reason the "do's" and "don'ts" of fundraising within diverse donor constituencies, and also be aware of the sensitivities and advantages of each mode.'
- 'This has provided me with a broader vision and outlook. This can be applied in different ways, as a support to the planning and resource mobilization team, and for direct application, on occasion.'
- 'It was highly relevant not only to my organization but to the entire nation, if the message gets across to them. Awareness of the same to NGOs and CBOs can vastly improve development service in Pakistan and can make organizations self-reliant.'
- 'I feel confident to materialize some of my projects in future, particularly the projects for which foreign funding is not available.'

NILOY BANERJEE, INDIA
Head, National Local Resource Mobilization Network, India

Overall, the handbook is an extremely useful and timely publication, providing a very good summary of experiences from various situations. A reader can potentially save on time and years of trial-and-error based lesson learning by reading this handbook in detail. The use of case studies is very appropriate as illustrations of the cases serve to very competently illustrate the contentions of the text.

By putting a host of ideas and experiences between two covers, the publication also serves a critically felt need in collating diverse experiences – another process that would take an individual years of work to gather.

There is clear intrinsic value in such a publication. The fact that some organization has actually attempted to put together such a publication is laudable in the first place given that fundraising, by definition, tends to be selfish or, from an organizational point of view, self-serving. A publication like this, by triggering discussions around it, also serves to seed a clearing house for the sharing of experiences and information among organizations within the civil society sector. The added value is that dialogues may take place between organizations that may otherwise be 'competitors', ie, organizations that target the same donor base or have similar activities.

As a handbook that is not context specific, the publication sets itself an ambitious task of being all things to all people in varying contexts. For the Indian context, it still makes a very relevant case by and large despite its more omnibus brief of catering to the 'South'. This is clearly a strength of this handbook.

The language is lucid and free from technicalities or jargon.

Only the most dedicated fundraiser will have the inclination to read the handbook from cover to cover. But its specific value is that the reader can easily dip selectively into specific chapters for her/his area of interest or relevance. So, an organization that functions on resources drawn from a reserve or corpus fund can read only the relevant module.

As a handbook for CSO managers and fundraisers who are going to use it as a resource in their fundraising endeavours, perhaps the fully argued case for local resource mobilization risks over-egging the pudding. The assumption should be that people who are aware of these issues and believe that local resource mobilization is important will pick up this publication in the first place.

The treatment of microcredit is a little simplistic. There are frequent (and well-founded) misgivings about the high cost of supervision, the sustainability of the lending institution taking precedence over sustainability of the borrower. There is a frequently espoused view (eg Wood and Sharif) that the success of the Grameen Bank model of microlending is successful mostly due to the efficiency of the field level staff in securing payback of loans. In that light, the suggestion that a CSO that revolves credit and generates some surplus to take care of overheads could well set a model for local resource mobilization, is not viable. The World Bank's calculation of the Subsidy Dependence Index (SDI) of the Grameen Bank is about 30 per cent. Most microcredit programmes do tend to have a fairly high cost of supervision and would not be viable without aid infusion (which, in my opinion, also explains why no Grameen has come up in India or the African continent, though many pilots have been tried). As opposed to that, self-help groups that rotate lending around a pooled savings scheme is a better model of local resource mobilization. The treatment of microcredit is a little simplistic in Chapter 13. Finally, new institutional forms of philanthropy, such as the 'community foundation', could be added.

Roberto Calingo, Philippines
Executive Director, Philippine Business for Social Progress

The greatest value of the handbook is the way in which it offers a menu of options for sustainable financing strategies that an organization may find appropriate. The cases provide concrete examples, that aid the reader/CSO in considering those options. Additionally, the handbook confirms recent discussions by Philippines Business for Social Progress with Indonesian groups. For many CSOs there, we found that while ethical issues remain crucial, sustainable financing as experienced by a few Indonesian CSOs presents an opportunity for a speedier resolution of those ethical issues. For instance, if Bina Swadaya is able to earn income without losing its credibility among its stakeholders, it could encourage an advocacy CSO to do the same without losing its effectiveness with its publics. The question then is: how do we disseminate the information?*

Our experience in the Philippines is quite different. In the workshops we have conducted, whether CSOs should earn income is not much of an issue anymore. The greater need is how to decide on the strategy. The following is what the workshops have taught us.

Before arriving at the process of deciding which strategies are viable for them, the CSOs need to have a more realistic appreciation of their present and future financial situation. Participants who come to a workshop on financial sustainability have already accepted the idea that their current sources are unsustainable. Thus, a more useful starting point for them is to reflect on the current financial situation (how much they have, how are they able to generate these current resources) and analyse their financial future. By comparing their financial goals with current capacity, the CSOs are able to determine the gaps both in terms of the amount of resources needed and their capacity to generate them.

Having set their financial goals, and having been provided cases of successful financing strategies, the workshop participants wanted more detailed how-to inputs for each strategy. While it was desirable to respond to such needs, it was not possible to provide a step-by-step set of procedures for each strategy that would apply to all the participating organizations during the workshop. It was deemed more appropriate to cull the lessons from the experiences/cases provided, and ask the participants to try to relate their situation with the situation in the cases. As a training reference, therefore, the handbook could provide a more comprehensive summary

---

* Philippine Business for Social Progress, together with Bina Swadaya and Synergos Institute conducted a country workshop in Yogyakarta, September 2000, on Sustainable Financing for Civil Society Resource Organizations. CSROs are those CSOs that make grants or loans to organizations and individuals.

of the cases, and the intention of the Aga Khan Foundation to use the handbook as a way to collect, collate, and publish, via the Internet, case studies provided by users of the handbook is most welcome.

PBSP (Philippine Business for Social Progress) conducted an Endowment Building Workshop in September 1999, bringing in experience from South Africa, South America, Indonesia, and the Philippines. The workshop brought to the fore rich experience on how endowments are created and invested, generating tremendous interest among participants. The issues and questions raised following the cases presented indicate the range of information that needed to be written in a handbook form. Matters like when to decide whether to employ internal or external investment managers, how much discretion to give your investment managers, and how to convince donors to support building a CSO's endowment, are topics that the ongoing Internet database aspect of the handbook could cover. For handbook readers interested in our examination of these issues, please contact Philippines Business for Social Progress.

Mathew Cherian, India
Executive Director, Charities Aid Foundation (India)

This handbook is a very useful book for practitioners and those who will be entering the field of fundraising and resource mobilization. In India, where the bulk of the voluntary sector relies on grant funding, resource mobilization is not yet the lingua franca. However, the bulk of the religious philanthropic sector has been largely successful in mobilizing funds from supporters, pilgrims and associates. Some of the techniques mentioned in the handbook will be useful for both religious and non-religious associations.

It is necessary for all non-profit organizations to be aware and reorganize the historical and cultural history of traditional charity in India. The 'concept of giving' is seen as an extension of a religious activity and is not a response to social needs. Because Hinduism, and indeed all major religions represented in India, is based on philosophical and cultural values for the emancipation of the soul, the performing of good deeds, including acts of charitable giving, served the particular purpose of making people accept their material misery as their destiny.

Hindu mythology has models of extreme philanthropy like Raja Harishchandra who gave away everything to become a Dom who survives by burning people's dead bodies. Even today in Gujarat many times a rich diamond merchant or his son will become a Jain monk and throw crores of diamonds to the public in a procession. Richard Lannoy tells us of the great merchant guilds that funded the Ajanta and Ellora complexes, and supported large sanghas of Buddhist monks.

Gandhi utilized this principle of community collection to support his ashrams. Howsoever small the donation, it connects people to an idea. The *langar* or the food service in most big *gurudwaras* is a metaphor for Guru Nanak's Kartarpur commune where all worked together on the land and ate together.

The other stream of giving is about giving of yourself, your skill, your labour or *shramdaan* – the giving of effort, whether for community work like cleaning tanks or for your ashram or guru. The best functioning religious institutions in India are the *gurudwaras* where Sikhs from all classes sweep and look after the shoes – all considered lower class activities – and also cook the food for the *langar*.

Health was looked after by the local *vaid* or traditional healers, who prescribed giving as a cure for depression, angst, or *vairagya* (or meaninglessness of existence). Just experiencing pure giving is supposed to help one feel catharsis.

Why haven't Indian CSOs managed to tune into this major tradition of giving? A friend once remarked how India is like a big cake with icing on it. The cake and icing are in contact yet completely different in character.

Where does one begin to estimate the amount of 'giving' in a society? Gifting, granting without expectation of return; giving which seeks no self-gratification except to fulfil some abstract notion of helping someone somewhere, or just helping because it cleanses oneself of the constant desire to have or to consume. What percentage should one expect? Or is that not possible in an age of personal, corporate, excise, customs, and local taxation when one's social duty is fulfilled with one's payment of honest taxes. Taxes are the equivalent of grants from an individual to the state to keep the social infrastructure in place, to transfer income to the poorest, and for overall development. In a way every taxpayer feels that they have performed their philanthropic role.

How does one make individuals and whole communities feel the need to give more, not through a state apparatus but through a voluntary system, not civil legal pressure but moral pressure? In it is implied the need for the accepting agency to be more credible, less self-serving, more humane and sensitive, and less bureaucratic. The expectations are very high for purity, transparency and simplicity of operation; hence the desire to give can very easily be snuffed out by even small examples of waste or corruption in the CSO sector. The UN faces similar accusations from many donor countries. Even while giving to God, there is an expectation of return. Only highly effective gods or goddesses get funds. Millions of religious places lie in neglect, so even giving in religion has certain requirements of performance accountability.

The individual who feels unsure of the reason for his success in a chaotic, random society needs to stabilize his upward mobility trajectory and then needs to give. Usually the need to give is directly proportional to the luck or success in 'receiving' material rewards. People who give need to see the visible results of giving, which are easiest appreciated in terms of medicines given, sick people treated, students educated, trees planted or orphans looked after. It is more difficult to get funds for gender awareness, health research, mental illnesses, development and income generation activities which need a long-term vision. People tend to get tired of giving to causes, which are like 'black holes of universal suffering'. They never tire of giving to God, as God is seen as perpetually giving to them as individuals.

How does one turn funding from a perspective of community's needs or to compassion towards a sustainable social programme? Who can be the agency? Is it individuals who inspire trust, institutional CSOs, voluntary groups, or all of them together? What roads would we take in the Indian context? We will need to look at the case studies in Holloway's handbook to reflect on how fundraising is happening in the Indian context.

This book can be read by the practitioner as a reference text because the case studies give very useful and interesting insights. In our experience with Charities Aid Foundation, always we have been looking at means of fundraising that will increase the flow of resources to the voluntary sector. Any devices to do this will help the sector to stabilize its income. One of our devices has been payroll giving, patented as 'Give as You Earn'. This mechanism of deduction from people's salaries is being tried out in India in Delhi and Bangalore. It helps employees who donate to realize a tax deduction of up to 50 per cent. This helps employees working in factories and companies to donate easily, and also to get tax benefits, although less than 2 per cent of India's population pays tax on income. In future years, however, with a widening tax base it could be very important.

The issue of the tax drivers for giving has not been dealt with in this handbook at great length. Lobbying with the government for improved tax benefits for donations will help. This becomes more and more important as tax regimes in many countries do not favour philanthropy as much as in the United Kingdom, which has become very liberal with the new Labour Government's tax changes. Very often measures, such as tax breaks, help social organizations to access new money and unlock resources that are hidden from the public domain. This could have been dealt with in greater length as it could definitely provide a fillip to local resource mobilization in developing economics.

The interesting aspect of the handbook is the separation and classification of various techniques. It will be useful both for the newly initiated as well as the experienced practitioner.

Noshir H Dadrawala, India
Executive Secretary,
Centre for Advancement of Philanthropy

It has been a pleasant and rewarding experience leafing through Richard Holloway's guide to resource mobilization entitled *Towards Financial Self-reliance*.

I had the pleasure of listening to Richard Holloway at the 8th Asia Pacific Fund Raising Workshop held in Manila, and what I appreciate both in his talks and writings is the clarity of thought, depth of research, and the wide array of experience that he draws on.

Towards Financial Self-reliance is an excellent resource book both for the amateur and the professional 'Southern fundraiser'.

The author indicates that the handbook is directed internationally at CSOs in the South (ie developing countries), many of which have become dangerously dependent on foreign funding. He is so right in his assessment. World Bank figures indicate that 50 per cent of the funds for voluntary organizations in India come from foreign donors, 30 per cent from local contributions, and 20 per cent from the Indian Government. The bulk of foreign funds from bilateral and multilateral agencies are channelled through government and, to that extent, are indistinguishable from government funds. It is only the funds of foreign funding organizations like Oxfam, Ford Foundation, Terres Des Hommes, etc that flow directly to private voluntary effort, albeit with government permission. Holloway is of the opinion that the existing pattern of foreign funding support to voluntary organizations is not sustainable. It is a statement one cannot dismiss easily.

Foreign donors are often deemed a good source of start-up funds for fledgling programmes that find it difficult to gain support locally from the government or corporations. Foreign foundations are usually known to be more willing to take risks.

Also, in a developing country like India, a foreign foundation grant carries a certain prestige that is believed to enrich the public image of the grantee – for example, support from the Ford Foundation seems to confer greater stature and public esteem.

However, raising support from foreign foundations has its disadvantages. The size of the foreign grant is often determined by conditions that are external to the needs of the applicant: the total funds available, the competition with other grantees, and the general guidelines for grant size set by the foreign foundation. Applicants may need to look for grants from a number of foundations before they can raise all the funds that are required to carry out their entire project.

Often, foreign donors set rigid timetables for proposal submission and grant approval – the timing may not necessarily conform to a voluntary organization's need for funds. More often than not, voluntary organizations miss their opportunity because they are not on time.

Foreign foundations also, are less likely than other sources to renew grants for organizations, and grantees cannot determine easily in advance whether the foreign funder will decide to renew their support. It is thus difficult for an organization that depends narrowly on foreign foundation support to plan more than a couple of years ahead. In other words, as Holloway asserts, foreign funding does not and probably cannot promote sustainability.

In this work, Holloway explores a variety of domestic resources that are potentially available to Southern voluntary organizations, but that have not been researched or tested adequately. Many of them are worth considering, provided they do not violate various laws governing voluntary organizations in the country.

Holloway's ideas are obviously not the last word on the subject, for resource mobilization is an ongoing and evolving process. He has paved a few paths, however: some we may tread with excitement and some with caution. More paths will be paved over the years. And as long as voluntary organizations continue to exist, new paths will have to be made, discovered, tried out, rejected or accepted.

RAJEEV DUA, SOUTH ASIA
Chief Executive Officer, SAFRG
AND
MURRAY CULSHAW, SOUTH ASIA
Consultant, Former Director, Oxfam, India*

The South Asia Fund Raising Group (SAFRG) is a lead organization in South Asia committed to developing and promoting the concept of resource mobilization, enhancing awareness and understanding about it, and building the capacities of organizations to implement them successfully. In order to strengthen the handbook, it undertook a process of consultation covering three countries – India, Bangladesh and Nepal – to provide expert feedback on the draft text, as well as to assess the market for it. SAFRG is taking an active role in distributing the handbook and the accompanying trainer manual in the South Asia region.

SAFRG found that Richard Holloway's handbook is quickly seen by practitioners as a remarkably useful and a comprehensive effort. The general impression of diminishing foreign sources of funds for the non-profit sector makes this handbook relevant and indispensable for practitioners and those who will be entering the field of resource mobilization aiming at self-sufficiency.

As fundraisers we have a responsibility to make connections between the 'givers' in society and the 'causes' that these people can give to and be involved in. However innovative we may get in our approach, the fundamentals are that fundraising is not just about money or targets to be met. It is about fulfilling the 'need'. It is about providing people with opportunities to participate. It is about making friends. Its non-negotiable aspects include integrity, accountability and transparency.

One of the major infirmities of CSOs in South Asia is their limited capability to tap local resources. With a regular flow of easy funds from foreign organizations, most CSOs have ceased to consider the possibility of exploring potential opportunities in the domestic arena. Possibilities definitely exist, and Indian citizens do want to

---

* Rajeev Dua, the Chief Executive Officer of the South Asia Fund Raising Group (SAFRG), introduces a South Asian SAFRG three-country review of the handbook. The report on

give and get involved, but they need to be given attractive opportunities by credible organizations.

In India, charity and religious philanthropy have been an integral part of the social framework. Industrialization resulted in a more focused concept of philanthropy. Industrialists like Jamshedji Tata redefined the scope of charity from disaster relief to an effort to address the root causes of social ills and problems. In the late 19th and early 20th centuries, the private charitable contributions for the freedom movement and social reform increased. Gandhiji further emphasized social philanthropy and community participation for the social betterment and self-reliance of communities. In post-independence India, with the emergence of the welfare state, the role and responsibility of the state for social and economic development increased. But the inability of the government to address effectively the complex and vast scope of developmental needs resulted in growing dissatisfaction. In the 1960s, this gap gave an impetus to individual and group initiatives to respond to the challenges by focusing on social concerns. The non-profit sector has gradually grown in number and activities. Furthermore, the development of concepts of social responsibility, social capital and social investment help in understanding the role, responsibilities and alternative mediums of support from various sectors of the society in enabling meaningful development. Congruent to the evolving under-standing of philanthropy is the expanding potential of resource mobilization for the non-profit sector. Food banks in Maharashtra, and the Ralegaon Sidhi experience have demonstrated the potential in community support. Similarly, the issue-based support that was mobilized during the Kargil war and the cyclone at Orissa are examples of the inherent scope of individual philanthropy.

The growing concern now is for financial self-reliance and the long-term sustainability of voluntary organizations or development effort (or what the handbook calls civil society organizations). Richard Holloway endeavours to provoke thinking about solutions. In India, debate and practical initiatives have been underway since 1980. However, the movement needs to be much more widespread. Current efforts in India by the Charities Aid Foundation, the Aga Khan Foundation, the Local Resource Mobilization Network, and others to explore dimensions of what has been termed 'diaspora giving', networking and the potential of support from small and medium traders and businesses are steps in this direction. Also,

India was prepared by a team including Murray Culshaw of Murray Culshaw Advisory Services (MCAS), Roshni Sharma from Aga Khan Foundation (India), and Jasreet S Mahal and Nidhi Bhasin from SAFRG. The Nepal report was written on the basis of a visit to Nepal on 12–15 June 2000 by Rajeev Dua and Murray Culshaw. And the Bangladesh report was also based on a Rajeev Dua-Murray Culshaw field visit, from 15–18 June 2000. These visits were made possible through grants from Aga Khan Foundation (India) and the Ford Foundation's New Delhi office.

there is a move towards systematizing the process by understanding and creating avenues of channelling diaspora giving, addressing the issues of transparency and accountability, and developing a universally accepted credibility rating.

The handbook is based on the premise that voluntary organizations are a vital element of society and, thus, that their capacity to mobilize resources in order to sustain and expand their activities is a necessity. This we agree with. However, the underlying assumption that civil society organizations are solely dependent on grants from foreign agencies is not so valid in India. Although CSOs in India are heavily dependent on government and international agency grants, many organizations are raising resources from a range of opportunities within Indian society. Some encouraging examples are:

- Lok Kalyan Samiti, which has not taken any foreign funds for expanding its eye care programme since 1990. It has developed very imaginatively direct mail support from a large donor base spread across India.
- Hindu Mission Hospital, Chennai, with its intense experience in fundraising, has demonstrated the potential traditional methods and occasion-related solicitation.
- As a pioneer in public resource mobilization, Child Relief and You (CRY) conducted innovative campaigns to access individual philanthropy through its range of popular stationery products.

Understanding the need for institutional strengthening, the Ratan Tata Trust has adopted an endowment policy.

With the belief in the positive role of business in bringing about social changes in Indian society, the Business Community Foundation (BCF) and the Confederation of Indian Industries (CII) are promoting the understanding and adoption of socially responsible business policies.

The handbook is relevant, however, both for organizations that are heavily dependent on foreign sources of income and organizations that have begun to diversify their sources of income, and now need to be more systematic and more effective in what they are already doing.

Overall, the handbook highlights the need for a culture change within organizations that are grant-dependent from international sources. It begins to explore ways and means of bringing about this pivotally important change of attitude. It argues that the shift from foreign to indigenous sources requires the public and corporate sector to be educated (we prefer the idea of dialogue), and challenged to support the efforts of voluntary organizations.

India's very large and vibrant voluntary sector has not yet been mapped. There is, therefore, hardly any publicly available information on the number of organizations and the patterns of income. The degree of self-reliance of the sector, or indeed of individual organization, remains unknown. This gap in information will soon close. Research is underway to determine the size of the sector (monetary value as a percentage of gross domestic product, and employment within the sector). It is being conducted by Participatory Research in Asia (PRIA) within the framework of the Johns Hopkins Comparative Non-Profit Sector Study Project. Initial findings are due for release in early 2001.

Other research was conducted during 1999 by the Charities Aid Foundation (CAF) and Voluntary Action Network, India (VANI).

The history of philanthropy in Nepal can be traced back to the Vedic period.* The 117 Sukta of Mandak 10 of the Rig Veda (5000 BC) is named Dhananna Dana Sukta and is dedicated to the glory of wealth and food donations; and the Bhagavad Gita (from the same period) recognizes three types of donations: Satvic – holy; Rajasic – with strings; and Tamasic – wrongfully done.

An inscription on a column facing the Buddhist chaitya (shrine) of Chabhil shows that 1700 years ago a simple woman donated her ricefield to feed the Buddha Sangha (the Buddhist priest community).

So, over the centuries Nepalese society built temples, centres of learning, and helped members of its own society in many ways. Various practices continue today – for example, the noble tradition of 'Gathi' (providing service without expecting returns), in society such as ... 'pranali gathi' for providing drinking water for travellers, 'arogyashala gathi' for treating sick people, and 'margon marjon gosht' for cleaning walking trails.

In the 1960s and 1970s the international aid system arrived, led by persons with no knowledge of Nepalese tradition and Nepal society, resulting in aid and grants that invariably disregarded traditional and long-established systems of caring and sharing. This aid system now supports several thousand CSOs that live from grant to grant, and are concerned about what happens when the current grant finishes. And international CSOs have begun to be concerned about the sustainability of the programmes they have supported.

Despite this, there are a few (and there may be many more) Nepalese people and organizations who have taken a conscious decision to work within the framework of Nepalese support. The following illustrate what must be just a few of the initiatives that exist.

In 1990, the Child Development Society (CDS) was established as a result of the international 'Child Rights'. Its focus is on child labour in the carpet industry. CDS started by working on health issues of children at work. Gradually it became possible to release children from work and place them in schools. Since the society's establishment about 3000 children have been drawn into non-formal education, and now about 550 children attend regular schools. Four staff work on rights and

---

* For a fascinating collection of ancient and modern insights into philanthropy, see the January 2000 booklet by Tewa, 'Twice blessed – the art of giving'.

advocacy issues. CDS receives international aid for the bulk of its US$17,000 budget. A conscious effort is made to raise local resources, however. A staff member said that obtaining the involvement of friends and people was a real benefit, and just working towards self-reliance generated self-confidence. Now about US$3000 is raised through donations and various activities, including:

- Life members, now 120, all from within Nepal, contribute US$14.5 each, which goes to build an endowment. The interest now amounts to about US$170 per annum.
- Candles and greeting cards are being made and sold.
- Land has been given for a new centre; and bricks have been offered to build the centre.
- CDS has a volunteer 'fundraising and media publicity' committee.

Manushi was established in 1991 to promote arts and crafts, and is self-sustaining through its activities. Ten staff members are employed, with responsibilities for designing, marketing, and accounting, and for the promotion of self-help groups, and saving and credit programmes among the groups.

In 1996, Tewa (meaning 'help' or 'support') was registered to increase the self-reliance of the Nepalese community by inculcating the habit of donating regularly, with a special focus on women. Tewa began with help from outside Nepal, but within two years took a policy decision manage with the funds it could raise within Nepal. It has since raised NRs3.2 million (US$45,700) and has made grants to 80 groups working on women's issues. Tewa now has 100 volunteers and 500 local donors.

Tewa trains its volunteers for three days before they begin to help and fundraise; Tewa is planning a microphilanthropy programme with the support of Unniti Foundation, New Delhi,* and produces leaflets and annual reports in Nepalese and English. Tewa has recently produced a beautiful booklet on philanthropy 'Twice blessed – the art of giving' in English and Nepalese. One staff member said: 'I feel proud to be a member of Tewa because of its reliance on support within Nepal'; another said that the long-term nature of the support beginning to come meant that 'Tewa is now free of the worry of project grants'.

The general view of the CSO representatives we met in Nepal was that the handbook and the trainer manual are information-intensive documents and could be very useful for the sector. A widening group understands the importance of local resource mobilization as a strategy for increasing sustainability.

---

* The Unniti Foundation's established 'microphilanthropy' project is also being run in India and in Bangladesh (with BRAC). The project aims to promote the idea of responsible philanthropy, including volunteering, among 'ordinary' individuals.

The Bangladesh CSO community in its present form is of comparatively recent origin, having grown up after the War of Liberation of 1971 and the subsequent establishment of the Republic of Bangladesh. Despite this comparatively short history, Bangladesh is known today for its innovative and large-scale approaches to combating poverty, and its successes in such areas as microenterprise and microcredit, primary education, health, and family planning. However, a seriously high level of poverty remains, with most social indicators figuring below other developing countries. The extensive network of CSOs that exist in Bangladesh offers a tremendous resource potential, which is being drawn upon to tackle the nation's vast development needs.

A 1992 estimate indicates that the 30 largest CSOs in Bangladesh received 80 per cent of the foreign funds given to CSOs, 60 per cent of which was controlled by eight of the CSOs (Davies, cited in PACT/ PRIP, undated). This 80 per cent appears to be ever increasing. Another estimate indicates that the total amount of foreign funds spent by the ten leading national CSOs equalled about 68 per cent of the total foreign funds released by the NGO Advisory Body in 1993–94.

This concentration of donor funds persists, as donors continue to channel a large proportion of funds to CSOs that have demonstrated programme effectiveness and management capacity. For example, in 1998–1999, just 8 CSOs (out of 1200) received 90 per cent of aid to the CSO sector, and BRAC's budget is 55 per cent of the budget of these 8 CSOs and accounts for 45 per cent of all CSO expenditure.* This polarized distribution of foreign resources and rapid growth of the larger CSOs is believed to be restricting the growth of the smaller local and innovative CSOs. A further consequence of this distinctive pattern of CSO growth and financing is that the growth of local resource mobilization by CSOs has so far been on a very limited scale.

Bangladesh's giant CSO conglomerates however, have been leading global pioneers in one of the approaches highlighted in the handbook – earned income through commercial ventures. The setting up of commercial ventures to fund the work of the CSO from profits is a feature of the larger CSOs. For example, BRAC, PROSHIKA, the Association for Social Advancement (ASA), and Grameen Bank, which are all registered under the Societies Registration Act of 1860, have set up commercial ventures, including retail outlets, cellular telephone services, Internet services, printing, cold storage, and garments units. Other smaller CSOs have also chosen to run small-scale business activities such as bakeries and tree nurseries. Some CSOs, however, are ambivalent about this way of earning revenue, feeling that it will deflect them from their social development mission.

The Government of Bangladesh, with support from bilateral and finance institutions such as the Asian Development Bank, has been financing microcredit

---

* See the report 'Partners in Development – a review of big NGOs in Bangladesh commissioned by DFID', early 2000.

programmes of CSOs through a specialized agency Palli Korma Shahayak Foundation (PKSF), which was established in 1990 as a non-profit company. The major objective of PKSF is to help the rural poor access resources (primarily microcredit) through its partner organizations that are usually local CSOs.

Linking with the banking sector, a growing number of CSOs are turning to nationalized commercial banks and agricultural banks to replenish their revolving funds – for example, Grameen, Swanirvar Bangladesh and PROSHIKA. Such linkages are possible for programmes that generate returns.

Contractual partnerships with government may currently be the most promising source of finance. Technically speaking, these do not represent domestic resources, however, as the funds are predominantly of foreign origin.

The sale of development-related services is emerging as a promising source of income for CSOs, particularly the big and specialized agencies. The services that earn income are mainly training, consultancy, and research.

Contributions from business and industry do not so far appear to be a significant source of funds for CSOs. Private business in Bangladesh has not yet developed a tradition of corporate philanthropy or corporate social investment. This should improve if the government introduces fiscal incentives.

Fundraising appeals to the general public are made by welfare organizations like orphanages and homes for aged persons, and a few organizations raise funds through such methods as public collections, sponsored events and public lotteries, as practised by the Sports Council and BIRDEM. Fundraising events have tax implications, and permission has to be sought from the Secretary, Internal Resource Division. These forms of fundraising are not yet popular among CSOs working on development issues.

Individuals frequently show their social responsibility through *zakat*, an Islamic injunction to give, amounting to 2.5 per cent of total wealth.

Bangladesh does not have an enabling fiscal policy environment. There is no provision of any exemption on donations given for charitable purposes. While in theory all CSOs are exempt from corporate taxes, since the early 1990s a number of large CSOs have been issued income tax assessment notices. The CSOs have so far refused to pay and have appealed to the tax tribunal. The major point of dispute relates to the showing of 'profit' from commercial ventures in financial statements of accounts. The tax authorities are arguing that this profit is taxable. The CSOs are arguing that the profit is being used for charitable and developmental activities. Richard Holloway suggests an excellent approach to this problem on p33. The dispute in Bangladesh is unresolved.

Government–CSO relations tend to be tempestuous. A recent phenomenon in the evolution of CSOs has been the inclusion by some CSOs of lobbying and advocacy activities designed to change the government's public policy. The government is rather thin-skinned about criticism, and tends to stereotype CSOs as lacking accountability, duplicating each other wastefully, relying too much on foreign funds, and spending too much money on their operations. CSOs also tend towards a simplistic view of government thinking as rigid, bureaucratic, and control-driven in its regulatory approach, unable and unwilling to appreciate the differences in approach and style of a CSO project management, and unwilling to differentiate between CSOs with a proven track record of performance and less committed CSOs.

In the early 1990s the Private Rural Initiatives Project (PRIP)* (under the leadership of Richard Holloway) conducted a number of workshops and produced manuals with a view to promoting self-reliance and corporate–CSO cooperation. While this laid the foundation for considering the issue, it is not clear to what extent practical initiatives emerged. However, there is growing interest in seeking more local resources among the following groups:

- Participants in the South Asian Fund Raising Group's (SAFRG) annual conferences over the past few years. Participation has grown each year – 40 persons from Bangladesh attended the 11th Conference held in Calcutta in November 1999.
- The 147 NGO members of the Bangladesh Fundraising Group (BFRG), which has conducted a series of workshops throughout the country. For these five- and six-day workshops, a comprehensive manual in Bengali has been prepared, and so far 280 persons have attended five workshops, and 70 trainers have also been trained.
- Those aware that the flow of aid is diminishing. Certainly the funds available to the smaller CSOs are decreasing (because the larger CSOs, as mentioned above, are capturing the foreign aid).

There is no doubt that the importance of local resource mobilization as a strategy towards increasing sustainability is being understood by a widening group. And now, with a very active BFRG, the issue will receive increasing practical encouragement. The Holloway handbook will be an important resource to advance this process.

Z I FAROOK, BANGLADESH
Executive Director, Bangladesh Fundraising Group

In Bangladesh, many CSOs have good programming knowledge; what they lack is expertise and a sound fundraising programme. Such CSOs will actively use the Richard Holloway handbook as an effective tool to raise funds locally.

Most of the ways of mobilizing resources mentioned in the handbook, are extremely useful. Indeed, some are already in use by local fundraising practitioners.

---

* PRIP began as a project of the US NGO PACT; it is now known as PRIP Trust.

The issues that need to be addressed in order to facilitate effective resource mobilization are:

- The development of a positive attitude among the public towards social development programmes run by CSOs.
- Policy dialogue with the government, donor agencies, and members of the civil society in favour of local giving to support development projects. The Bangladesh Fundraising Group offers one platform for this policy dialogue.
- Foreign financial agencies can cooperate with the BFRG to assess whether a CSO has potential for local fundraising.

ANWAR FAZAL, MALAYSIA
Senior Regional Advisor, The Urban Governance Initiative, UNDP, Malaysia

Richard Holloway's compilation of ideas and approaches towards self-reliance meets a very important need at these times of dwindling aid. I have found three important principles useful in resource mobilization, all of which are confirmed by the handbook.

1   The best way of raising funds is not to need them.
2   Use hitch-hiking or 'smart partnerships' (depending on whether you prefer a hippie or a corporate term). Link with people who have the resources and means – other people's premises, new outlets, volunteers – instead of spending scarce funds on these.
3   Many of our communities have rich traditions of philanthropy. 'Mapping' the resources in our own communities, cities, countries, and drawing from them, opens the door to adapting old ways of public support to today's 'new issues'.

The book also suggests a range of strategies and methods that will be most helpful to groups working in the public interest, and for the public good. Combining it with a website, a network of local contacts and training packages, will enable the wide dissemination and application of this good work. I shall certainly use it in my capacity-building programmes.

DOROTHY K GORDON, GHANA
Executive Director, Integrated Resources Group

Effective resource mobilization implies accountability. One aspect of the development of NGOs and other CSOs in sub-Saharan Africa that causes real concern is the distortion in the focus of accountability that has resulted from over-dependence on external funding. In many cases the donor agenda has come to take precedence over the real needs of target beneficiaries. Unlike their counterparts in Latin America and Asia, very few formally registered CSOs in Africa have developed locally generated financial resources.

It is against this background that the news that donor funds are drying up – one of the central messages of this book – can be seen as a good thing, especially if it means that taking up the challenge to develop a strategic approach to domestic resource mobilization offers the hope of greater accountability to the people that Southern CSOs intend to serve.

Unfortunately, in some cases the real issue is not that funds are drying up but that the terms under which CSOs can access funds increasingly reflect the kind of subcontracting relationships that one would normally find in the private sector. This kind of 'partnership' approach, favoured by multilateral lending institutions working in sub-Saharan Africa, makes it more and more difficult to distinguish between commercial institutions and those of the third sector. By becoming mere contractors, these organizations have in practice set aside 'public benefit' as their goal. Accountability in these cases is clearly focused on the primary 'client' who pays for a specific service.

This situation reinforces distortions, as well-located air-conditioned offices and luxury four-wheel drives become prerequisites for 'credible' organizations. As the author of this manual so rightly points out, 'resources are not neutral or value free'. The availability of this type of 'funding' is a powerful force that pulls organizations away from domestic resource mobilization.

Apart from these very real external forces, there exist considerable internal constraints. In a continent that is still poor in skilled human resources, the new 'professionalism' of third-sector institutions imposes requirements of oral and written fluency in English (or some other colonial language), good knowledge of modern management techniques, including strategic planning, and an understanding of what outsiders understand, by impact, performance, etc. Skilled individuals of this type do not come cheap and even when 'grown' within an organization, poaching by head-hunters makes it difficult to retain them.

Of course, there is the cheaper alternative – a foreign volunteer – paid for by a donor but who can act as a bridge between the organization and outside partners. This has been one very sore point with local organizations. The impression is that for donors (or development partners, as they like to be called these days), any foreigner is honest until proven guilty and can access funds with relative ease. On the other hand, Africans are virtually always seen as crooks until they prove themselves otherwise. The end result is that individuals with good ideas are often frustrated in their efforts due to their lack of ability to 'talk the talk'.

Apart from these general concerns that are linked with the foreign dominance of what constitutes good practice in the area of third-sector activities, there are specific concerns that make many of the extremely logical and well thought-out options presented in the handbook of marginal relevance to African organizations – at least for the immediate future. It would have been good if the boiling down of the information that went into the current handbook had included some experience from West Africa in addition to that from South Asia, Central Europe, and Jamaica. No doubt in addition to the highly informative boxes on case studies, actual feedback from practitioners on this continent in all its diversity will inform subsequent editions.

One key concern relates to the legal frameworks for third-sector activities, which on the African continent often fall far short of the ideal. In my own country, Ghana, the existing legislation is such that most third-sector organizations register as companies that are limited by guarantee and then specify that they will be operating not-for-profit. There is no question of formal registration as a foundation. Of course, this does not preclude one from calling one's organization a foundation, but the regulatory framework as far as finances are concerned remains that of a company that is limited by guarantee. This touches on the viability of the reserve fund and endowment approach set out in the handbook.

The fact that the regulatory framework is more tied to private-sector needs means that CSO involvement in activities to generate wealth is subject to misinterpretation. Is every failed businessperson operating a CSO? There is little pressure on CSOs to fulfil the legal obligation to submit accounts to the accountant-general's office. The system of checks and balances to support organizations in really remaining not-for-profit once they start running income-generating activities is rather weak.

There are a number of well-recognized issues in relation to domestic resource mobilization that also affect the viability of income-generating activities on the continent. The macroeconomic instability and poverty that plague many African economies mean that the pool of businesses of potential major donors is relatively limited. Also, macroeconomic instability has been the death of many microcredit programmes as inflation makes the amounts available meaningless and exchange-rate depreciation erodes foreign seed capital. Naturally, the not-for-profit organization that launches income-generating activities is just as subject to the pressures that the volatile economic climate imposes on the survival of the average businessperson. These very real risks come to supplement concerns that are related to the potential for being diverted from one's mission, and the challenge of acquiring the necessary business management skills.

While accessing existing wealth and generating new wealth will mean that organizations will have to figure out how best to deal with some of the systemic issues raised above, there is great potential for organizations to capitalize on non-financial resources.

Historically, grass-roots organizations (GROs) and other membership organizations have shown how effectively this can be done, at least as far as volunteer time is concerned. Indeed, they have also demonstrated how using national, as opposed to official, languages in their fundraising messages and demonstrating results on the ground can inspire even the poorest to make a contribution.

It is these types of organizations that often have no option but to depend on domestic resource mobilization that must be given the opportunity to access the valuable knowledge contained in the handbook. Their intuitive understanding of suitable approaches to domestic resource mobilization could be enriched by this exposure. An additional gain would be reduced vulnerability and dependency on 'pretender' CSOs that see third-sector activities merely as lucrative employment opportunities.

However, if the handbook is to reach the GROs, it may be necessary to use alternative presentations such as audio-visuals using local languages in order to overcome the barriers that are linked to language and literacy. There are, in fact, infinite possibilities for 'rolling-out' the valuable lessons contained in the handbook, and at the same time ensuring that subsequent editions will have even more practical examples of best practice from around the world.

Successful resource mobilization is not easy, and this handbook comes as a valuable guide in charting a viable course that no doubt will inspire many, and at the same time give them the tools to make change for real public benefit.

DANIEL Q KELLEY, USA AND LATIN AMERICA
President, Global Work-Ethic Fund

I have been asked to comment on this book as one who advises a variety of CSOs on local and international fundraising. I spend most of my time in Latin America, so my observations are coloured by this region, but my work in Africa, Asia and Eastern Europe has only impressed upon me that human nature is the same everywhere. Each culture, each country, each community has known the warm and cold currents that ebb and flow in the human heart: the North, to use this book's terminology, has no monopoly on giving, and the South is not the realm of the stingy. The charitable impulse is everywhere, although historical and economic circumstances channel it in different ways. Latin America's generosity to family and friends is legendary.

When it comes to civil society, Richard Holloway's sketch of the general circumstances that have shaped its finances in the South applies to Latin America. Many poor people, a small middle class, and a few wealthy families have occupied the landscape under the shadow, first of a giant crown, then of an all-present government of whatever stripe. Some of the wealthy have founded – and controlled, as is their wont – charitable organizations, and some have constantly supported the initiatives of others, mostly those of religious groups, principally those of the Catholic Church. This generosity and this dedication have done much good, but the starting point – the concentration of political power and disposable income in the hands of a very few people – held little room for the flowering of civil society.

Yet civil society *seems* to have blossomed over the past 30 years. CSOs have been cropping up in ever more variety all over Latin America. The phenomenon is more than Latin American; it is worldwide. And it is positive. But there remains a question that is at the heart of this fine book: what is to keep the flowers from fading?

There is reason for concern. The author warns us that many CSOs are foreign aid junkies in line for ruin. If the foreign foundation and government money dries up – and such is the trend – the addicts will stagger and collapse. To the extent that the drug keeps flowing, it will, as bureaucrats phrase it, modify behaviour. The people say it nicely: he who pays the piper calls the tune. The danger lies in a CSO's pawning its mission for money just to survive.

Holloway's bugaboo is the foreign institution. Mine is big business. Our different spectres rise from our different regions: his, mainly Africa and Asia; mine, mainly Latin America. The effects are the same: dependency and behavioural modification. There are CSOs that put up anything for sale, even their self-respect. For the most egregious example I have ever seen, I will turn to my own country, the USA. It took place in 1998, during the half-time of an important college basketball game. The television audience was huge. An insurance company and a CSO selected a man from the stands and offered him the following proposition: if you sink a three-point basket, the company will donate a million dollars to the CSO Institute for Breast Cancer Research. If you miss, it will donate US$50,000. The guy gets in position, takes a deep breath, he dips, he shoots, and – CLAANG! Sorry, girls! Better luck next time! Oh, here's US$50,000. We wish we had more, but we had to pay another CSO, the National Collegiate Athletic Association, a million dollars to host this disgraceful publicity stunt.

Certainly, most CSOs have more self-respect than the ones I have just cited – most corporations, too. A growing number in Latin America, both domestic and transnational, make genuine efforts to improve their communities, often partnering with an outside CSO. But a corporation's agenda rarely matches a CSO's. What is more, Latin America is witnessing the worldwide trend towards 'strategic philanthropy'. Corporations always wanted some publicity when they funded a CSO, but, more and more, they make sure they get it in a way that furthers a specific business interest of theirs. Often, they want to use the good name of a CSO to sell their products.

I don't blame companies for trying to use CSOs to generate wealth. After all, without profits, the non-profits would only have 'non'. And who can blame the CSOs? A reporter once asked Willy Sutton, who finally landed in jail after making a world record robbery, 'Why do you rob banks?' Willy replied, 'That's where the money is'. The larger CSOs in the region, particularly Brazilian and Mexican ones, are learning how to negotiate good deals for themselves. Unfortunately, the scope of this book has not allowed the author to include much detail on the subject.

Holloway hints that CSOs should group together to learn how to be tough negotiators. I would emphasize this: they must work together in networks and professional associations for this and many other reasons. If only they shared data on every deal they make with companies, they would quickly learn how to price their services to the business sector, and all would benefit.

Unfortunately, Latin America remains a somewhat low-trust society. To be clearer about it, the region's civil society suffers from too much secrecy and too many squabbles. This is understandable, given that CSOs either have sprung from the few sources of power and wealth, or they have to compete for access to them. Over the last decade, cooperation among CSOs has increased, but much more needs to be done for civil society to truly flourish. In particular, CSOs must join together to convince ordinary citizens to contribute money to the CSO of their choice.

This returns us to Holloway's timely warning that 'big money' creates an unhealthy dependence. Certainly, the multilateral institutions, the international foundations and the bilateral agencies should heed Holloway's plea that donors should not straitjacket spontaneity. 'Civil society' should not be an 'outsourcing society'. They should help CSOs to diversify their sources of income so that they spread their wings and fly to their impossible dreams; they should not kill civil society by their kindness. Although the danger for Latin America is no longer the foreign donor but the business sector, it would be preposterous to demand that it should stop doing what it does best: creating wealth, often by outsourcing, including to CSOs.

The true danger, in any case, is not dependency on institutional donors. In all the developing and transition countries I know, civil society has always looked *up* for support, up to the crown, the government, the church, foreign foundations, foreign governments, and now transnational corporations. Civil society, apparently flourishing, has not sunk its roots *down* into the hearts of the man and woman in the street. In the words of Jesus, 'Where your heart is, there is your treasure'. The 'civil' of 'civil society', as the author points out, refers to the citizenry. If their hearts were in it, they would pay for it. Not exclusively, of course – just a lot.

It is the job of CSOs, alone and in groups, to tap into the hearts of the citizens as they tap into their treasure. This is more than a question of diversifying a CSO's income, a strategy that Richard Holloway promotes and elucidates in this valuable book, and which I heartily endorse. It is a question of the very legitimacy of civil society.

Ezra Mbogori, East and Southern Africa
Executive Director, MWENGO, Zimbabwe

I have no doubt in my mind that the availability of resources for sustained operations remains the Achilles heel for most, if not all, CSOs in the Eastern and Southern Africa region. I speak from personal experience whenever I get the opportunity to describe the agonizing that most CSO practitioners go through in trying to ensure that their creative programming proceeds as planned. Often, the one critical factor that determines whether this will be the case or not is the availability of resources. This reality, coupled with the unpredictability of the choices of traditional donor sources as we know them, has led to a much more focused look at the prospects of local resource mobilization by CSOs.

Over the past ten-or-so years, I have been involved in one way or another in attempting to provide CSOs with an orientation to local resource mobilization. The biggest part of this has been the regional domestic resource mobilization workshops that are conducted annually in collaboration with international and national CSOs in different countries of the region. What I have found to be remarkable at each of these events is the extent to which each event attracts a far greater level of participation than was planned for. Many reasons have been extended for this. Some participants, it is said, attend the workshops out of sheer desperation, as their traditional sources dry up and they need to find, as fast as possible, alternative ways of filling the gap that inevitably arises. The example comes to mind here of a workshop participant whose organization had been plunged into a crisis by a major disagreement with their only donor. This participant was seeking to identify possible new sources that would afford them a measure of independence from what they now realized was a rather domineering donor. Even the idea of diversifying their funding sources had not occurred to this organization before their chief executive attended this workshop. There are also those who come to these events to upgrade their skills, and, equally important, to network with their peers and colleagues. They recognise what value there is in exchanging ideas and experiences on the practice of local resource mobilization, but also see the need to strengthen consciously the body of knowledge that exists in this area. As a community of actors, we all obviously need to get involved in the business of creating conditions that will unlock the immense resources that undoubtedly exist in the operating environments for our work.

This handbook constitutes a rich resource of material that speaks to both the operating environment as well as to the diverse skills that are necessary for domestic resource mobilization. Given the possibilities it presents, I feel compelled to disagree with Richard Holloway over how best to use the book. Let me explain this briefly.

In the example I have cited above regarding the CSO participant who is driven to a resource mobilization workshop by sheer desperation, the suggestion that the handbook is a stand-alone reference on 'how to', or a companion to the four-day workshop version of the course available through the trainer manual, fits squarely into the unrealistic expectation that the problems of a CSO in this area could be solved quite rapidly, maybe as soon as it has mastered the range of skills presented in the handbook. I know I am stretching the implication here, but the point I want to make is that there really is no substitute to the systematic building up of relationships, the profiling of the sector, and the gradual development of a culture that appreciates and supports the CSO sector. All this takes time. There are no quick fixes. So, rather than confine the handbook to the role of a reference text, I would like to suggest that this becomes an important reference for all those who may be involved in local resource mobilization, all the time.

As one works with the material presented here, the supporting material on the website becomes a crucial additional resource. I understand that the website will provide regular updates on field experience, and achievements (or lack of these) in the operating environment for philanthropy. If this is the case, the gap that I see requiring specific action to fill is that of ensuring access to the web for those smaller CSOs that currently do not have such access. I would imagine that it is they that will probably need most the information presented. I might suggest here that this is a challenge that should be discussed with CSO support organizations in different regions. I know that this remains a worrisome issue for many of us who continue to seek appropriate ways of strengthening the sector.

The current challenge is thus to distribute this material as widely as possible to all intended users. Aga Khan Foundation will need to get the website up rapidly enough to facilitate a dynamic discussion on who does what, when and how, as this relates to domestic resource mobilization. The opportunity of testing ideas and describing results thereafter is certainly an attractive proposition for those who will get to interact electronically. It will be useful to encourage the less adventurous CSOs to explore new avenues and to take bolder risks as they try to create new possibilities for resource mobilization. The task I see ahead for all of us is that of understanding our environment – and I mean all aspects of it – much better than is the case at present. In Eastern and Southern Africa, for example, there is a great deal yet to be done in terms of presenting a compelling argument for incentives that will stimulate increased philanthropy. The CSO sector also needs to create systematically new relationships with other sectors. Finally, there is our basic understanding of the money economy and how we might manipulate it better to suit our purposes. Having developed our understanding on all these fronts, we then have to translate this improved understanding into opportunities for gaining support.

The new networks that are attempting to build this capacity in Eastern and Southern Africa will find this handbook, as well as the trainer manual, a most useful set of resources.

As a concerned and interested CSO practitioner, I have every confidence in the potential of this publication, and both embrace and commend it wholeheartedly to all those who seek to embark on the road to respectable sustainability. In the end, it is our creativity, our commitment to people-centred development, and our passion for a better world that will bear us out as a worthwhile sector.

SITHEMBISO NYONI, ZIMBABWE
Founder, Organization of Rural Associations for Progress, Zimbabwe

In the face of today's globalization, the need for CSOs to mobilize their own resources cannot be overemphasized. Globalization has a tendency to assume shared global values about what resources are needed and how they are to be used. It has concentrated resources – especially finance, technology, and other skills – in the hands of a few global financial and economic actors. As a result, the resources that are available to Southern CSOs from Northern donors have decreased, and continue to do so. Although good things have been achieved through overseas assistance, Southern CSOs have had to put up with a lot of disadvantages associated with foreign aid. This includes donor conditionality. CSOs have had to manage aid under largely inflexible conditions. They have been expected to take care of and maintain donors. This has left less time for envisioning and managing their own development processes, including the generation of their own local resources. Further, this has robbed local CSOs of relationships with their governments, local communities and the business sector.

In developing the art and skills to raise funds from foreign donors, unfortunately the local CSOs have tended to develop a style and language that is responsive and problem-based rather than responsive and solution-oriented. Most fundraisers make project proposal presentations in a way that so often describes the problem that they end up thinking and feeling that they are part of the problem rather than of the solution. This is usually done in order to appeal to the donor's heart and to gain sympathy in a way that unlocks their safes. For a disaster this is acceptable, but for development, some fundraising techniques that exclude people's own solutions and different forms of resources can be disempowering and counter-productive.

Local or indigenous resource mobilization is therefore of necessity, not only to raise money but also to empower and liberate local CSOs in a practical way.

For development to be sustainable, local resource mobilization is a necessity. Although an enabling environment does not exist in Zimbabwe and in the region, there are still a few issues that need to be addressed in order to facilitate effective resource mobilization:

- Dependency mentality needs to be addressed. Many people continue to look towards the outside not only for resources but, more often than not, for solutions to their problems.
- Corporations need to be encouraged to donate to charitable organizations, using tax rebates for such donations as an incentive.

- There is a need to cultivate a culture of giving, especially from among the urban middle classes and the low-income bracket. Rural Zimbabweans give a lot more, no matter how poor they are. Most of them share both life and their meagre resources in cash or kind.
- Our media need to focus more on encouraging local giving. There is still a tendency to highlight foreign giving at the expense of local expressions of philanthropy.
- There has to be a deliberate government policy to give grants to CSOs. Currently, the Government of Zimbabwe only supports cooperatives and small enterprises for specific projects. It needs to have a budget for general CSO support, either to provide funding or technical support, without controlling CSO operations.

There are unique advantages to local resource mobilization and the handbook leads directly to them. Three of the chief advantages are:

1 The process of defining a resource beyond money makes the members of a project or CSO see and discover as central their own local knowledge, solidarity, unity of purpose, time, ideas, labour, creativity and skills. These are often taken for granted when money is put first.
2 Engaging locals in resource mobilization helps the group to realize the potential in people to contribute to a cause in whatever way they can. It builds confidence and a sense of responsibility and fulfilment in those involved.
3 Fundraising can be a vehicle to develop chains of trust, cultivate values and a culture of giving, all of which may bring lasting social change and sustainability.

This book is therefore going to be a very important and powerful development tool for Southern CSOs. The fact that it makes for easy reading and suggests 12 different approaches to resource mobilization make it useful to organizations and individuals. It will enrich those who have started the process and assist the beginners. ORAP has been involved in local resource mobilization, and we shall find such a book a very practical companion. Local resource mobilization is not only an art but also a skill. It thus needs creative imagination and experience, as well as an ability and willingness to learn from others.

In our experience, the following have proved essential and distinct conditions to resource mobilization:

1 It is important for organizations to be of good repute, of the highest integrity, to be respected and trusted by the public to do what they say they will do with the resources they raise.
2 Have a clear vision of what you want to do, clear steps how to get there, and well-defined resources for implementation.

3   Such a vision could be targeted towards a specific group of people – say, women, the disabled or the poor in general. But it needs to connect with wider social concerns. Is this something that a wide range of our society would do if they had the time to do it themselves?

4   Before going public, first select a small group of people – women and men of integrity from different sectors – with whom to share your vision. Such people can then go and approach their colleagues in different sectors on behalf of the organization.

5   Assume that every individual wants to contribute and then provide an opportunity for people to give.

6   Make those who give feel a part of your success.

7   Seek cooperation from as many different kinds of citizens in your country as possible – government, business, communities, and religious groups. In development, everybody has something to give.

8   Be prepared to put your own resources first – time, ideas, skills, money, etc.

9   Define resources as widely as possible to enable as many people as possible to participate, and divide what is to be given into manageable amounts to include the smallest donors and community participation.

10   Don't overgeneralize – make people feel that what they have given, no matter how small, is special and needed.

11   There is a need for rootedness and greater legitimacy. By whose mandate is the organization mobilizing the needed resources?

12   Indigenous resource mobilization is not a quick fix. It takes time and patience. Resource mobilization can be an event or a long on-going process. Even a one-time fundraising event takes time to prepare and manage.

ELKANAH ODEMBO, EAST AFRICA
Director, Centre for Promotion of Philanthropy and Social Responsibility

The CSO and civil sector in Kenya and the East Africa region has been concerned with the issues of resource mobilization for some time now. This is indicated by the large numbers of CSOs and CBOs that have attended various fundraising and resource mobilization workshops over the last six to eight years. The Kenya National Council of CSOs organized the very first workshop on fundraising (in partnership with the then International Fund Raising Group, now Resource Alliance) in the mid-1990s. Since then, many training workshops have taken place. A significant number of these have been regional, but several have been national.

While Kenya clearly has the oldest and best-established CSO sector in the region, the issues and context are quite similar throughout East Africa.

In Kenya, as with the region, we have seen trends of declining aid; increasing poverty; a receding state; the mushrooming of CSOs and CBOs; greater democratic space; a general (even if weak) recognition by the state of the potential role of CSOs in development and poverty reduction.

There is no doubt that in Kenya there is tremendous competition for resources and funds. It is also the case that the public is more critical of the role of CSOs, and is demanding greater transparency and accountability. This means that CSOs will find it quite challenging to mobilize resources from the public, both individual and corporate. The handbook therefore will be extremely valuable to those CSOs that have started the 'soul searching', and are clear about their role in development and truly want to make a difference. The numerous 'briefcase CSOs' will no doubt perish because they will not and should not exist in a competitive world where the market will determine the survival of factors whether for-profit or not-for-profit.

Some of the resource mobilization measures mentioned in the handbook are particularly relevant in East Africa. Among the most promising is the admonition to create wealth through partnerships with the private sector. CSOs must look at the private sector as a partner rather than as a donor. Partnership needs to be well thought out and long term.

Individual giving also has great potential. But individuals would best be reached through the various professional groups and/or corporate institutions. This is where there is likely to be disposable income. The extremely wealthy are difficult to access and even more difficult to involve. A lot of wealth has been acquired through corruption and dubious means, and this appears to be a deterrent. People who have acquired their wealth corruptly will sometimes give for political gains, but most prefer to stay out of the public eye for fear of being subject to public scrutiny. Many do not pay taxes and would be reluctant to be involved in formal giving.

In-kind resource mobilization has potential, particularly among professionals in Kenya. However, this requires organization and capacity on the part of the CSOs or CBOs. This is one area in which CSOs would need assistance.

Debt swap and debt conversion could result in large amounts of resources being accessible to CSOs and CBOs. But CSOs and CBOs in Kenya still lack the necessary recognition by government to benefit from debt conversion. This method needs to be tried with a few of the large recognized CSOs taking the lead and entering a dialogue with government and donors. As pressure mounts for debt relief, Kenya, like most debt-burdened countries in Africa, needs clear strategies as to how debt resources could be applied. CSOs will have to demonstrate their ability to put these large resources to good use in addressing basic needs and social development.

Resources from a cash-strapped government are an unlikely source for CSOs. In-kind government support in the areas of legislation and policy are the most that CSOs might realistically expect. Social investment is still a very new idea in the region. Microcredit programmes by CSOs have mixed results. The impact on the beneficiaries must remain the priority. Any diversion in objectives is likely to result in a weakened and less effective credit programme. Use of the Internet would be too far-fetched at this point. Most CSOs are not online and the Internet is a facility that is commonly used by international CSOs and CSO consultants only. In general, the number of local Internet users, though growing, is still small.

In East Africa, several issues require careful attention to create a more positive general climate for local fundraising efforts:

- The existing dependency on foreign aid has developed over the years that must be overcome. There needs to be a change of attitude in government and among citizens about where resources for development should come from.
- CSOs and CBOs should develop effective self-regulation to set minimum standards of good practice.
- The tax system needs to be dramatically improved – eg to widen the tax base and eliminate corruption – and tax incentives for giving in the public interest need to be instituted.
- We need programmes to recognize and celebrate individuals and corporations that demonstrate exemplary social responsibility. These might be combined with national campaigns to promote social responsibility.
- Economies must grow and wealth must be generated, and this requires fiscal discipline and good economic governance. The rule of law must be applied and government must provide an efficient regulatory framework.
- Governments should facilitate and encourage NGO and private-sector partnership.

MARIANNE G QUEBRAL, PHILIPPINES
Executive Director, Venture for Fund Raising

The trend of diminishing foreign institutional grants to the non-profit sector makes this handbook an indispensable resource for those seeking alternative and indigenous sources of monies for civil society. In our work in the Philippines and other areas in the region, we have found that this trend has caused real fear for organizations dependent on foreign funds. Exploring alternative sources of income – particularly the potentially large, untapped individual gift market – continues to be a challenge to these organizations because the skills, knowledge and resources are not readily available.

It is indeed fortunate that the author and organizations such as the Aga Khan Foundation recognize the need for such resources and have published this handbook. Also, to address this need in other parts of Asia, Venture for Fund Raising*

---

* Venture for Fund Raising is a non-profit organization that aims to promote financial sustainability in the Philippine and Asian non-profit sector. It offers practitioner-driven training and consulting services, and is engaged in research and public information programmes.

(Philippines) is conducting research on the gift markets in the Philippines, Thailand, Indonesia, Pakistan, India, Bangladesh and Nepal. The research is a two-part study that (1) documents successful, replicable fundraising experiences of non-profit organizations, and (2) surveys households on the motivations for giving, preferred causes and donation sizes. Research findings, which will be made available through the Holloway handbook website, will give non-profit organizations a better grasp of the gift market landscape and enable them to draw lessons from the proven successful mechanisms used in these Asian countries. This knowledge will point organizations towards a more strategic, structured and effective approach to resource mobilization, to build a culture of sustainability.

The discussions in the handbook also show a growing awareness of the structures and processes that are relevant to resource mobilization. While these are not unknown to Asian non-profit organizations, their use has not been optimized.

We have observed that indigenous non-profit organizations will benefit from the following:

1   The documentation of successful resource mobilization practices of small, medium and large-scale non-profit organizations. This information will help in the process of shifting from dependence on grants to achieving a diversified, sustainable funding structure. In collecting and posting such case studies in an ongoing way, the Aga Khan Foundation is making a distinctive and strategic contribution.
2   Provision of how-to manuals, such as this one, that will guide organizations step-by-step in strategizing, implementing and evaluating resource mobilization campaigns.
3   The organization of lobby groups to develop an environment that is conducive to resource mobilization, especially in the areas of tax write-offs, institutional transparency and accountability.

Organizations that venture into fundraising inevitably open their doors to a larger public putting to test the legitimacy of their claims for support, and demanding organizational efficiency, transparency and accountability. This implies change in all aspects of the organization, more often than not in areas that do not seem to be related directly to fundraising, but are part of the institution's development as a whole. The giving public has a predisposition to give; as such, an organization needs only to set itself up and prepare to 'make the ask', translating the public's goodwill into a donation response. We see that this 'ask' is but the tip of the iceberg, and the real financial sustainability work begins with honest reflection on the organization's reason for existence, followed by goal-setting and an assessment of its fundraising capacity. This handbook is an invaluable resource for the next steps – planning and implementing an institutional resource mobilization programme.

Vijay K Sardana, India
Chief Executive Officer, Aga Khan Foundation (India)

I would like to begin by complimenting Richard Holloway for his frank and challenging propositions presented in the handbook. I was struck by Holloway's statement of belief:

> *If civil society organizations pursue a mission and perform functions that are valuable to society, if they communicate this well to the public, business and government, and if they undertake well thought out efforts to obtain the resources needed to perform these functions, then, in most circumstances, such resources will be available.*

Part of the strategic analysis will mean considering the risks to their organizations of pursuing an alternative financing approach; will they be deviated from this mission? Will they be able to acquire the management skills necessary? Are they prepared for the increased accountability and transparency to the public?

There is a huge need for more active citizen participation in public benefit activities and this shall translate into more civil society organizations. The credo is, however, that if you do good work, and if you are competent at requesting support for your good works, you will likely be supported by the resources of your own country – with such support perhaps supplemented by foreign funding, but in no way dependent on it.

Respecting, Valuing and Acknowledging People's Contributions

In community projects, people's organizations make a sizeable contribution that too often goes unnoticed and unaccounted for. Donors tend to ignore the contribution made by the community and focus primarily on the contribution they are making to the outputs of the project funded by them. Let us take an example of a health centre in a village. After two years of community organization work with health facilities operating from makeshift premises, the community decides to construct a Primary Health Centre (PHC) in the village. A wealthy landlord, owning 20 acres of land, decides to donate 2 acres to the Village Development Committee (VDC). A project proposal is prepared for getting the PHC funded from the NGO, Star Integrated Development Foundation (SIDF). The proposal lists all the items for which funds are required from the SIDF. The total funding requirement comes to Rs100,000 (US$2380). This excludes Rs25,000 (US$595) which the people's organization will mobilize from the community. In the current funding scenario, the cost of the project will be considered as Rs125,000 (US$2976). What is missing from the narration is the value of the land donated by a wealthy landlord, the 6 cart-loads of sand collected by the villages from the nearby river for use in the construction of the health centre, and the community's 120 person days of labour.

All these contributions can be calculated easily and added to the cost of the project. After monetizing the land at, say, Rs10,000 (US$238), converting 6 cart-loads of sand, equivalent to one truck-load which would otherwise cost Rs1000 (US$24), and also valuing 120 person days of labour at the rate of Rs50 person/day (US$1.20), the cost of labour will come to Rs6000 (US$143). Thus, the value of in-kind contribution in this construction project comes to Rs17,000 (US$405), which otherwise goes unnoticed and unaccounted for. In any calculus geared towards financial self-reliance, these costs must find a place. In India, if proper records of such contributions are maintained, and the rationale for valuation adequately provided and explained, chartered accountants are now prepared to include these costs in the audited statement of accounts. In this way the actual total value of effort and contribution will be rendered visible.

Including Non-resident Citizens

Non-resident citizens are becoming interested in donating resources for the development of their country. Some available data show that the bulk of the money is being directed to family trusts and villages where the non-resident citizen has roots, as they have a sense of familiarity with the local community. It is time now for CSOs to explore and start tapping this source as more and more non-resident citizens are on the lookout for reliable and credible intermediary organizations. A recent example in India is of the Naandi Foundation, set up in Hyderabad, Andhra Pradesh. Reportedly, the Naandi Foundation intends to channel the resources from the Telugu-speaking non-resident Indians living in the USA.

Including Traders and Small Businesses

Developing partnerships with businesses is becoming fashionable. But all the talk and effort is focused on developing partnerships with the organized sector. There is need to learn from and to mobilize resources from traders and small businesses. The potential is large, but the thinking is nowhere close to the potential. I would like to suggest systematic research focusing on traders and small businesses. The resources that are potentially available from them include human, material, technical (for example, training in marketing skills or assistance in promoting rural products), and financial. The strategy should be to mobilize all these various kinds of resources and not just money. There is a need to develop an approach for tapping into the charity of traders / small businesses. The time has come to explore the potential of this segment.

Tapping the Middle Class

There is great potential for mobilizing resources from the middle class in any society. Existing research shows that in some Western countries most donations are from individuals, while the reverse is believed to be true for India, although there are no reliable data. There is definitely a need for research to be carried out on individual giving trends. The question that CSOs need to ask themselves is that if corporations can reach the middle class (approximately 300 million in India) and influence their buying decisions, then why cannot CSOs initiate a similar process and understand as well as influence their philanthropic decisions? It is imperative for the voluntary sector to find ways of tapping the philanthropic potential of this large unexplored mass of people.

Mobilizing In-kind Contributions

Professionals from different disciplines are looking for ways to volunteer their time, from two hours to a day a week. The mechanism to match the availability of the volunteer pool with the requirements of CSOs is generally lacking. The United Nations Volunteer Programme in India plans to create a local mechanism in collaboration with local CSOs for using the skills of specialist and untrained volunteers with CSOs/NGOs. The Internet could be a very useful tool for initiating such an activity, and particularly for matchmaking the volunteer with the CSO. Another example is of a Delhi-based NGO in India, Youthreach, that has started to offer such a service, and is constantly on the lookout for professionals/individuals who have expertise in certain areas and have the inclination and time to make contributions to community development initiatives.

Collection of clothing and equipment has been going on for some time. However some industries are able to donate new equipment. For example, the information technology sector is willing to give away hardware and train CSO personnel in the use of computers. In India, the South Asian Fund Raising Group, which needed a bicycle for the use of its messenger, obtained one in the form of a donation. Tata Infotech donated ten computers to the CSO Deepalaya for use in a school.

Accountability and Transparency

Accountability in CSOs continues to be externally imposed, generally by the donor community and the government. The CSO sector is at a crossroads; its credibility is at stake. The need of the day is to identify and ensure participation of all stakeholders. I find the language of the marketplace helpful here. Who are the 'customers' of any particular CSO? Beneficiaries are demand customers. Donors are supply customers. Staff are facilitating customers. People at large are credibility building customers. CSO accountability should begin with the demand-side customers, the beneficiaries.

The potential to mobilize resources locally in India is tremendous. The greatest challenge for CSOs is to develop the skill of asking the public for funds. If they learn to ask, there is no reason why they cannot mobilize resources even from the ordinary person in the street.

The voluntary sector communicates well within its own network, but has been very poor at its work and achievements to the outside world. Therefore, the immediate need for CSOs is to communicate effectively to the other sectors and to individuals; to learn to market themselves.

Mark Sidel, India
Associate Professor of Law, Research Fellow, University of Iowa

Richard Holloway's handbook is a superbly detailed and commendably practical guide to assist Southern CSOs in the development of effective and energetic resource mobilization. These comments focus first on the distinct and complex tasks that Holloway has set for his handbook. They then address briefly how CSOs can seek to interact with the 'new philanthropy' that is emerging not only in the North but in some areas of the South, using developments in India and what I term the 'new Indian philanthropy' as an example.

There are two distinct tasks to the work that Holloway has set for himself, and some authors would not handle them both well. Holloway has done so. The first task is to outline and suggest practical approaches to traditional methods of resource mobilization. These include individual giving, revenue from earned income, resources from government, dealing with foreign development agencies, and other reasonably well-known means of developing resources for programmes and sustainability.

Holloway addresses these effectively. He does not overgeneralize in an attempt to provide material that would be useful for CSOs around the world – a potential pitfall that this work clearly avoids. But, also commendably, his handbook does not swing too far in the other direction of overspecification, or providing commentary that is so detailed and tied to a particular context that it would not be usable beyond that and closely related environments.

Beyond traditional sources of resources mobilization, Holloway also sets himself the task of outlining and suggesting approaches to considerably less traditional sources of sustainability for CSOs. These include corporate giving, building endowments and reserve funds, debt conversion, and aspects of social investment. Here the task is to explain the sources of funds and sustainability that may be new to some organizational and individual readers, in a way that can lead to creative thinking about accessing these sources of support and sustainability, in particular local, national and regional contexts. Here Holloway also succeeds admirably, and this handbook is likely to become a key source of information and approaches to these newer, less traditional resources.

The world of resource mobilization and financial self-reliance is always changing. In India – a key site for experimentation with organizational sustainability and financial independence from foreign donors, government and others – CSOs and other organizations are just beginning to experience the complexities of interaction with what we might call the 'new philanthropy'. Since these developments are too new to have been included in Holloway's handbook, I will outline them very briefly here, and then invite interested readers to contact knowledgeable colleagues in India, or me, for further information.

We are now seeing the rapid development of newer forms of individual philanthropy emanating from the areas of India that have been most strongly touched by the 'new economy' of information technology, software and hardware development, biotechnology, and other fields. In rapidly growing cities and corporate centres such as Bangalore and Hyderabad, significant wealth is being created for managers and professionals at a range of these companies. Some of this wealth is in cash form (through salaries and bonuses), but much of it is in the form of stock options, many yet to be exercised.

In Bangalore, corporates such as Infosys and Wipro Technologies lead this trend, both in corporate growth and in new forms of giving that are emerging from the rapid creation of wealth in a relatively few hands. The giving that is emerging from these newly wealthy and the new middle class is diverse; it is focused; it is often anti-institutional and anti-intermediary, and it is growing with exceptional speed and with the needs that rapid growth brings.

The diversity of the 'new Indian philanthropy', as I call it, is quite real. In the leading Indian cities of the 'new economy' – Bangalore and Hyderabad – charitable and philanthropic giving is channelled through individual gifts, through self-generated collections of donations, and volunteer time by employees who are organized on a horizontal basis, through corporate giving and volunteer programmes, through corporate foundations, through family foundations (which need to be distinguished from corporate foundations), through payroll giving, and in other ways. Understanding the diverse channels of the new giving is a key task for CSOs that wish to engage with it – a diversity in the forms of giving, but also a diversity in the individuals and companies that are engaged in financial support. It is a serious mistake to reduce the 'new Indian philanthropy' to the work of certain individuals or certain companies, for that loses a forest of useful giving for a few tall trees.

The 'new Indian philanthropy' is also considerably more focused than the relief and charitable giving of the past. Primary education is a key programming goal of much of the new giving, for the individuals and corporations that are active in this area have determined that primary education is a key baseline for sustainable development in India. There is also focused giving for higher education (almost entirely from individual resources), and for infrastructure and service development in Bangalore (from both corporate and individual resources, epitomized by the Bangalore Task Force), but the strong focus on primary education within the 'new Indian philanthropy', at least at its current initial stages, is quite clear.

Several examples will suffice to outline this trend. At the Azim Premji Foundation, the family foundation now under development by the chair of Wipro Technologies and one of the world's wealthiest individuals (at mid-2000), primary education is the key programming focus. That focus is mirrored in the corporate giving and volunteering programmes that are growing with Wipro itself, one of India's fastest growing and most successful 'new economy' corporates.

The 'new Indian philanthropy', at least as it is currently developing in Bangalore, also seeks to eschew dependence on intermediary institutions (such as CSOs that carry on onward funding) that separate donors from specific projects at the grass-roots level. In Bangalore 'new Indian philanthropy' prefers, for the most part, to interact directly with projects, and often bypasses intermediaries that can play a funding and reporting role to provide support directly to projects at the grass-roots. A sense of a strong, at times defiant anti-institutional and anti-intermediary approach comes through clearly in conversations with leaders of the 'new Indian philanthropy'.

But that 'new Indian philanthropy' also has needs that may conflict with its strongly held anti-institutional and anti-intermediary views. Software exports alone from Bangalore are expected to grow more than eight times over the next ten years to over US$80 billion per year, for example, creating substantial additional wealth and, we can expect, substantial additional giving – not to speak of hardware development, biotechnology, other services, and the growth of domestic as well as international markets. Already the new philanthropists of Bangalore understand that their desire to work directly with the grass-roots – to give funds directly to a specific school or day-care centre, often multiplied by 20 such institutions in 20 direct approaches – may be overtaken by the giving that will emerge from a rapidly growing economy.

The 'new Indian philanthropy' in Bangalore will be defined, over the next 5–15 years, by the conflict between these new givers' strongly held anti-institutional and anti-intermediary views, and their strong need for implementation, reporting, accountability and leveraging of funding from other domestic and non-resident Indian sources of giving. How these diverse goals and approaches are resolved in ways that provide an effective and efficient means for philanthropic and charitable giving will fundamentally define much of the 'new Indian philanthropy' and the new Bangalore philanthropy.

It may be that new forms of effective, efficient, credible, accountable and leverageable institutions emerge to assist in the efficient programming of the new Indian philanthropy and the new Bangalore philanthropy. Already explorations of lean, corporate-supported community foundations that are closely tied to the values of social justice, social development and diversity are underway in such new giving centres as Bangalore, Ahmedabad, and Pune. In Hyderabad four major corporations representing both new and old economies have formed a new foundation, with support from the state's chief minister, to undertake jointly development projects and to leverage additional domestic and overseas Indian funds.

So we may see various approaches to the clear anti-institutional and anti-intermediary sense of many of the new Indian philanthropists, as well as their strong sense that, as the new Indian economy grows, ways will need to be found to imbue the new philanthropy with efficiency, effectiveness, accountability, credibility, and an ability to leverage substantial additional funds at home and abroad.

These developments are too new to have been addressed in Richard Holloway's exceptionally useful handbook. But CSOs in India – particularly those working in and seeking support from areas of rapid growth – will need to understand and address the changing concerns and values of the 'new philanthropy'. They will not find it easy to do so, because the new philanthropy raises challenging, even hostile questions of the economic efficiency in small voluntary organizations; of the management, financial and social sector skills of CSO managers and personnel; and of the true, measurable economic and social returns from education, health and other projects.

Embedded in the 'new Indian philanthropy' is a fundamental challenge (if yet not fully voiced) to the very structure of the Indian voluntary sector in thousands of small organizations with overlapping goals and highly inefficient, redundant structures of staffing, infrastructure and internal operating costs. The 'new Indian philanthropy' and the new Bangalore philanthropy will directly challenge the traditional organizational and personalized structures of the Indian voluntary sector.

From their distinct perspective, the 'new Indian philanthropy' will ask, without any apology whatsoever, why every CSO and voluntary sector manager seems to have his or her own small organization, and will question aggressively the enormous economic, social, political and other inefficiencies that result from what they consider an 'old economy' structural approach to social justice and social development. The Indian voluntary sector, and voluntary sectors in other parts of the world that seek to engage and access the 'new philanthropy' will need to be prepared to address these direct challenges to their traditional modes of structure and operations.

PAIBOON WATTANASIRITHAM, THAILAND
Director General, Chief Executive Officer,
Government Savings Bank, Thailand

Richard Holloway's publication is easy to understand, and provides a vast array of experience and lessons learned from countries around the world. It provides an excellent conceptual framework for the various approaches to resource mobilization. More importantly, however, Richard addresses the critical question of why organizations need to shift to the local citizen base away from foreign aid. The case for Thailand provides an excellent example.

In Thailand, where the economic crisis has persuaded only a small percentage of foreign donors to return, CSOs are thinking about and implementing new ways to generate and mobilize resources, particularly through government and philanthropic institutions. Equally important are those CSOs that are working together to create forums and consortiums for dialogue, and to improve on current strategies.

The Holloway handbook will not only be helpful in stimulating the discussion of these approaches but will provide some useful examples and experiences from around the world for comparison.

ERNA WITOELAR, INDONESIA
Minister of Settlements and Regional Infrastructure, Indonesia

This handbook offers to its readers a menu of useful approaches, complemented by rich case study material that is relevant to the Indonesian experience. Holloway's book offers to its readers clarity, depth and a wide array of experience. More importantly, however, through the discussion of moving towards financial self-reliance, this book provides the ethical grounding that remains crucial for Indonesian CSOs.

By practising self-reliance, CSOs can maintain their independence. Being independent from the government makes the CSOs more effective in their advocacy work. More independence from donors enables CSOs to be more flexible in their programmes, and more able to respond to grass-roots' needs. For too long the Indonesian CSOs, like CSOs in many developing countries, have been dependent on foreign donors. Even though this injected some cash into civil society, many CSOs have failed to maintain their sustainability after the donor's support ended. This handbook will encourage and enable CSOs to drive for their self-reliance, sustainability and independence.

DANIEL YOFFE, ARGENTINA AND LATIN AMERICA
Professor, School of Education, Universidad Austral, Argentina

Richard Holloway's work is an excellent exercise of approximation and systematization of the strategies needed by civil society organizations to mobilize.

Although the handbook centres its attention on the CSO that is dedicated to development issues and characterized by extreme dependence on an international financing resource (Northern CSOs or governments), his message is equally valid for the ample world of organizations known as 'voluntary sector', 'third sector' or 'independent sector'.* I certainly intend to draw from the reflections obtained from reading this excellent work tool in my own writing and our training programmes.

In its last part, the handbook points out that, after developing all the strategies to obtain the necessary funds, 'It is very important to remember that any of these alternative strategies will require serious changes in the structure and management of the CSO.' In our experience, this subject constitutes, maybe, one of the most complex challenges faced by organizations and those who have the responsibility to help in this search.

One of the ideas that has permitted us to widen the consciousness of the Latin American region's CSO leaders is the existence of a clear relationship between the organization's various sources of resources and its human resources.

In our training programmes we say, 'You tell me what human resources you have, and I'll tell you to what sources you have access', or 'You tell me what sources you want to reach, and I'll tell you what human resources you need.' Let us see some examples.

If a CSO expects to tap a local government resource, this means that it counts among its human resources people who can both elaborate projects that appeal to public officials, and lobby for them.

If we consider private giving, we must distinguish between individuals or corporations. We have learned that one needs to segment the market further, into small, medium or great contributors. The approach to the small ones will be substantially different from that to the big donors.

Dependence on a specific source puts the organization and its mission's continuity at risk. On the other hand, an organization's sustainability will be determined by the degree of its resource diversification. Therefore, it is a credo for us that the base of sustainability is in the diversification of the resources. Given what we have learned about the human resource requirements for resource mobilization, this implies the need for diverse skills within a CSO's human resource pool.

Moreover, obtaining the support of a source of resources is more than obtaining the resource itself. It implies a form of social validation of the organization and its mission. This permits one to attain new 'validations' or sources of resources. In synthesis, the sources are synergistic among themselves, and attaining one of them is a step towards the opening of a new one.

---

* *The Emerging Sector Revisited*, Lester Salamon, Helmut K Anheier and collaborators, Johns Hopkins University, Institute for Political Studies, Center for Civil Society Studies, Madrid 1999.

In the 1990s with the opening up of the economy, the reform of the state, and the emergence of CSOs, a process of change began in Argentina in which financing opportunities, both public and private, expanded. Within this context, the organizations dedicated to development issues, human rights and the environment the main solicitors of resources from international cooperation – were compelled to seek local resources because of the new priorities of the international sources. This produced some initial experience from which to draw lessons that may be of interest to practitioners of indigenous resource mobilisation elsewhere.

Here, for example, the sale of services is well established. There were problems with service activity leading to distortions in an organization's social mission. The key seems to be in attracting voluntary human resources with experience in the business world. These individuals, who are vested in the mission and limited by their status as volunteers, permit the organizations to overcome such obstacles.

Turning to individual giving, we can cite some interesting data generated by Gallup Argentina in the years 1997, 1998 and 1999. When measuring people's confidence in a series of institutions to make programmes that can help to solve the country's social problems, the study revealed that six out of ten people (58 per cent) trusted non-profit organizations to solve the social problems. A significant percentage (81 per cent) considered that non-profit organizations are more necessary today than five years ago. The study also showed that 20 per cent of the population does voluntary work and 30 per cent expressed interest in doing so in the coming year.

Society is highly predisposed to collaborate with non-profit organizations with time and money: 62 per cent of the population makes some kind of donation. This divides into donations to formal organizations (45 per cent) and directly to the beneficiaries (17 per cent). Apart from the economic cycles, fundraising through individuals has increased. The case of small contributors constitutes a notable experience wherein are combined the use of massive communications media, telemarketing and the use of credit card automatic debits. These procedures not only produce results but also start to model a conduct in society that impacts on other groups, corporations and large contributors.

Public financing of the non-profit organizations tends to grow with the changes to the social economic model that are occurring, and the handbook makes an excellent description of the risks and benefits for both sides in this relationship. In Argentina, the last 16 years of democracy have lessened the traditional mistrust between the public and the non-governmental sector. Furthermore, during the last two governments, an important group of CSO leaders has entered the public function, facilitating contact between the sectors. An important threat to this process is corruption and the political use of public funds.

The last years have produced an important amount of research, diffusion and training in the field of corporate philanthropy. Society's demands on this sector, which has received important economic benefits, are greater every day. In view of this, companies are starting to establish long-term policies with donations and budgets for marketing and human resource departments linked with CSOs. The handbook should help CSOs especially to overcome the cultural differences with corporations that inhibit effective partnership.

In conclusion, I wish to underline the importance of this handbook as a guide for action, as well as to trigger the necessary reflection that is implied in the mobilization of resources for the common good. I believe that Richard Holloway has done an excellent job, managing to reconcile the simple with the profound in this complex subject. I hope that our Spanish-speaking South will have the opportunity to read, in its own language, this important contribution to financial self-reliance.

IFTEKHAR ZAMAN, BANGLADESH
Executive Director, Bangladesh Freedom Foundation, Dhaka

One of the primary objectives of CSOs is to contribute to the empowerment and self-reliance of the citizens with and for whom such organizations are created to work. There can be no empowerment or self-reliance for CSOs without ensuring their sustained citizen access to financial resources. Hence, concern for the financial self-reliance of CSOs is as old as their origins. Richard Holloway's handbook presents a set of practical guidelines on ways such organizations can mobilize resources. The merit of the work is that it offers a handy collection of the practices followed by NGOs and other CSOs in the developing world.

The author tells us that he had always felt that there was a 'lack of conceptual framework for CSO resource mobilization work' and sets out through this handbook 'to change the way that civil society organizations think'. The conceptual basis is that CSOs in the South are 'dangerously dependent' on foreign funding, and that it is not sustainable. However, one needs to point out that the roots and rationale of this dependence lie less in the South than in the North, which is also the principal stakeholder of the continued dependence of the South on the North.

Many of the listed ways, like profits from income-generating and microcredit programmes, are as old as the concept of CSOs and CSOs in the developing world, especially in Bangladesh and other South Asian countries. Not only the big players in the field, which are by now national and international models, but also many relatively smaller and local level CSOs have adopted these ways of resource development with greater or lesser success. From this perspective the handbook provides hardly any directions to 'change the way citizens' organizations think'.

The report is nevertheless a valuable addition to the literature on the subject. It would be more helpful if it also focused on ways to contribute to the enabling environment for the proposed methods of domestic resource development. Of particular importance is, for instance, the institutional and policy environment that is conducive to promoting corporate sector contributions, indigenous foundations, individual and institutional philanthropy, the conversion of debt, etc. Without a proper incentive and regulatory mechanism that is designed to be CSO-friendly, the success of such efforts would remain only limited. In many of the countries to which this report is addressed, there has always been a fairly rich tradition and culture of giving and sharing; what is lacking is a conducive environment with a strategic vision to revive and strengthen such practices.

With respect to profit-making ventures by CSOs also, which is a growing area of debate in many countries, it is also necessary to consider various legal and fiscal measures that would ensure a 'level playing-field' before such practices bounce back in various forms, like tension between the corporate sector and the CSOs, as well as between CSOs themselves. While these were not clearly within the scope of this handbook, hopefully Holloway's future contributions will address such issues.

Commentator Biographies

Qadeer Baig, is acting director of the NGO Resource Centre, a project of the Aga Khan Foundation in Pakistan. He holds a London School of Economics Master's degree in the 'Management of NGOs'. Because of his experience, Qadeer Baig is frequently invited by government, donors and NGOs as a resource person to facilitate workshops and sessions on issues related to NGO management and the enabling environment for citizen action. He is also called upon to work for other capacity-building NGOs across South Asia and East Africa (director@ngorc2.khi.sdnpk.undp.org).

Niloy Banerjee is the head of the National Local Resource Mobilization Network in India. The Network aims to engage society at large with the broad aim of promoting philanthropic giving for development action. Niloy Banerjee has been assistant director of the National Foundation for India, where his area of focus has been philanthropy and resource mobilization. He is a core member of the Institutional and Capacity Development Network that advises the Development Assistance Committee of the Organization for Economic Cooperation and Development (OECD). On behalf of the Network, he has recently completed a detailed analysis of community capacity development by the microfinance industry in Bangladesh. Niloy Banerjee's other work has been in the area of trade, aid and debt, and he is the co-author of a paper analysing the impact of external debt on the development process in South Asia (niloyb@nfi.ren.nic.in).

Roberto Calingo is the executive director of the Philippine Business for Social Progress (PBSP), the country's largest and oldest corporate-led social development foundation. He developed PBSP's Five-year Development Strategy (1996–2001) that became the basis for its grant programmes, corporate membership, and resource mobilization. He also directed the formulation of Area Resource Management (ARM), a flagship programme of the foundation. He holds a Master's degree in Development Management from the Asian Institute of Management (AIM) in Makati (bcalingo@pbsp.org.ph).

Mathew Cherian is at present the executive director of the Charities Aid Foundation (India). After graduating in Civil Engineering from Birla Institute of Technology and Science (BITS), Pilani, he worked with rural communities in Mahrashtra. Mathew Cherian later completed his post-graduate degree in Rural Management from the Institute for Rural Management, Anand (IRMA) in Gujarat, and was from the very first batch of the Institute. In a long career with NGOs, he also was country representative for Oxfam and programme manager for Plan International in India. He has served as a consultant (voluntary agencies) for the government of India. He currently serves as visiting faculty at the Indian Institute of Foreign Trade and with other organizations (cafindia@vsnl.com).

Murray Culshaw is a strong advocate of indigenous resource mobilization. Mr Culshaw was Director of Oxfam in India from 1989 to 1994, during which period he helped Oxfam to consider the implications of fundraising in India. Since 1995 Murray has been running a consultancy service based in Bangalore specializing in fundraising consultancy and training; and in conducting related research and producing publications for and about the voluntary sector in India. His latest publication is *Getting Started in Fundraising* – a practical guide for organizations in India, which he has co-authored with Michael Norton of the United Kingdom (murray@vsnl.com).

Noshir H Dadrawala, a lawyer by training, has been involved in the field of philanthropy for nearly 15 years and has been the executive secretary of the Centre for Advancement of Philanthropy since its inception. He is an International Fellow of the Centre for the Study of Philanthropy, which is affiliated to the City University of New York. He is the editor of the Centre for Advancement of Philanthropy's bi-monthly journal, *Philanthropy*. He has presented research papers at international forums both in India and the US, and has delivered talks at a number of seminars and conferences. He is a founder-member of the Indian Centre for Philanthropy based in New Delhi, a member of the Governing Council of the India Sponsorship Committee, and an adviser to the Bombay Community Public Trust (centphil@bom7.vsnl.nt.in).

Rajeev Dua is a retired pilot from the Indian Air Defence Corps, and an information technology professional with a law degree from the University of Delhi. He has been in the field of social welfare as a grass-roots reformer for about a decade. He initiated an NGO called PRAGATI in 1993 that specializes in women's empowerment through entrepreneurship development, and has implemented a number of income-generating programmes and innovative initiatives in the hills of Uttar Pradesh (Kumaon and Garhwal). He is presently an adviser to PRAGATI, consultant on microenterprise development to the Aga Khan Foundation, and chief executive officer of the South Asia Fundraising Group (safrg@vsnl.com).

Z I Farook received a Master of Social Science degree from Rajshahi University in Bangladesh in 1980. His specialty in organizational management and strategic planning development and networking has been honed over 22 years of work in the NGO movement in Bangladesh. He is well known as a development trainer in

Bangladesh, having started his development career with Oxfam as a trainer in 1978. He now serves as the Executive Director of the Bangladesh Fund Raising Group (prip.org@bangla.net).

Anwar Fazal is senior regional advisor, The Urban Governance Initiative (TUGI), United Nations Development Programme (UNDP), based in Kuala Lumpur, Malaysia. He was formerly President of the International Organization of Consumers Unions (IOCU) based in the Netherlands, and chairman of the Environmental Liaison Centre International (ELCI) based in Nairobi, Kenya. He has been a founder or prime mover of some 20 local, national and global citizens' networks, including the Consumers Association of Penang (CAP) and the World Alliance for Breast-feeding Action (WABA). He is a recipient of the Right Livelihood Award, popularly known as the Alternative Nobel Prize (anwar.fazal@undp.org).

Dorothy K Gordon is the executive director of the Integrated Resource Group, an organization that focuses on the capacity enhancement of CSOs. In 18 years as a development practitioner, her international experience has involved her with third-sector institutions in Africa, Asia and Latin America as a donor, manager and adviser. International consulting assignments for a range of policy, research and training institutions include work for the Economic Commission for Africa and other UN bodies, the Centre for Social Policy Studies and other national think-tanks, as well as individual NGOs and CBOs. She is a member of the recently established Ghana Institute of Fund Raisers and recently participated in the Task Force on National NGO Policy (dorothyg@ghana.com).

Daniel Q Kelley, after receiving degrees in City Planning from Massachusetts Institute of Technology and Harvard, became the executive director and fundraiser for a community centre for Mexican and African American workers and their families in Chicago. An expert in corporate real estate finance, he stayed active in educational and youth projects while a consultant in Chicago and Houston. He now combines his business and non-profit experiences as President of the Global Work-Ethic Fund, which provides strategic planning services to CSOs in developing and transition countries, advising them on local and international fundraising. Mr Kelley is the author, in Spanish, of *Más Dinero Para Su Causa*, a fundraising manual for Latin American CSOs, and is the co-editor of the scholarly journal *Cooperación Internacional*. He is on the International Development Committee of the US-based Association of Fund Raising Professionals and a member of the Board of Directors of the Worldwide Responsible Apparel Program (WRAP), which certifies factories for compliance with standards of safety, ecology and human rights (info@global fund.org).

Ezra Mbogori is currently the executive director of MWENGO, a reflection and development centre for NGOs in eastern and southern Africa, based in Harare,

Zimbabwe. Over the past 20 years, Ezra Mbogori has worked with several NGOs that are involved in a range of relief and development initiatives in Africa. He has also undertaken consultancy assignments for NGOs as well as multilateral organizations on issues that affect the life and work of NGOs. He sits on the governing boards of several organizations, including CIVICUS and the Resource Alliance (formerly the International Fund Raising Group) (ezra@mwengo.org.zw).

Sithembiso Nyoni founded the Organization of Rural Associations for Progress (ORAP) in 1980 and served as its executive director until 1995. ORAP is a rural development movement with a membership in Zimbabwe of 1.5 million. Sithembiso Nyoni has received numerous international awards for her work with ORAP, including the 1993 Right Livelihood Award. An active international campaigner on issues of social justice, she has at various times headed four different international movements. From 1995, Sithembiso Nyoni has served as a Member of Parliament for her home constituency in Bulawayo, also holding two consecutive ministerial positions, most recently Minister of State in the President's Office Responsible for Economic Ministries (orapzenze@acacia.samara.co.zw).

Elkanah Odembo is the Director of the Centre for Promotion of Philanthropy and Social Responsibility (CPPRS), recently established in East Africa with the support of the Ford Foundation. The centre aims to promote local resource mobilization and corporate partnerships for social development in East Africa. Prior to the establishment of the centre, Elkanah worked for two years as a Ford Foundation consultant on the Africa Philanthropy Initiative, which brought together indigenous Ford Foundation grantees to share and distill lessons and experiences from emerging community foundations in Africa. For ten years, until 1998, Elkanah served as the East Africa Representative for World Neighbours. He joined World Neighbours from AMREF, where he was Research and Training Programme Officer for six years. Elkanah holds an MSc in Epidemiology and Health Research (eOdembo@fordfound.org).

Marianne G Quebral is executive director of Venture for Fund Raising. A pioneer in fundraising and a graduate of The Fund Raising School, Marianne Quebral managed the largest non-profit direct mail campaign with over one million letters sent annually, generating a total income of 85 million Philippine pesos in less than four years. Formerly the Resource Development Officer of the United Nations Children's Fund (UNICEF), she conducted the first survey of the nature of gift-giving attitudes in the Philippines. Marianne Quebral also has extensive experience in special event management and corporate solicitation campaigns (www.venture-asia.org).

Vijay K Sardana has a first degree in Agricultural Engineering and Master's degrees in Business Administration and Management. He started his career in 1967 with the Rockefeller Foundation, New Delhi, as an agricultural engineer. He then served Action for Food Production (AFPRO), New Delhi, for over 14 years in different senior positions. Vijay Sardana joined Foster Parents Plan International as Country Director for India in 1983 and left Plan International in 1993, as the Regional Director for South Asia. Later he worked as a freelance consultant for about two years with a number of bilateral and other aid agencies. In March 1994, he joined the Aga Khan Foundation (India) as chief executive officer. Currently, Vijay Sardana, apart from being the chief executive officer of the Aga Khan Foundation in India, holds a number of volunteer positions as trustee and committee member for a number of development organizations (akfind@nda.vsnl.net.in).

Mark Sidel served until mid-2000 as the Ford Foundation's first overseas programme officer, working full-time on philanthropy and the non-profit sector, directing a rapid expansion of the foundation's work to support philanthropy and the non-profit sector in India and South Asia from the Ford Foundation's New Delhi office. Beginning from September 2000, Mark Sidel assumed the posts of associate professor of law and research fellow, Obermann Center for Advanced Studies, University of Iowa (mark-sidel@uiowa.edu).

Paiboon Wattanasiritham is currently director general and chief executive officer of the Government Savings Bank, a state-owned, socially committed development bank. Having served in the past as president of the prestigious Foundation for the Thailand Rural Reconstruction Movement Under Royal Patronage and also as chair of the NGO Coordinating Committee on Development, Paiboon Wattanasiritham is now still active in the NGO sector by being, among others, adviser to the Development Support Consortium, chair of the Thai Development Fund Foundation, and executive committee member of the Asia Pacific Philanthropy Consortium (paiboon@gsb.or.th).

Erna Witoelar is now, after more than two decades as an NGO activist, the Minister of Settlements and Regional Infrastructure in the Indonesian cabinet. She was the founder and first executive director of WALHI, the Indonesian umbrella network of environmental NGOs. She was also the founder of Friends of the Environment Fund, which started corporate fundraising to support small NGOs far from the capital in places not reached by international donors or corporates. Erna Witoelar has also been active in the consumer movement, was president of the Indonesian consumer support movement, YLKI, and later became president of its world federation, Consumers International. Her latest NGO post before joining the government was as executive director of the Asia Pacific Philanthropy Consortium, where she promoted and facilitated NGOs' public fundraising through workshops and training. Erna Witoelar is a chemical engineer from the Bandung Institute of Technology, and finished her postgraduate studies in human ecology at the University of Indonesia, Jakarta (erna@witoelar.com).

Daniel Yoffe is a professor at the School of Education at the Universidad Austral. He is also a professor at the Post Graduate Program in Management for Nonprofits at the Universidad de San Andres, Buenos Aires, Argentina and Universidad Di Tella. Daniel Yoffe has served as a consultant for the International Red Cross Federation (Southern Cone: Argentina, Chile, Bolivia and Paraguay), and currently is director of the Fund Raising School at the Center for the Study of State and Society (CEDES) for Argentina and Chile. He is also a resource development consultant for various universities and institutions, and is a member of CEDES.

Iftekhar Zaman is executive director of the Bangladesh Freedom Foundation, Dhaka, and holds a PhD in economics. Before joining the foundation in May 1999, he served for four years from May 1995 as executive director of the Regional Centre for Strategic Studies, Colombo, Sri Lanka. He previously worked as research director of the Bangladesh Institute of International and Strategic Studies, where he has been employed since 1982. He is a core group member of the Program for Promoting Nuclear Non-proliferation, New York and Southampton; a member of the international committee of the Washington-based Council on Foundations; a member of the executive committee of the Asia-Pacific Philanthropy Consortium; advisory group member of the Dialogue and Research Monitor, Joint Center for Asia Pacific Studies, York University, Toronto; and a member of the independent group on South Asian Cooperation, Dhaka. Iftekhar Zaman's main interest areas of research and publication are development, security and South Asia regional cooperation (edbff@bdcom.com).

Further Reading

The readings suggested here are specifically for organizations in the South and East (developing countries and countries in transition). There are many publications on the general topic of resource mobilization and its different applications in North America and Europe but, for the most part, they are not directly relevant to the situation of organizations in the South, principally because the culture, tax regulations and laws are different. In some cases, books from the Northern experience are listed if they are of special merit, or if nothing else is available on that topic based on Southern experience.

For an extensive bibliography of Indian and Northern literature, see *A Guide to Resource Mobilisation for Voluntary Organisations in India* by the South Asia Fundraising Group (2000).

PART ONE: SETTING THE SCENE

Sustaining Civil Society – Strategies for Resource Mobilisation, edited by Bruce Shearer and Leslie Fox, CIVICUS (1997)

The World Wide Fundraiser's Handbook – a Guide to Fundraising for Southern NGOs and Voluntary Organisations by Michael Norton, Directory of Social Change, UK, in collaboration with the Resource Alliance, London (1996)

Towards Greater Financial Autonomy – a guide for voluntary organisations and community groups by Piers Campbell and Fernand Vincent, IRED, Geneva (1989)

NGO Funding Strategies by Jon Bennet and Sarah Gibbs, INTRAC, Oxford (1997)

A One Day Orientation to Alternative Financing by Richard Holloway, Pact Zambia, Lusaka (1996)

Striking a Balance – enhancing the effectiveness of non-governmental organisations working in the field of international development by Alan Fowler, Earthscan, London (1997)

The Emerging Sector Revisited by Lester Salamon and Helmut Anheier, Johns Hopkins University Centre for Civil Society Studies, Baltimore (1999)

Current data and analysis are available from the centre's website, listed below under Resource Organizations.

A Guide to Resource Mobilisation for Voluntary Organisations in India by the South Asia Fundraising Group, India June (2000)

Más Dinero Para Su Causa, 2000 (Spanish) by Daniel Q Kelley, Panorama Editorial, Mexico (2000) and *Dinheiro Para Sua Causa* (Portugese) by Daniel Q Kelley, Textonova Editora, Brazil (1995)

Apoyo Financiero:como lorarlo? by Maria Elena Noriega and Murray Milton, Mexico (1995)

Growing your Organisation: a sustainability resource book for NGOs by Susan Pezzullo, International Youth Foundation, Baltimore, USA (2000)

International Fund-raising for Not-for-Profits – a country by country profile by T Harris, John Wiley & Sons, New York (1999). This book is very expensive!

Handbook for Resource Mobilisation by the Institute for Development Research, Boston (2000). A comprehensive treatment of the subject, based on a training course.

Part Two: Ways of Mobilizing Resources

Chapter 4: Revenue from Earned Income

'Earning Income through Trade and Exchange' by Horacio Morales Jr in *Sustaining Civil Society – Strategies for Resource Mobilisation* edited by Shearer and Fox, CIVICUS (1997). This contains further case studies, lists for further reading, and resource organizations.

New Directions in NGO Self-Financing by Lee Davis, Social Change and Development Occasional Papers 1997, The Johns Hopkins University School of Advanced International Studies (SAIS), Washington (1997)

'Income Generation' in *The World Wide Fundraiser's Handbook – a guide to fund-raising for Southern NGOs and Voluntary Organisations* by Michael Norton, Directory of Social Change and Resource Alliance, London (1997). This contains a list of further reading and resource organizations.

Grassroots Development, vol 19, no 2 (1995). (A journal of the Inter-American Foundation.)

Generating Revenue by the International Federation of the Red Cross and Red Crescent Societies, Geneva (1995)

A Handbook on the Good Practices for Laws relating to Non-Governmental Organisations by Leon Irish, World Bank and International Centre for Not-for-profit Law (ICNL) (1997) (Available on ICNL website, listed below under Resource Organizations.)

The Charity as a Business by Clutterbuck and Dearlove, Books for Change, Bangalore, India (1996)

Life Beyond Aid: Twenty Strategies to Help Make NGOs Sustainable by Lisa Cannon, Initiative for Participatory Development (IPD), Johannesburg (1999)

Chapter 5: Indigenous Foundations

'Foundation funding: venture capital for civil society' by Elan Garonzik, and 'Building Indigenous Foundations that Support Civil Society' by Bruce Shearer in *Sustaining Civil Society – Strategies for Resource Mobilisation* edited by Shearer and Fox, CIVICUS (1997). (This contains more case studies, lists of further reading and resource organizations.)

'Foundations' in the *World Wide Fundraiser's Handbook – a guide to fundraising for NGOs and Voluntary Organisations'* by Michael Norton, DSC and Resource Alliance, London (1997)

'Building Foundations' in *The Unit of Development is the Organisation, not the Project* by Richard Holloway, SAIS/JHU, Washington, DC (1997)

The Process and Techniques of Foundation Building: Experience from Eight Organisations in Africa, Asia, and Latin America, The Synergos Institute, New York (1996)

Autonomous Development Funds, special issue of Development Dialogue (1995):2 from the Dag Hammarskjold Foundation

Directory of Indian Donor Organisations by the Indian Centre on Philanthropy, Delhi (1999)

Directory of Donor Organisations in Pakistan by the NGO Resource Centre, Karachi (September 1998)

Philanthropy in Pakistan, The Aga Khan Development Network, Geneva (2000)

Foundation Building Sourcebook: A practioner's guide based upon experiences from Africa, Asia, and Latin America by DuPree, A Scott and David Winder with Cristina Parnetti, Chandni Prasad, and Shari Turitz, The Synergos Institute, New York (2000)

Chapter 6: Individual Philanthropy

'Individual Philanthropy' by Daniel Q Kelley and Susan Garcia-Robles in *Sustaining Civil Society – Strategies for Resource Mobilisation*, CIVICUS (1997)

Section 4.1 in *The WorldWide Fundraiser's Handbook – a guide to fundraising for Southern NGOs and Voluntary Organisations* by Michael Norton, DSC and Resource Alliance, London (1997)

Resource Development Handbook, International Federation of Red Cross and Red Crescent Societies (1994)

Más Dinero para su Causa/Dinheiro para sua causa by Daniel Kelley, Global Work Ethic Fund (2000)

'Building Grass-roots Citizens' Organisations' by Fernando Vincent and William Leclere in *Sustaining Civil Society – Strategies for Resource Mobilisation*, CIVICUS (1997)

Intermediary NGOs: the supporting link in Grassroots Development by Thomas Carroll, Kumarian Press, USA (1992)

Towards Greater Financial Autonomy – a guide for voluntary organisations and community groups by Piers Campbell and Fernando Vincent, IRED, Geneva (1989)

Striking a Balance – enhancing the effectiveness of non-governmental organisations working in the field of international development by Alan Fowler, Earthscan, London (1997)

'The Dimensions of Individual Giving in Pakistan', in *Philanthropy in Pakistan*, Aga Khan Development Network, Islamabad (2000)

How to Raise Rps 10 Million year after year by K S Gupta, OEU Networking Group Trust, Delhi (1999)

Philanthropy and the Dynamics of Change in East and South East Asia edited by Barnett Baron, East Asia Institute, New York (1991)

Diaspora giving from the United States as a funding source for indigenous philanthropic and non-profit institutions by Mark Sidel, Ford Foundation, India (1997)

Getting the Message Across – guide for CSOs on the use of media by F Mwaffcsi and R Mafula, East African Support Unit for NGOs, Arusha, Tanzania

Funding Civil Society in Asia – Philanthropy and public-private partnerships by F B Baron, Asia Foundation, San Francisco (1997)

Philanthropy in Pakistan – A Report of the Initiative on Indigenous Philanthropy by the Aga Khan Foundation, Islamabad (2000)

Chapter 7: Building Grass-roots Organizations

'Building Grass-roots Citizens' Organisations by William Leclere and Fernando Vincent, in *Sustaining Civil Society – Strategies for Resource Mobilisation*, CIVICUS (1997)

Intermediary NGOs: the supporting link in grass-roots development by Thomas Carroll, Kumarian Press, USA (1992)

Towards Greater Financial Autonomy – a guide for voluntary organisations and community groups by Piers Campbell and Fernando Vincent, IRED, Geneva (1989)

Striking a Balance – enhancing the effectiveness of non-governmental organisations working in the field of international development by Alan Fowler, Earthscan, London (1997)

Chapter 8: Resources from Government

'Public Resources from Government' by Gonzalo de la Maza, Richard Holloway, Fadel N'Diame in *Sustaining Civil Society – Strategies for Resource Mobilization*, edited by Shearer and Fox, CIVICUS (1997)

The State and the Voluntary Sector by John Clark, HRO Working Paper 12, World Bank, Washington, DC (1993)

Handbook of Good Practices for Laws Relating to Non-Governmental Organisations by the International Center for Not-for-Profit Law, World Bank, Washington, DC (1997)

Pursuing Common Goals – strengthening relations between government and development NGOs by the World Bank, Dhaka, UPL, Dhaka (1996)

Reluctant Partners by the Overseas Development Institute, London, Routledge, London (1993); plus three other books in the set: *NGOs and the State in Asia, NGOs and the State in Africa, NGOs and the State in Latin America*

Confrontation, Co-operation or Co-optation; CSOs and the Ghanaian State during Structural Adjustment by Ian Gary, ROAPE 68, London (1996)

Non-Governmental Organisations: guidelines for good policy and practice by the Commonwealth Foundation, London (1996)

Non-Governmental Organisations in Bank-Supported Projects by Gibbs, Fumo and Kuby, Operations Evaluation Department, World Bank, Washington, DC (1998)

Decentralized Government and NGOs – issues, strategies, and ways forward by D Rajasekhar, Concept Publishing Company, Delhi (1999)

Development programmes and NGOs – a guide on central government programmes for NGOs in India by N L N Reddy and R Rajasekhar, Books for Change, Bangalore, India (1997)

NGO–Government Relations by Rajesh Tandon, PRIA, Delhi (1989)

Circle of Power: An enabling framework for civil society in Southern Africa edited by Owen Stuurman and Riann Villiers, Development Resources Centre, South Africa (1997)

Chapter 9: Resources for Sustainability from Foreign Development Agencies

'The Direct Funding of Southern NGOs by Donors – new agenda and old problems' by Bebbington and Riddell, *Journal of International Development* (1995)

Striking a Balance – enhancing the effectiveness of non-governmental organisations working in the field of international development by Alan Fowler, Earthscan, London (1997)

How New Funding Mechanisms could be used to support Civil Society – a preliminary study of existing experience by Leslie Fox, Synergos Institute, New York (1994)

The Sustainable Financing Series from the Africa Bureau of USAID, Washington (1997): 'Sustainable Financing – background paper'; 'Endowments in Africa – a discussion of issues for using alternative funding mechanisms to support agriculture and natural resources management programmes'; 'Basic guide to using debt conversions'; 'Checkoffs (Voluntary Levies): new approaches to funding research, development, and conservation programmes'; 'Sustainable financing: framework, concepts, and applications'

'Autonomous Development Funds', *Development Dialogue,* no 2 (1995)

Working with NGOs – a practical guide to operational collaboration between the World Bank and non-governmental organisations by C Malena, World Bank, Washington, DC (1995)

Chapter 10: Resources from the Corporate Sector

'Engaging Corporations in Strengthening Civil Society' by Laurie Regelbrugge in *Sustaining Civil Society – strategies for resource mobilization* edited by Shearer and Fox, CIVICUS (1997)

'Company Giving' in *The World Wide Fundraiser's Handbook – a Guide for Southern NGOs and Voluntary Organisations* by Michael Norton, Directory of Social Change in collaboration with the Resource Alliance, London (1996)

Business as Partners in Development – creating wealth for countries, companies and communities by Jane Nelson, World Bank, UNDP, and Prince of Wales' Business Leaders Forum (1996)

Global Corporate Citizenship – rationale and strategies by Logan, Roy and Regelbrugge, Hitachi Foundation (1997)

Companies in Communities – valuing the contribution by M Tuffrey and D Logan, Charities Aid Foundation, Delhi (1999)

Corporate–NGO partnership in Asia Pacific by T Yamamoto and KG Ashizawa, Japan Centre for International Exchange (1999)

Corporate Responsibility – philanthropy, self-interest and bribery by D Roy, CAF and Kluwer Law International, USA (1998)

Promoting Corporate Citizenship – opportunities for business and civil society engagement edited by L Regelbrugge, CIVICUS, Washington, DC (1999)

'The Dimensions of Corporate Giving in Pakistan' in *Philanthropy in Pakistan*, Aga Khan Development Network Islamabad (2000)

Chapter 11: Building Reserve Funds and Endowments

Endowments as a Tool for Sustainable Development by Kathleen Horkan and Patricia Jordan, USAID, Washington (1996)

Endowments as a Tool for Financial Sustainability – a manual for NGOs by PROFIT, published by USAID (1994)

'Reserves and Investment' in *Towards Greater Financial Autonomy* by Fernando Vincent and Piers Campbell, IRED, Switzerland (1989)

Investment Opportunities for Charitable Organisations by N H Dadrawalla, Center for Advancement of Philanthropy, Mumbai (1993)

Beyond Fund-raising: New strategies for non-profit innovation and investment by K S Grace, John Wiley & Sons, New York (1997)

Non-profit Investment Policies: Practical steps for growing charitable funds by R P Fry (1998)

Chapter 12: Conversion of Debt

Debt Swaps for Sustainable Development: a Practical Guide for NGOs by Jurgen and Lambert, IUCN, SCDO and EURODAD (1995)

How the International Debt Problem Can Work for Development by Debt for Development Coalition, Washington, DC (1993)

Basic Guide to Using Debt Conversions by Elizabeth Dunn, Technical Paper 44 of USAID's SD Publication series (1997). (This contains a fine bibliography.)

Publications of the Debt for Development Coalition, including the Country Opportunity Series

Freedom from Debt – the re-appropriation of development through financial self-reliance by J B Gelinas, Zed Books, UK

Work against Poverty, Development Aid and Debt Conversion for Employment Guarantee in India by G Onnk, India Committee of the Netherlands, the Netherlands (1992)

Chapter 13: Microcredit Programmes

Maximising the Outreach of Micro-enterprise Finance – an analysis of successful Micro-finance programmes, USAID Programme and Operations Assessment Report 10, Centre for Development Information and Evaluation, Washington, DC (1995)

Financial Management of Micro-Credit Projects by Robert Peck Christen, ACCION (1995)

The New World of Micro-enterprise Finance – building healthy financial institutions for the poor by Otero and Rhyne, Kumarian Press, USA (1994)

Successful Rural Finance Institutions by Jacob Yaron, World Bank Discussion Papers, no 150 (1992)

Chapter 14: Social Investment

From Transition to Consolidation by Ann Hudock, JHU/SAIS, Washington, DC (1997)

Alternative Financing of Third World Organisations and NGOs by Fernando Vincent, IRED, Geneva (1995)

Programme Related Investment by Renz and Massarky, Foundation Center, New York (1995)

'New Sources of Borrowing for Charities' by M Hayday, in *Charity Finance Yearbook* (1997)

Mission Based Marketing by P Brinckerhoff, John Wiley & Sons, New York (1998)

Chapter 15: Use of the Internet

Nonprofit Toolkit Fundraising Software by Artswire, New York Foundation for the Arts Reuse (1999). From www.nptoolkit.org/forum.html

How Do We Select Fundraising Software? by Duff Batchelder, Management Solutions for Non profit Organizations from: www.allianceonline.org/faqs/frfaq7.html)

Exploring Online Fundraising for NonProfit Arts Organizations, from www.idealist.org/beth.html

UN Food Site Encourages Free Online Donations, Fundraising UK Ltd (28 July 1999). From http://www.fundraising.co.uk/news/9907/hunger.html.

Net Results, Lipman Hearne's monthly new media report. Issue 21: 'E-Philanthropy, part 2: Click and Give'. Back issues of *Net Results* are available on the website www.lipmanhearne.com. To subscribe to the newsletter, send an email to majordomo@listbox.com. In the body of the message, type 'subscribe NetResults'.

Elementary E-Philanthropy by Michael Stein from www.netaction.org

'Fund-raising on the Internet' by S A Abraham and S R Sreekanth in *A Guide to Resource Mobilisation for Voluntary Organisations in India*, SAFRG, Delhi (2000)

Fund-raising on the Internet by Howard Lake, Aurelian Press, UK (1996)

The Fund-raiser's Guide to the Internet by M Johnston, John Wiley & Sons, New York (1999)

Brave New World Wide Web by H Lake in *Professional Fundraising* (March 1997)

'Charity begins at the Homepage' by H Lake in *Trust Monitor* (June 1995)

'Cybergifts' by A Corson-Finnerty in *Library at Charity Village* (March 2000)

'Electronic Mail as a Fund-raising Tool' by H Lake in *Journal of Non-Profit and Voluntary Sector Marketing* (October 1996)

'E-Mailing for Donations' in *Join Together Online* (September 1998)

'Free Space in Cyberspace' by M Demko, *Chronicle of Philanthropy*

'Fund-raising in Cyberspace' by M Green in the *Grantsmanship Center Magazine*

'Fund-raising on the Internet' by M Johnston in *Professional Fundraising Magazine* (September 1995)

'Legacy Fundraising and the Internet' by H Lake in *Smee and Ford Limited's Codicil* (May 1996)

PART THREE: DECIDING WHICH WAY TO GO

Resources for Success – A Manual for Conservation Organisations in Latin America and the Caribbean by The Nature Conservancy (1996) (This book covers some of the same ground as the present handbook but helps also with strategic planning and financial management.)

The Virtuous Spiral: a guide to sustainability thinking and practice for non-governmental organisations in international development by Alan Fowler, Earthscan, London (August 2000) (An invaluable resource.)

Getting Started on Fund-raising by Michael Norton and Murray Culshaw, SAGE Publications, Delhi (1997)

Financial Sustainability Strategies for NGOs (2 vols) by the Institute for Development Research, Boston, USA (2000) (A comprehensive treatment of the subject, based on a training course. A series of technical assistance packages developed to assist consultants and technical assistance advisors working with NGOs to help them achieve greater financial assistance and institutional autonomy.)

The Unit of Development is the Organisation Not the Project by Richard Holloway, SAIS, the Johns Hopkins University, Washington, DC (1996)

Resource Organizations

Part One: Setting the Scene

The Resource Alliance
(previously the International Fund Raising Group (IFRG))
295 Kennington Road
London SE11 4QF,
United Kingdom
Tel: 44 (0) 207-587-0287
Fax: 44(0) 207-582-4335
Email: contact@ifrg.org.uk
Web: www.ifrg.org.uk

Comparative Nonprofit Sectors Study Project
Center for Civil Society Studies
Johns Hopkins Institute for Policy Studies
3400 North Charles Street
Baltimore MD 21218-2688
USA
Tel: 1-410-516-4523
Fax: 1-410-516-7818
Email: cnp@jhu.edu
Web: www.jhu.edu/~cnp

Ashoka: Innovators for the Public
1700 North Moore Street, Suite 2000
Arlington VA 22209
USA
Tel: 1-703-527-8300
Fax: 1-703-527-8383
Email: info@ashoka.org
Web: www.ashoka.org

PART TWO: WAYS OF MOBILIZING RESOURCES

Chapter 4 Revenue from Earned Income

Non-Profit Enterprise and Self Sustainability Team (NESsT)
Jose Arrieta 89
Providencia Santiago
Chile
Tel/Fax: 56-2-222-5190
Email: nesst@igc.apc.org
Web: www.nesst.org

The Philippine Business for Social Progress (PBSP)
3/F Magallanes cor Real Street
Intramuros
Manila
Philippines
Tel: 63-2-527-7741 to 50
Fax: 63-2-527-3743
Email: bcalingo@pbsp.org.ph

Chapter 5 Indigenous Foundations

Asia Pacific Philanthropy Consortium (APPC)
Jl Dharmawangsa Raya 50
Kebayoran Baru
Jakarta 12160
Indonesia
Tel: 62-21-726-1860, 724-4204
Fax: 62-21-726-2834
Email: appc@netscape.net
Web: www.asiafoundation.com/events/news-appc1.html

Institute for the Development of Philanthropy (IDEPH)
Puerto Rico Community Foundation
Royal Bank Centre, Suite 1417
Hato Rey, Puerto Rico 00917
USA
Tel: 1-787-754-2623
Fax: 1-787-751-3297

National Center for Non-Profit Boards (NCNB)
1828 L Street, NW
Suite 900
Washington DC 20036-5104
USA
Tel: 1-202-452-6262
Fax: 1-202-452-6299
Email: ncnb@ncnb.org
Web: www.ncnb.org

The Synergos Institute
9 East 69th Street
New York, NY 10021
USA
Tel: 1-212-517-4900
Fax: 1-212-517-4815
Email: synergos@synergos.org
Web: www.synergos.org

Chapter 6 Individual Philanthropy

Fundraising from the public is a profession in the North, with many organizations offering training, consultancies, computer programmes, research, journals, etc. Very few, however, have experience of doing the same in the South. Exceptions are:

The Resource Alliance
(previously the International Fund Raising Group (IFRG))
(for contact details see p216)

National Center for Non-Profit Boards (NCNB)
(for contact details see above)

Charities Aid Foundation (CAF)
Kings Hill, West Malling
Kent ME19 4TA
United Kingdom
Tel: 44 (0) 1732-520000
Fax: 44 (0) 1732-520001
Email: enquiries@caf.charitynet.org
Web: www.cafonline.org

Venture for Fund Raising
Unit 2801 Jollibee Plaza Bldg, Emerald Avenue
Ortigas Centre Metro Manila
Philippines 1605
Tel: 63-2-634-8889/90
Fax: 63-2-637-3545
Email: info@venture-asia.org
Web: www.venture-asia.org

Finlay Craig Consulting
Lochside Guest House
Main Street
Arrochar
Argyll G83 7AA
Scotland
Tel/Fax: 44-1301-702-467
Email: fcraigcons@aol.com

Global Work Ethic Fund
1521 16th Street, NW
Washington DC 20036
USA
Tel: 1-202-232-1600
Fax: 1-202-318-0876
Email: info@globalfund.org
Web: www.globalfund.org

Murray Culshaw Advisory Services (MCAS)
139/4 Domlur layout, Domlur
Bangalore – 5600071
India
Tel: 91-11-080-5543770, 556-0003
Email: murray@vsnl.com

Chapter 7 Building Grass-roots Organizations

Inter-American Foundation (IAF)
901 North Stuart Street, 10th floor
Arlington, VA 22203
USA
Tel: 1-703-306-4301
Fax: 1-703-306-4365
Web: www.iaf.gov

Innovations et Reseaux pour le Développement (IRED)
3 Rue de Varembé, Case 116
1211 Geneva 20
Switzerland
Tel: 41-22-734-1716
Fax: 41-22-740-0011
Email: ired@worldcom.ch
Web: www.ired.org

RAFAD Foundation
CP 117, Rue de Varembé, 1
1211 Geneva 20
Switzerland
Tel: 41-22-733-5073
Fax: 41-22-734-7083
Email: rafad@onetelnet.ch
Web: www.fig-igf.org

International Center for Not-for-Profit Law
733 15th Street, NW, Suite 420
Washington DC 20005
USA
Tel: 202-624-0766
Fax: 202-624-0767
Email: infoicnl@icnl.org
Web: www.icnl.org

Chapter 8 Resources from Government

NGO Unit
Social Development Department
World Bank
1818 H Street, NW
Washington DC 20433
USA
Tel: 1-202-477-1234
Fax: 1-202-477-6391
Web: www.worldbank.org

International Center for Not-for-Profit Law
(for contact details see p220)

Commonwealth Foundation
Marlborough House
Pall Mall
London SW1Y SHY
United Kingdom
Tel: 44 (0)20 7930-3783
Fax: 44 (0)20 7839-8157
Email: geninfo@commonwealth.int
Web: www.commonwealthfoundation.com

Chapter 9 Resources for Sustainability from Foreign Development Agencies

Innovations et Reseaux pour le Développement (IRED)
(for contact details see p220)

New Programme Initiative
USAID
Washington DC 20523
USA
Web: www.info.usaid.gov/pubs/npi

Centre for Development Information Exchange
c/o USAID
Washington DC 20523
USA
Web: www.info.usaid.gov

INTRAC
PO Box 563
Oxford OX2 6RZ
United Kingdom
Tel: 44 (0) 1865-201851
Fax: 44 (0) 1865-201852
Email: intrac@gn.apc.org
Web: www.intrac.org

Chapter 10 Resources From the Corporate Sector

Businesses for Social Responsibility
609 Mission Street (2nd floor)
San Francisco CA 94105
USA
Tel: 1-415-537-0888
Fax: 1-415-537-0889
Web: www.bsr.org

The Conference Board
845 Third Avenue
New York, NY 10022
USA
Tel: 1-212-759-0900
Fax: 1-212-980-7014
Web: www.conference-board.org

The Hitachi Foundation
1509 22nd Street NW
Washington DC 20037
USA
Tel: 1-202-457-0588
Fax: 1-202-296-1098
Web: www.hitachi.org

The Prince of Wales Business Leaders Forum
15–16 Cornwall Terrace
Regent's Park
London NW1 4QP
United Kingdom
Tel: 44 (0) 207-467-3600
Fax: 44 (0) 207-467-3610
Email: info@pwblf.org
Web: www.csrforum.com

Partners in Change
E-270, Greater Kailash – II
New Delhi 110-048
India
Tel: 91-11-641-8885,6,7
Fax: 91-11-623-3525
Email: pic@actionaidindia.org

Southern Africa Grant Makers Association (SAGA)
PO Box 31667,
2017 Braamfontein,
South Africa
Tel: 27-11-403-1610
Fax: 27-11-403-1689
Email: saga@wn.apc.org

Ethos Brazil
Rua Francisco Leitao, 469 – Conj 1407
CEP: 05414-020
São Paulo/SP
Brazil
Tel/fax: 55-11-3068-8539
Web: www.ethos.org.br

INTRAC
(for contact details see p221)

Chapter 11 Building Reserve Funds and Endowments

Innovations et Reseaux pour le Développement (IRED)
(for contact details see p220)

Ford Foundation
320 East 43rd Street
New York NY 10017
USA
Tel: 1-212-573-5000
Fax: 1-212-351-3677
Email: office-communications@fordfound.org
Web: www.fordfound.org

Chapter 12 Conversion of Debt

Debt for Development Coalition
EURODAD (European Network of Debt and Development)
Rue de Joncker 46
B-1060 Brussels
Belgium
Tel: 32-2-543-9060
Fax: 32-2-544-0559
Email: info@eurodad.ngonet.be
Web: www.oneworld.org/eurodad

Swiss Coalition on Development Organizations
Monbijoustrasse 31
CH-3001
Berne
Switzerland
Tel: 41-31-390-9330
Fax: 41-31-390-9331
Email: mail@swisscoalition.ch
Web: www.swisscoalition.ch

Chapter 13 Microcredit Programmes

The Microcredit Summit Campaign
440 First Street NW, Suite 460
Washington DC, 20001
USA
Tel: 1-202-637-9600
Fax: 1-202-637-3566
Email: info@microcreditsummit.org
Web: www.microcreditsummit.org

ACCION International
120 Beacon Street
Somerville, MA 02143
USA
Tel: 1-617-492-4930
Fax: 1-617-876-9509
Email: info@accion.org
Web: www.accion.org

The SEEP (Small Enterprise Education and Promotion) Network
1825 Connecticut Avenue NW
Washington DC 20009
USA
Tel: 1-202-884-8392
Fax: 1-202-884-8479
Email: dekanter@seepnetwork.org
Web: www.seepnetwork.org

Innovations et Reseaux pour le Développement (IRED)
(for contact details see p220)

RAFAD Foundation
(for contact details see p220)

Chapter 14 Social Investment

INAISE (International Association of Investors in the Social Economy)
Rue Haute 139, Box 3
B-1000 Brussels
Belgium
Tel: 32-2-230-3057
Fax: 32-2-230-3764
Email: inaise@inaise.org
Web: www.inaise.org

Innovations et Reseaux pour le Développement (IRED)
(for contact details see p220)

RAFAD Foundation
(for contact details see p220)

Chapter 15 Use of the Internet

www.changemakers.net
www.charityvillage.org
www.internet-fundraising.com

Online fundraising mailing list: This list is offered by Michael Gilbert of the Gilbert Center in Seattle. To subscribe, send email to autoshare@gilbert.org (from the address at which you wish to be subscribed) with the words 'sub fundraising' (without quotes) in the body of the message. To learn more about the Gilbert Center, visit http://www.gilbert.org

Chronicle of Philanthropy (http://philanthropy.com): you can get an advanced look at the Chronicle of Philanthropy via weekly email bulletins. The service includes headlines and brief information. For more information, check out the website or send a message to Chronicle-request@philanthropy.com

Part Three: Deciding Which Way to Go

The Nature Conservancy
4245 North Fairfax Drive, Suite 100
Arlington, VA 22203-1606
USA
Tel: 1-703-841-5300
Web: www.tnc.org

Inter-American Foundation (IAF)
901 North Stuart Street, 10th floor
Arlington, VA 22203
USA
Tel: 1-703-306-4301
Fax: 1-703-306-4365
Web: www.iaf.gov

South Asia Fundraising Group
A-97 (GF), Defence Colony
New Delhi –24
India
Tel: 91-11-465-4453, 465-4570
Fax: 91-11-465-4571
Email: safrg@del3.vsnl.net.in

Index

Managing for Change

Leadership, strategy and management in Asian NGOs

Ian Smillie and John Hailey

'Managing for Change *is the first serious comparative study of how NGOs can and do succeed in the resource-poor, often unstable and, at times, openly hostile environments of South Asia'*
Alan Fowler, author of *Striking a Balance: A Guide to Enhancing the Effectiveness of NGOs in International Development* and *The Virtuous Spiral: A Guide to Sustainability for NGOs in International Development*

'*Very well written. . . mercifully free of jargon. It is consistently clear, well structured and accessible to a non-expert. This will be a very useful guide and a valuable contribution to the literature'*
Michael Edwards, Director, Governance and Civil Society Unit, Ford Foundation, author of *Future Positive: International Co-operation in the 21st Century*

Managing for Change addresses the key operational issues facing NGO managers, drawing lessons from the reality of Southern NGOs. It explores areas such as the formation of strategy, effective NGO leadership, the handling of donor relations, staff motivation and development, and the management styles most appropriate to crises and change. Well written and engaging, clear and comprehensive, this is an essential sourcebook for practitioners, professionals and scholars.

Ian Smillie is a development consultant and co-author of *Stakeholders: Government–NGO Partnerships for International Development*. **John Hailey** is Deputy Director of Oxford Brookes University Business School and a co-founder of the International Training and Research Centre (INTRAC).

Published in association with the Aga Khan Foundation Canada

Paperback	1 85383 722 9	£16.95
Hardback	1 85383 721 0	£45.00

Orders to EARTHSCAN
FREEPOST 1, 120 PENTONVILLE ROAD, LONDON N1 9BR
Fax: +44 (0)20 7278 1142
email: earthinfo@earthscan.co.uk

www.earthscan.co.uk

The Virtuous Spiral

A guide to sustainability for NGOs in international development

Alan Fowler

'This book provides an international perspective on the future role of development NGOs and integrates a breadth of research and a wide range of practical examples, of value to practitioners and academics alike'
JOHN HAILEY, Director of Research, Oxford Brookes University Business School

The Virtuous Spiral offers practical guidance on how organizations in international development can achieve sustainability by focusing on three interactive facets: their work must be enduring; continuity of funding must be ensured; the organization must remain viable. When realized these facets lead to a 'virtuous spiral' through which the organization moves ever-closer towards genuine sustainability.

Paperback   1 85383 610 9   £14.95

Striking a Balance

A guide to enhancing the effectiveness of NGOs in international development

Alan Fowler

'An immensely useful tool for NGO leaders in development'
John D Clark, *Senior NGO Specialist, The World Bank*

Striking a Balance offers both analysis of and a practical guide to how NGDOs can achieve sustainable, people-centred development through sustainable organizational design, competent leadership, appropriate external relationships, mobilization of finance and measurement of performance.

Paperback   1 85383 325 8   £14.95

Orders to EARTHSCAN
FREEPOST 1, 120 PENTONVILLE ROAD, LONDON N1 9BR
Fax: +44 (0)20 7278 1142
email: earthinfo@earthscan.co.uk

---

www.earthscan.co.uk